The *Oxford English* Programme 4B

John O'Connor
Celeste Flower
Paul Roberts

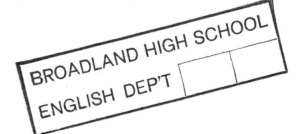

Oxford University Press

Oxford University Press, Walton Street, Oxford OX2 6DP

Oxford New York Toronto
Delhi Bombay Calcutta Madras Karachi
Kuala Lumpur Singapore Hong Kong Tokyo
Nairobi Dar es Salaam Cape Town
Melbourne Auckland Madrid

and associated companies in
Berlin Ibadan

Oxford is a trademark of Oxford University Press

© John O'Connor, Celeste Flower and Paul Roberts, 1992
First published 1992
Reprinted 1992

ISBN 0 19 831177 X

Printed and bound in Italy

Contents

Module 2   The Process of Writing

Module 3   Non-literary Forms

Introduction

Books 4A and 4B of *The Oxford English Programme* are designed for use in Years 10 and 11, as you work towards GCSE or Years S3 and S4 for Standard Grade. Using the language of the National Curriculum, they are aimed at Key Stage 4.

The National Curriculum

The National Curriculum thinks of English in terms of three 'Profile Components': Speaking and Listening; Reading; and Writing. It also lists what students should know, understand and be able to do at different 'Levels' of attainment.

The Oxford English Programme at Key Stage 4 has been devised so as to cover all the detailed requirements of the National Curriculum, but at the same time (and just as importantly) offer materials and activities that will be exciting and enjoyable.

The structure of The Oxford English Programme

As there is so much in the English curriculum at this Key Stage, this part of the programme is made up of two books rather than one. We have done this in order to give full and detailed coverage of the areas you need to be familiar with at GCSE or Standard Grade level.

We do not expect that you should begin with Module 1 of Book 4A and work your way through to the end of Book 4B. Nobody develops their ability to use English in such a mechanical, step-by-step way. Moving from module to module, you might be writing a radio play one day, talking about dialects the next and organising a charity event the week after!

The books and the modules

Book 4A gives particular emphasis to literature. In Module 1, **Forms of Narrative**, you will encounter a variety of the ways in which people compose written stories – from diaries to folk-tales; travel writing to short stories – and have the opportunity to experiment with these forms yourself.

Module 2 focuses upon **Poetry**, looking at the different effects that can be achieved through its many features and the forms that it can take.

Media Scripts is the title of Module 3, which offers examples of plays written for radio, film, theatre and television; and encourages you to write and direct your own.

Book 4B directs your attention more towards language. Module 1 is called **Knowledge about Language**. In this you will consider how the English language has changed over the centuries and how it continues to be rich in its variety today.

Module 2 examines **The Process of Writing**, asking you to think about the different purposes of writing (for example, to convey information, or to persuade people) and contains an important unit on planning and drafting.

Newspapers and advertising are a major feature of Module 3, **Non-literary Forms**. It also looks at the types of language used by specialists, such as scientists or historians, when writing for different audiences.

There are cross references between all the modules, to show how work you are involved with in one might be linked to or helped by work in another. For example in Book 4A, work on dramatic monologue in the Poetry module on pages 84-87 would lead well into the unit on scripted monologue on pages 154-158 in the Media Scripts module.

Each module concludes with a special Feature that gives you the opportunity to put into practice in a longer assignment the knowledge, understanding and skills that you have acquired.

Module 1 Knowledge about Language

Objectives

The material and activities included in this module aim to help you acquire more knowledge about language by:

◆ presenting you with both historical and current information about the English language in its many forms
◆ offering a wide range of examples which illustrate the many varieties of spoken and written English
◆ enabling you to develop opinions about your language and other people's through experimentation, deduction and practical research

The growing language

The foundations of English

The words we use most

1 Which would you say were the commonest words in written English? Discuss this question in pairs and write your ideas down.
2 A statistical analysis of the following newspaper article will produce the answer.
   a) You may find it easiest to work in small groups and to identify *five* or *six* of the words that are most frequently used here.

You could then compare findings with those of other groups in the class.
   b) If you are willing to do the counting, though, the passage will, in fact, reveal *ten* of the most commonly used words in written English. When you have completed your analysis, check your results with other groups'.

The future of the country in the hands of a man of iron

THE newly elected President of the republic is Mr Samuel Vednadze, who came to prominence when he was Minister for Trade and Industry in 1990. It is likely that he will remain leader for the foreseeable future, and certainly while the opposition is in as disorganised and confused a state as it currently is.

However, the problem of the economy is a serious one and Mr Vednadze, with experience in finance for a number of years in appropriate ministries, believes that he is in a unique position to solve it, as his address to yesterday's meeting of the U.N. Security Council made abundantly clear.

His central argument was that he was elected to see to it that inflation was curbed, that the food supply was maintained and that the cost of living was held steady. He acknowledged that this was as difficult and demanding a job as existed anywhere in the continent and that for the present time there was a crisis of confidence in the country. But he was resolute, he said, and claimed to have the will of the people behind him.

Vednadze knows, and his people understand, that the most important thing of all now is to unite, to identify a common cause in which to believe, a cause for which they care, for which they are prepared to fight. This is Vednadze's reason for carrying on for the immediate future.

In the weeks to come it is certain that Mr Vednadze is the man to watch and that inflation will be the major enemy of his efforts to stay in power for the time it takes in order to finish the job. A man of iron requires room to expand and to contract.

Examining word origins

Where do these ten commonest words come from? How long have they been in the language?

Actually most of them are present in these fragments of Old English – also known as Anglo-Saxon – that date from the Eighth to the Eleventh centuries.

To locate the words it helps to understand that:
þ and ð can be replaced by **th**
æ can be replaced by **a**
ƿ can be replaced by **w** } but these two are not used
ȝ can be replaced by **g** } in most books of Old English printed today

- First try to locate some of the commonest words, which in some cases are in slightly different forms.
- Then see if you can translate any of the phrases in the scripts.
  (The first three lines have already been translated, to start you off.)
- Finally, compare your translation with the version at the foot of this page.

said = told
with = by;
West Sea = Atlantic

Sio cwen sæde him spella of heora land
The queen told him stories of their land
He sæde þæt he bude on þæm lande
He said that he lived on the land
norþƿeardum ƿið þa ƿestsæ
northward with the West Sea

þæt Estland wæs eal ƿeste
on his aȝnum lande is se betsta hƿælhuntað
he sæde þæt he ofsloȝe syxtiȝ
on tƿam daȝum in ƿintra ond in sumera

þa preostas læddon þone
kyninȝ to anum treoƿe
for eorlum

Translation: The queen told (said) him stories of their land
He said that he lived in the land
northward by the Atlantic (West Sea)

...the east land was all waste
in his own land is the best whale-hunting
he said that he killed sixty
in two days...in winter and in summer

the priests led the king to a
tree in front of the earls.

Some connections with modern English:
spella = stories
bude = bide, abode
ofsloȝe = slew

Old English Literature

The most famous piece of literature in Old English is an epic poem, with over 3000 lines, called *Beowulf*. It is the story of a warrior hero's three great combats: first with the evil monster, Grendel; then with Grendel's mother; and finally with an enraged dragon.

You may have read a modern version of the story – perhaps Rosemary Sutcliff's *Dragon slayer*.

This passage describes Beowulf's triumphant departure from the Danish shore and the journey back across the sea to his own country, the land of the Geats.

It has been translated word-for-word. As you read, look at the notes which explain the special features of Old English poetry.

Beowulf

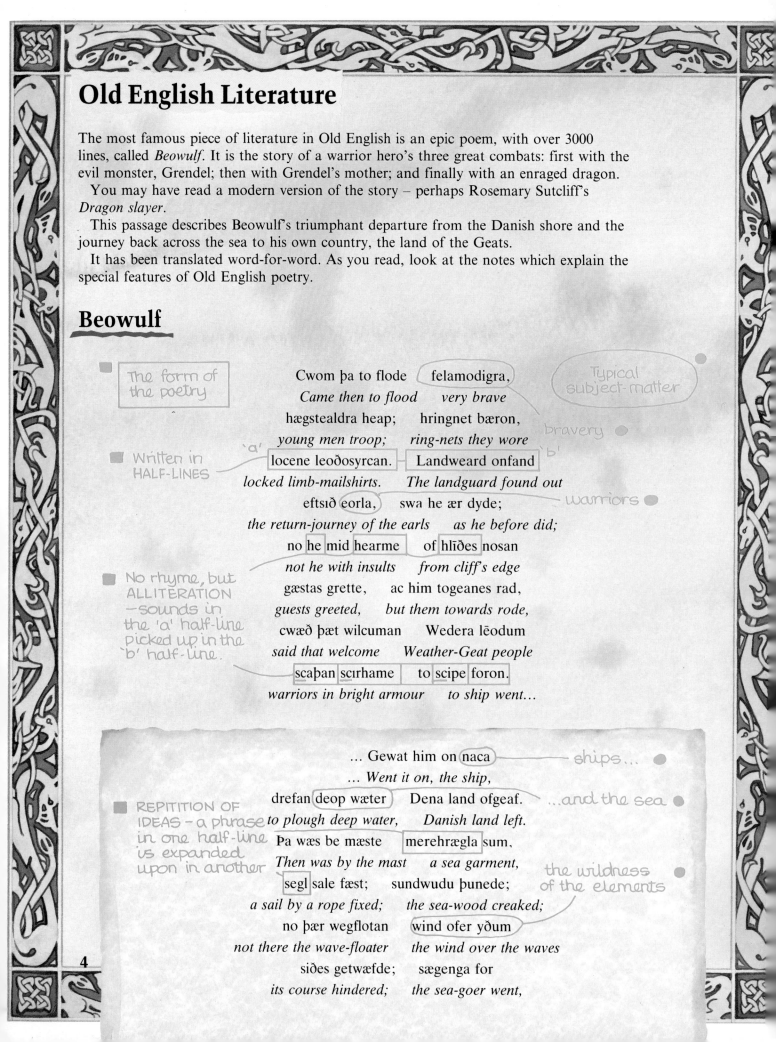

The form of the poetry

Written in HALF-LINES

No rhyme, but ALLITERATION – sounds in the 'a' half-line picked up in the 'b' half-line.

Typical subject-matter

bravery

warriors

Cwom þa to flode   felamodigra,
Came then to flood   very brave
hægstealdra heap;   hringnet bæron,
young men troop;   ring-nets they wore
locene leoðosyrcan.   Landweard onfand
locked limb-mailshirts.   The landguard found out
eftsið eorla,   swa he ær dyde;
the return-journey of the earls   as he before did;
no he mid hearme   of hlīðes nosan
not he with insults   from cliff's edge
gæstas grette,   ac him togeanes rad,
guests greeted,   but them towards rode,
cwæð þæt wilcuman   Wedera lēodum
said that welcome   Weather-Geat people
scaþan scırhame   to scipe foron.
warriors in bright armour   to ship went…

REPITITION OF IDEAS – a phrase in one half-line is expanded upon in another

ships…

…and the sea

the wildness of the elements

… Gewat him on naca
… Went it on, the ship,
drefan deop wæter   Dena land ofgeaf.
to plough deep water,   Danish land left.
Þa wæs be mæste   merehrægla sum,
Then was by the mast   a sea garment,
segl sale fæst;   sundwudu þunede;
a sail by a rope fixed;   the sea-wood creaked;
no þær wegflotan   wind ofer yðum
not there the wave-floater   the wind over the waves
siðes getwæfde;   sægenga for
its course hindered;   the sea-goer went,

4

Invention of KENNINGS – made-up compound words, designed to make us think of a familiar object in a new way.

fleat famigheals | forð ofer yðe,
floated the foamy-neck, | *forward over the waves,*
bundenstefna | ofer brimstreamas,
the bound prow | *over the ocean stream,*
þæt hie Geata clifu | ongitan meahton,
until they the Geats' cliffs | *perceive might,*
cuþe næssas; | ceol up geþrang
the known headlands; the boat | *(up) pressed forward*
lyftgeswenced, | on lande stod.
wind-pushed, | *on to land stood.*

rugged scenery

More about Kennings:

In the examples here, 'mere' (sea) is joined to 'hrægle' (garment) to create a new way in which to think of a sail: a sea-garment. In a similar way, a ship is 'sund wudu' (sea-wood), 'sægenga' (sea-goer) or, most imaginatively 'famigheals' (foamy-neck).

Anglo-Saxon poets loved to create new kennings. A minstrel might be 'hleahtor-smiþ' (laughter-smith).

There was a whole vocabulary of kennings to describe the sea. At one point it might be the 'hwæl-weg' (whale-way); at others the 'swan-rad' (swan-road), bæþ-weg' (bath-way) or 'flod-weg' (flood-way).

This modern verse translation of the same passage has many of the same features as the Anglo-Saxon original.

They came then to the sea-flood, the spirited band
of warrior youth, wearing the ring-meshed
coat of mail. The coastguard saw
the heroes approaching, as he had done before.
Nor was it ungraciously that he greeted the strangers
from his ridge by the cliff, but rode down to meet them:
how welcome they would be to the Weather-Geats, he said
to those shipward-bound men in their shining armour…
…Out moved the boat then
to divide the deep water, left Denmark behind.
A special sea-dress, a sail, was hoisted
and belayed to the mast. The beams spoke.
The wind did not hinder the wave-skimming ship
as it ran through the seas, but the sea-going craft
with foam at its throat, furled back the waves
her ring-bound prow planing the waters
till they caught sight of the cliffs of the Geats
and headlands they knew. The hull drove ahead,
urged by the breeze, and beached on the shore.

Michael Alexander

Writing your own

Try writing your own modern English poem using some of the features of Old English poetry.
Remember that:

- it is written in half-lines with a steady rhythm
- it uses **alliteration**, with sounds in half-line 'a' echoed in half-line 'b'
- ideas are repeated and expanded upon
- familiar objects are described in new ways with the formation of **kennings** – invented compound words that create an unusual image

You might base the story of your poem on a news report, a legend or a story of your own invention.

For more on epics in English Literature see the Narrative module in Book 4A, page 30 for an extract of Sir Thomas Malory's *Le mort d'Arthur*.

The changing language

Changing spellings

When we compare Old English with its Modern English version, one of the most obvious differences is in spelling.

> **Est** has become **East**
>
> **Eorl** has become **Earl**
>
> **þintra** has become **Winter**

> In pairs, make a list of some of the more interesting spelling changes that have taken place using evidence from the first set of Anglo-Saxon fragments on page 3. For more on changes in spelling and the question of spelling reform see Unit 5, pages 51-53.

The changing alphabet

There have been changes to the alphabet too. We have already seen that Old English contained letters that have since been lost:

- þ   known as **'thorn'** } both of which did the same job as Modern
- ð   known as **'eth'**   } English **'th'**
- æ   known as **'ash'**   – which was like the **'a'** in 'cat'
- ƿ   known as **'wyn'**   – modern **w**
- ȝ   known as **'yogh'**   – modern **g**

A careful reading of the first Old English fragments will also reveal which letters we have today which were not used then. There are four. Try and decide which ones they are.

Changes in meaning

In the first line of the fragment was the word 'spella', meaning 'stories'. In Modern English a 'spell' is something rather different, as is the idea of 'spelling'. It is only in the current word 'gospel' that the original meaning of 'story' can be seen.

Invasions of words

The people who spoke and wrote Old English originally came from Northern Europe in the middle of the Fifth century.

The **Jutes** settled in what is now Kent and the Isle of Wight.

The **Angles** settled in the East and North.

The **Saxons** settled in the South and West, later called Wessex (from West Saxons).

These invaders were themselves to experience three major word invasions that would transform the language in the centuries that followed as shown on the map opposite.

Where did they come from?

Each of the common English words in this box derives from one of these languages:

- Scandinavian – brought over by the Vikings
- Latin – brought over by Christian missionaries to the Anglo-Saxons or some time later by Norman scholars
- French – brought over by Normans before and after 1066

Use a dictionary to identify the origin of each word and write it in the appropriate column in a table like the one below.

city	band	toast	rotten
guess	dance	sky	scab
race	both	mat	they
soldier	index	collar	river
outlaw	gap	battle	lamp
giant	freckle	bucket	pain
school	axle	awkward	skull
rule	cap	elephant	lobster
candle	offer	slaughter	people
sock	leg	window	use

From Scandinavian	**From Latin**	**From French**

Use of dictionaries

You will find it useful to become familiar with larger dictionaries and the ways in which their entries are organised

For this research in particular, smaller dictionaries will not contain the information that you require.

This entry is from *The Concise Oxford Dictionary* and shows the word's origin (or **etymology**) quite clearly.

In this case, ON stands for Old Norse, the Scandinavian language spoken by the Vikings.

awk´ward, a. Ill-adapted for use; clumsy (person, thing); bungling; embarrassing; difficult; dangerous, to deal with. Hence ~ISH¹ (2) a., ~LY² adv., ~NESS n. [f.obs. adj. *awk* backhanded, untoward (ME, f. ON *afug* turned the wrong way) + -WARD]

Middle English

from Old Norse

Threesomes, trios and triplets

One particular feature of all this 'borrowing' (not a very accurate term, since there was never any intention to pay anything back!) is that English has frequently picked up a new word from French or Latin, when there was already a perfectly good one in existence.

For example, Old English had a word from which we get the verb *ask*. But, not satisfied with that, we have borrowed *question* from French and *interrogate* from Latin.

1 Discuss the difference between *ask*, *question* and *interrogate*. You will probably find that it helps to place each one in a sentence first. There are other words of Old English origin that have near **synonyms** in words borrowed from French and Latin.

2 Look at the following table and discuss the different shades of meaning for the words in each 'set' of three.

1 Old English	2 French	3 Latin
ask	question	interrogate
kingly	royal	regal
fast	firm	secure
forebear	parent	ancestor
rise	mount	ascend
holy	sacred	consecrated
time	age	epoch
folk	person	people

(Note: some of the words in the middle column were originally Latin; the point here is that they came to us in their French forms.)

3 Now compose three short paragraphs. In the first, use all the Old English words in Column 1. In the second, use all the French words in Column 2 and in the third, use all the Latin words in Column 3.
You will need to think carefully about a story-line that contains all the vocabulary, and you will probably have to change a few endings. For example:
His *royal* Highness was yesterday *questioned* about the difficulties of being a *firm parent* in this *age* of...
The aim is to illustrate the very different tones that the Old English, French and Latin vocabulary can give to the language.

4 When you have finished writing these paragraphs, discuss whether it is possible to make any generalisations about the use of these words from different languages. For example, do we tend to use the three groups of words in different contexts, registers or for a particular effect?

Synonyms are words that have the same or similar meanings.
For example:

glad	happy
kill	slay
serpent	snake

These words seem at first sight to mean the same thing; but there are occasions when we would certainly use one rather than the other. (Can you imagine wishing someone a 'Glad Birthday!'?)

Meaning changes over time

One of the most interesting – and sometimes the most puzzling – things that can happen to a word is that its meaning can change over the years; puzzling, because we often cannot see why this change should have taken place.

In some words, however, it is possible to look back through time and work out what has happened...

The scavenger's tale

Old English had a verb **sceawian**, which meant 'to survey' and the Vikings had a very similar word with the same meaning.

By the time the word had reached the Middle English, a **scavager** was a particular kind of surveyor: an inspector of imports.

This **scavager** also had the responsibility for making sure that the town was kept clean.

And over the years the name **scavager** became associated, no longer with the inspector, but with the person who actually carried the rubbish away.

It was not long before a **scavager**, now written **scavenger**, was the name given to any person who went around picking through rubbish of any kind.

And in Modern English it has come to mean an animal that feeds on dead 'rubbish', or carrion.

When words change in meaning over the centuries, they can change in one of several ways.

1 They can take on a less pleasant or less favourable meaning, e.g. the history of the word 'scavenger'.
We might call this **decline** in meaning.
2 They can take on a more pleasant or more favourable meaning, e.g. Latin 'nescius' which originally meant 'ignorant' and has come down to us as 'nice'.
We might call this **elevation** in meaning.
3 They can take on a narrower or more specialised meaning, e.g. Old English 'deor', which meant any kind of animal has become a particular kind, a 'deer'.
We might call this **narrowing** of meaning.
4 They can take on a broader or less specialised meaning, e.g. Latin 'salarium', which meant money given to Roman soldiers to enable them to buy salt, has become 'salary', a wage.
We might call this **broadening** of meaning.

Analysing changes in meaning

The following Modern English words have all changed meaning over the centuries. Each one has experienced one of the processes described above, i.e. decline, elevation, narrowing or broadening.

fine	hound	journey	treacle	sly
starve	awful	silly	panier	fame
villain	luxury	meat		

Using a detailed etymological dictionary, write a brief history of each word, stating which process has taken place and, where possible, outlining one or two of the most interesting stages in the change of meaning.

Middle English

Old English did not become Middle English overnight. But, by the end of the Fourteenth century, the poet Geoffrey Chaucer was writing in a language that looked like this:

The Miller was a stout carl for the nones;
Ful big he was of brawn, and eek of bones.
That proved wel, for over al ther he cam,
At wrastlinge he wolde have alwey the ram.
He was short-sholdred, brood, a thikke knarre;
Ther was no dore that he nolde heve of harre,
Or breke it at a renning with his heed.
His berd as any sowe or fox was reed,
And therto brood, as though it were a spade.
Upon the cop right of his nose he hade
A werte, and theron stood a toft of heris.
Reed as the brustles of a sowes eris;
His nosethirles blake were and wide.
A swerd and bokeler bar he by his side.
His mouth as greet was as a greet forneys,
He was a janglere and a goliardeys,
And that was moost of sinne and harlotries.
Wel koude he stelen corn and tollen thries;
And yet he hadde a thombe of gold, pardee.
A whit cote and a blew hood wered he.
A baggepipe wel koude he blowe and sowne,
And therwithal he broghte us out of towne.

Geoffrey Chaucer

carl — man, 'churl'
for the nones — especially
eek — also
proved wel — that had been well tested
the ram — a ram would often be first prize at country fairs.
knarre — fellow
harre — hinge
nolde — could not
cop — tip
bokeler — buckler, shield
forneys — furnace
janglere — loud talker
goliardeys — teller of dirty stories
harlotries — obscenities

This is the description of the Miller, from *The general prologue* to *The Canterbury tales* .

With the aid of the handwritten notes, rewrite the description in Modern English.

Reading it out

A good deal of Chaucer's language becomes easier to understand when it is read aloud. As you might expect, pronunciation has changed as much as spelling and grammar, and a Modern English accent will not do it justice.

1 Look at these rough guidelines on how to pronounce Chaucer's English. Then practise some readings in pairs with each of you taking a section of the description of the Miller.
- Pronounce '**a**' as in modern English 'f**a**r'
  '**e**' like the sound in 's**ay**'
  '**i**' like the sound in 'm**e**'
  '**u**' like the sound in 't**o**'
  ('**o**' is near enough to the modern sound).
- Final **-e** is usually pronounced as if there were **-er** on the end, or like the **-a** in 'sof**a**'.

Read the lines confidently and don't worry about getting it exactly right.

2 When you are happy with your reading, you could try recording it.

The growth of dialects

Despite all the changes that the invasions brought about (see the map on page 7) the dialect differences in Old English survived through to Middle English, though we give Middle English dialects different names as this map shows.

Putting detail on the map

In Old English, the West Saxon dialect had had a high status because it was the language of King Alfred's powerful and influential Wessex.

But over the centuries things changed. To work out which of the Middle English dialects became the most influential, you will need to do some research in your school or local library. In your research, try to find out where the following places were in the late Fourteenth century and put them in on your version of the map.

- Write a **P** for the main centre or centres of population.
- Write a **C** for the centre of court life.
- Write two **L**s for the centres of learning.
- Write **W**s for the areas benefiting from the growing wool trade.
- Write **pp** for the position of Caxton's first printing press.

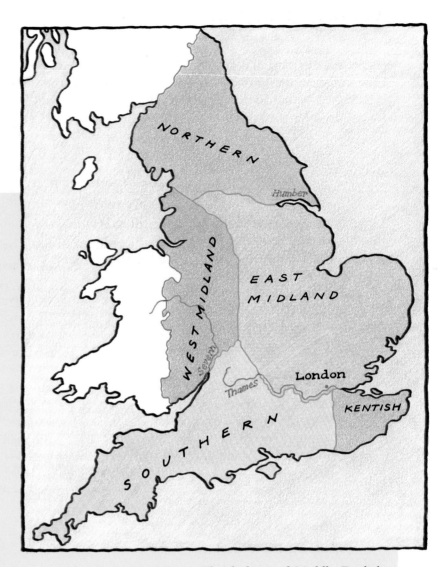

The dialects of Middle English

Each of these factors contributed to the growth of East Midlands as the major dialect of Middle English, as did its position between the extremes of North and South. This is a comment from a man called John of Trevisa, writing in the 1380s (when Chaucer was composing *The Canterbury tales*):

> ...men of myddel Engelond, as hyt were parteners of þe endes, understondeþ betre þe syde longages, Norþeron and Souþeron, þan Norþeron and Souþeron understondeþ eyþer oþer.

> ...men of middle England, as it were partners of the ends, understand better the side languages, Northern and Southern, than Northern and Southern understand each other.

11

Changes in grammar

As an introduction to some of the ways in which the English language has changed over the centuries, look at these three extracts from the Bible.

Extract **A** was written by John Wyclif in the late Fourteenth century; extract **B** is from the Authorised Version of 1611 and extract **C** is from the New English Bible of 1961.

A

A man hadde two sones; and þe ȝonger of hem seide unto his fadir: 'Fadir, ȝyve me a porcioun of þe substance þat falliþ me.' And þe fadir departide him his goodis. And soone aftir, þis ȝonge sone gederide al þat fel to him, and wente forþ in pilgrimage in to a fer contré; and þer he wastide his goodis, lyvynge in lecherie.

B

A certain man had two sons:

12 And the younger of them said to *his* father, Father, give me the portion of goods that falleth *to me*. And he divided unto them *his* living.

13 And not many days after the younger son gathered all together, and took his journey into a far country, and there wasted his substance with riotous living.

C There was once a man who had two sons; and the younger said to his father, 'Father, give me my share of the property.' So he divided his estate between them. A few days later the younger son turned the whole of his share into cash and left home for a distant country, where he squandered it in reckless living.

Comparing the extracts

1 What are the major similarities between the three in terms of language? In pairs, list:
   ● the words which are spelt the same in the three passages
   ● phrases which are built up in similar ways, e.g. 'and þe ȝonger of hem seide unto his fadir...And the younger of them said to his father...and the younger said to his father...'

2 What are the most striking ways in which the language has changed? Use a chart like the one below to record some of the more interesting examples of these changes.

	Wyclif Bible	**Authorised version** 1600 - 1700	**New English Bible** 1961
Different spellings			
Different ways of phrasing ideas			

Shakespeare's grammar

The two characters in this short extract from Shakespeare's *A midsummer night's dream* have both been the victims of magic.

  Bottom, the weaver, is totally unaware of the fact that he now has an ass's head in place of his own; and Titania, Queen of the fairies, has had a spell cast upon her that will make her fall in love with the first creature she sees when she awakes. Naturally, it is Bottom who wakes her up... with his appalling singing!

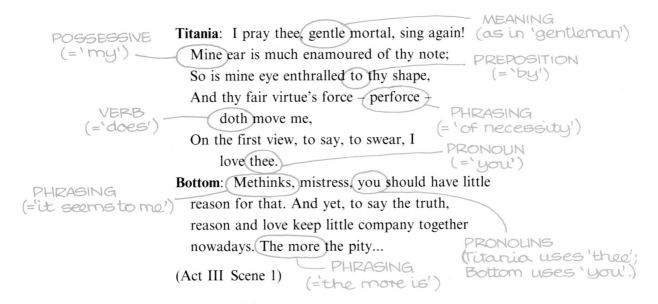

POSSESSIVE (='my')

MEANING (as in 'gentleman')

PREPOSITION (='by')

VERB (='does')

PHRASING (='of necessity')

PRONOUN (='you')

PHRASING (='it seems to me')

PRONOUNS (Titania uses 'thee'; Bottom uses 'you'.)

PHRASING (='the more is')

Titania: I pray thee, gentle mortal, sing again!
Mine ear is much enamoured of thy note;
So is mine eye enthralled to thy shape,
And thy fair virtue's force – perforce –
doth move me,
On the first view, to say, to swear, I
love thee.
Bottom: Methinks, mistress, you should have little
reason for that. And yet, to say the truth,
reason and love keep little company together
nowadays. The more the pity...

(Act III Scene 1)

Group discussion

Shakespeare wrote his play almost four hundred years ago and, not surprisingly, the language has changed in those four centuries.

  In groups of 3 or 4, look at the speeches as they are printed above and the notes written in around them.

1 Using these, talk about some of the differences between Shakespeare's language and our own.
2 Then make brief notes under the following headings.
   Changes in:
   pronouns   possessives
   verbs   meaning
   prepositions   phrasing
   (Phrasing is a deliberately vague heading! It covers a number of very different kinds of change.)

Assignment

Using the extracts from the 1611 version of the Bible, *A midsummer night's dream*, and whichever Shakespeare play you are familiar with at the moment, write an essay on some of the interesting changes that have taken place in the English language since Shakespeare's time. You could structure your essay around the six areas of change considered in your discussion, i.e. pronouns, verbs, prepositions, possessives, meaning and phrasing.

13

Language and the Gulf

It seems rather tasteless to say that the horrific Gulf War of 1991 was 'an interesting time' for anybody studying language. But it is often in times of war and national crisis that development in language occurs.

During the Gulf War:
- new words and expressions were heard on television and radio or read in the newspapers
- letters and articles appeared in newspapers about these changes in the language
- we had an opportunity to compare the 'British' ways of saying things with the 'American' ways

The dictionary of war

This *Gulf-English dictionary* appeared in the Press in February 1991.

Gulf-English dictionary

An aid to communication with British and American forces
Beach, the: Saudi Arabia
Canaries: journalists who crowd hotel roofs to observe scud attacks on Saudi cities
Chicken Chernobyl: very hot curry, as eaten by Royal Navy
De-airing: knocking out enemy aircraft
Deconfliction: trying not to have so many planes in the air that they collide
Forget-me-not: condom (used to protect the rifle barrels from sand)
HRP: Human Remains Pouch, or body bag
Jib rats: reporters working through the Joint Information Bureau
KTO: Kuwaiti Theatre of Operations
MCB: Multiple Cratering Bomblets
Motion lotion: Petrol
MRE: Meals Ready to Eat (alternatively, Meals Rejected by Ethiopians)
Nagging machine: wife
Punch: effect from an aircraft
Rudolf Hess: a mess
Slud: effect of a chemical attack (Salivate, Lachrymate, Urinate and Defecate)
Switched-on cookie: a good soldier
Tow: Tube-launched, Optically tracked, Wire-guided (type of anti-tank missile)
Unhappy teddy: a depressed soldier

The Guardian 18 February 1991

Looking at the language

1 Discuss this 'dictionary' with a partner and list examples of:
   - racism/sexism
   - euphemism
   - acronym
   - grim humour
   - rhyming slang
   - neologism
2 Are there any new 'Gulf' expressions that you remember which are not recorded here? If so, add them to your list.
3 Use the article opposite to add further euphemisms, acronyms and neologisms to the list you made from the *Gulf-English dictionary*.
4 From the context and the examples provided, could you define what *portmanteau words* are?

   For more on language used in the media during the Gulf War see pages 130-131 in the Non-literary Forms module.

Euphemism is a mild or vague expression that is used in place of one that the speaker thinks too blunt, unpleasant or embarrassing, e.g.
   'I'm afraid she passed away last week.'
   'Where can I go to wash my hands?'
   'He's had a drink or two!'
Rhyming slang originated in London and is best explained by examples:
   china plate = mate
   tit fer tat = hat
   mince pies = eyes
Normally, only the first, non-rhyming part of the expression is used: we would talk of 'me old china', put on a 'titfer' and rub our 'minces'.
An **Acronym** is a word that is itself made up of the initial letters of other words, e.g. NATO, RADAR, AIDS
A **Neologism** is any new word or phrase invented to fill a gap in the language. Obviously, thousands of words which were once neologisms are now accepted parts of our vocabulary, e.g. gas (invented by a Dutch chemist in 1652) and of course words such as 'television', and 'video'.

   The word 'scud', which is used in the *Gulf-English dictionary* as part of a definition, would itself have needed explaining before the conflict.

Military words weasel a way into the language

From Edward Lucas in Washington

THE GULF war has driven military terms and neologisms into the public domain more prominently than at any time since Vietnam.

Some well-known euphemisms from those days are making a comeback, *collateral damage* (casualties not directly targeted by the attacker) being perhaps the most notorious example.

Some new ones are also being created. US troops in the Gulf are sustained by notorious military rations known as MREs, or Meals Ready to Eat - a partially dehydrated concoction of goodies packaged in flimsy foil pouches. The soldiers hate them so much that they have derisively renamed them Meals Rejected by Ethiopians.

A *berm* (a 'protective mound' of dirt used by the Iraquis in their fortifications) could gain currency among Scrabble players, if nowhere else.

A *revetement* sounds like a shady financial deal, and left a Pentagon spokesman speechless when he tried to explain it.

To *suppress* a target, when used by US officials, is a shade less precise than 'destroy' and means that the installation has at least been hit. The use of ambiguous, optimistic phrases is justified by the *weather*, which is an all-purpose excuse for not knowing (or maybe just not saying) what the allied bombs are actually doing (known in the trade as *BDA* — bomb damage assessment).

Other reasons for not providing the information journalists want (*specifics*) is to say that the issues raised are (new noun) *hypotheticals*.

Two new portmanteau words have made a debut: *scenario-dependent* (meaning depending on the circumstances) and *date-certain* (as in a plan that isn't), both used by the military when (perhaps not surprisingly) unwilling to provide the Press with detailed information about their future intentions.

Military operations and hardware are famous for the code-names and acronyms they generate.

No one seems to have worried very much that a *desert storm* is the most unfavourable climatic condition for a military operation, or that a *patriot* is not normally connected with last-minute attempts to bribe an ally.

But the *warthog* is an apt name for the ugly but effective A-10, and the chivalric connotations of *templar* are not far removed from its meaning of Tactical Expert Mission Planner (the military computer that revises the battle-plan).

The literary zenith (or maybe nadir) of the war so far came on Friday, when Lieutenant-General Charles Horner, Air Commander for Operation Desert Storm, was trying to explain how the air offensive was coordinated by 'a common air-tasking order'.

'It provides a sheet of music that everybody sings the same song off,' he elaborated.

The Independent 22 January 1991

This final cutting is an example of the importance that language holds for all of its users. For this letter writer, the neologism 'attrit' and the new meaning found for 'degrade' are not merely a matter of interest to people studying language:

From Professor Patrick Collinson (Professor of Modern History, University of Cambridge)

Sir: A minor thing to have come out of this war is a new transitive verb (at least, new to me), 'to attrit'; also a new use for the word 'degrade'. Both apparently mean to kill or maim enemy soldiers, retribution more excusable than the 'collateral damage' wreaked upon 'innocent civilians'.

That it has been found necessary, and possible, to inflict 'attrition' and 'degradation' on as many as 100,000 Iraqis while sustaining so little corresponding attrition in return may be, at one level, a remarkable triumph. At another it constitutes dismal failure, an indictment of our civilisation. Some of us will never be convinced it was necessary.

To say it must not be allowed to happen again may be to add to the triteness of recent public discourse. No matter. It must not be allowed to happen again.

The Independent 2 March 1991

For discussion

Words and phrases enter the language whether we as individuals like it or not.

1 Look through all Gulf words and phrases in the lists that you have made and discuss which of them you approve of and which you disapprove of. Consider:
   ● the idea that lies behind the word or expression
   ● how witty or clever it is
   ● how useful it is in filling a gap

2 Try to predict which of these neologisms will last and explain why. Discuss them and add more examples to the notes you have already made.

Listen Mr Oxford don

Me not no Oxford don
Me a simple immigrant
from Clapham Common
I didn't graduate
I immigrate

But listen Mr Oxford don
I'm a man on de run
and a man on de run
is a dangerous one

I ent have no gun
I ent have no knife
but mugging de Queen's English
is the story of my life

I don't need no axe
to split up yu syntax
I don't need no hammer
To mash up yu grammar

I warning you Mr Oxford don
I'm a wanted man
and a wanted man
is a dangerous one

Dem accuse me of assault
On de Oxford dictionary
imagine a concise peaceful man like me
dem want me serve time
for inciting rhyme to riot
but I tekking it quiet
down here in Clapham Common

I'm not a violent man Mr Oxford don
I only armed wit mih human breath
but human breath
is a dangerous weapon

So mek dem send one big word after me
I ent serving no jail sentence
I slashing suffix in self-defence
I bashing future wit present tense
and if necessary

I making de Queen's English accessory
to my offence

John Agard

Remember

Accent: the way in which people from different places and backgrounds pronounce words and sentences.

Dialect: the different forms of English used by people from different areas and different groups. This involves variations in grammar and vocabulary.

Group discussion

1. What is the Queen's English?
2. Who are 'dem' in line 1 of verse 6.
3. What is 'an Oxford don' and why is he writing to one?
4. The speaker's point of view is that of a wanted criminal, guilty of 'mugging de Queen's English'.
   Where has he been 'guilty' in this poem of:
   - splitting up syntax or mashing up grammar?
   - 'assault on de Oxford dictionary'?
   - 'inciting rhyme to riot?'
5. How might the Queen's English be an 'accessory' to his offence?
   (In law an accessory is someone who knows about the crime and possibly aids the criminal.)
6. 'Me not no...' '...on de run' 'I ent have...'
   '...yu syntax' 'I warning you...'
   'Dem accuse me...'
   What can you say about the language in which this poem is written and about John Agard's possible reasons for deciding to write in this way?

A language profile

Put yourself in the place of the 'language mugger' of John Agard's poem and write his language profile. Using details from the poem, fill in the following profile sheet. The opening entries might look something like this.

Language profile sheet

Section A

Name: *a simple immigrant*

Current home region: *from Clapham Common*

Earlier home regions: *the Caribbean*

'First' language (or 'mother tongue'): ....

Other languages: ....

Section B

	At home	In other situations (state which ones)
Current accent:		
Current dialect:		

Section C

What other people feel about my language:
  The kinds of people: Their attitudes:

Section D

What I feel about my language:

Your language profile

Using either a copy of the language profile sheet on page 17 or your own version, write your language profile.

If you choose to write your own profile sheet for use with a word processor, you could create whatever sections you want. It would also allow you to add or change details at a later date. In your language profile concentrate for the moment on speech rather than writing.

Before you write anything, discuss the following questions with a partner.

1 When you are talking with:
   ● teachers
   ● family
   ● friends
   ● other groups of people (it is up to you to choose who these other groups might be)
   a) How much and in what ways do you change the way you speak?
   b) How confident do you feel?
   You might find it helpful to draw up a grid like the one below.

2 Has your speech changed in recent years (perhaps because of moving house or changing school)?

3 Is there anything that you wish to change about the way you speak? If you wanted to change, would it be an easy matter?
   Now use what you have learned from the discussion to fill in your language profile.

Talking with:	Teachers	Family	Friends	Others (give details)
How much, and in what ways, do I change the way I speak?				
How confident do I feel?				

Influences on accent

There are a number of factors that will affect what accent we have. Three of the most common are social class, education and the place where we were born or live now.

Accent and social class

It is very difficult to define social class or say that someone 'belongs' to one class or another. Class seems to be determined by so many different factors. For example:
● how much money we earn
● what kind of 'lifestyle' we lead
● what job we do, if any
● what class we consider ourselves to be
It is certainly true, though, that many people make judgments about our class by the accent we use.

In the following excerpt from BBC's *Fawlty Towers* (an episode called 'A Touch of Class'), Basil, the hotel proprietor, encounters a casually dressed young man (Danny Brown) in the lobby.

Fawlty Towers

The reception bell rings. Basil goes to the reception desk; standing there is a very non-aristocratic-looking cockney, Danny Brown.

Danny: 'Allo! *(Basil stands appalled)* Got a room?
Basil: ...I beg your pardon?
Danny: Got a room for tonight, mate?
Basil: ...I shall have to see, sir...single?
Danny: Yeah. No, make it a double, I feel lucky today! *(smiling appreciatively at Polly, who is passing)* 'Allo...
Polly: *(smiling nicely)* Good morning.

Danny watches her as she leaves. He turns back to Basil who is staring at him with loathing.

Danny: Only joking.
Basil: No we haven't.
Danny: What?
Basil: No we haven't any rooms. Good day...
Sybil: *(coming in)* Number seven is free, Basil.
Basil: What?...oh...Mr Tone is in number seven, dear.
Sybil: No, he left while you were putting the picture up, Basil...
  (to Danny) You have luggage, sir?
Danny: Just one case. *(to Basil, pointedly)* In the car...the white sports...

  ...Manuel arrives.

Basil: *(slowly)* Er, Manuel, would you fetch this gentleman's case from the car outside. Take it to room seven.
Manuel: ...Is not easy for me.
Basil: What?
Manuel: Is not easy for me...*entender.*
Basil: Ah! It's not easy for you to understand. Manuel... *(to Danny)* We're training him...he's from Barcelona...in Spain. *(to Manuel)* Obtener la valisa...
Manuel: *Qué?*
Basil: *La valisa en el,* er, *auto bianco sportiv...y...a la sala...siete...por favor. Pronto.*
Manuel: Is impossible!
Basil: What?
Manuel: Is impossible.
Basil: Look, it's perfectly simple!
Danny: *(fluently)* Manuel – *sirvase buscar mi equipaje. blanco y lo traer a la sala*

Margin notes:

Brown speaks in a cockney working-class accent. This means that he pronounces some of his 'ts' as 'glottal stops' – the sound we make in the middle of 'football' (foo'ball). It is a standard sound in many world languages.

Basil speaks in a middle-class accent. What kind of tone should Basil use here?

What impression do we form of Brown from these early speeches?

What is Basil implying here?

Manuel is still learning English and has a strong Spanish accent.

Why does Basil translate Manuel's statement? For whose benefit?

What points might be made about Basil's attitude to accent and class?

Group work on accent

1 In groups of 4 or 5, read the passage through, and then discuss the explanatory notes written in the right-hand margin
2 a) Plan and rehearse a dramatised reading of the passage, with each of you taking on the role of one character.
  b) If possible, record it on tape and then discuss your performance, looking at the way you brought out the accents in particular. Was it easy to interpret the spoken quality of the accents involved from the written script?
3 Talk about the questions raised by the handwritten notes in the right-hand margin.

Accent and education

Many well known people have recalled the moment in childhood or adolescence – and sometimes as late as adulthood – when they made a conscious decision to change their accent. Usually this change was not forced upon them. They simply changed in order to fit in with the people around them or so as not to sound different.

In some cases people adopt a local regional accent – scientists and entertainers who go to work in the United States usually return with a pronounced American accent. Very often, though, people lose their regional accent and copy features of the 'standard' accent used by many of their teachers and the voices on television or radio.

This accent is known as **received pronunciation (RP)** and will be explored further later in this unit.

Perhaps the most famous story about a deliberate attempt to change an accent is George Bernard Shaw's *Pygmalion*, a play first produced in 1914.

Professor Higgins is an expert in accent and dialect. Having met the flower-seller Eliza Doolittle, he bets his friend Colonel Pickering that he can teach Eliza to change her accent so convincingly that she will pass for a duchess in London society.

In the extract below, we see Eliza before her transformation during her first lesson.

Higgins: Say your alphabet.

Liza: I know my alphabet. Do you think I know nothing? I don't need to be taught like a child.

Higgins: (*thundering*) Say your alphabet.

Pickering: Say it, Miss Doolittle. You will understand presently. Do what he tells you; and let him teach you in his own way.

Liza: Oh well, if you put it like that – Ahyee, bəyee, cəyee, dəyee –

Higgins: (*with the roar of a wounded lion*) Stop. Listen to this, Pickering. This is what we pay for as elementary education. This unfortunate animal has been locked up for nine years in school at our expense to teach her to speak and read the language of Shakespear and Milton. And the result is Ahyee, Bə-yee, Cə-yee, Də-yee. (*To Eliza*) Say A, B, C, D.

Liza: (*almost in tears*) But I'm sayin it. Ahyee, Bəyee, Cə-yee –

Higgins: Stop. Say a cup of tea.

Liza: A cappə tə-ee.

Higgins: Put your tongue forward until it squeezes against the top of your lower teeth. Now say cup.

Liza: C-c-c – I can't. C-Cup.

Pickering: Good. Splendid, Miss Doolittle.

Higgins: By Jupiter, she's done it at the first shot. Pickering: we shall make a duchess of her. (*To Eliza*) Now do you think you could possibly say tea? Not tə-yee, mind: if you ever say bə-yee cə-yee də-yee again you shall be dragged round the room three times by the hair of your head. (*Fortissimo*) T, T, T, T.

Liza: (*weeping*) I can't hear no difference cep that it sounds more genteel-like when you say it.

Higgins: Well, if you can hear that difference, what the devil are you crying for? Pickering: give her a chocolate.

Pickering: No, no. Never mind crying a little, Miss Doolittle: you are doing very well; and the lessons won't hurt. I promise you I won't let him drag you round the room by your hair.

Towards the end of the play, after her triumph in 'high-class' society, Eliza has learned far more than the business of speaking with a different accent as the following extract shows.

Liza: But do you know what began my real education?

Pickering: What?

Liza: (*stopping her work for a moment*) Your calling me Miss Doolittle that day when I first came to Wimpole Street. That was the beginning of self-respect for me. (*She resumes her stitching.*) And there were a hundred little things you never noticed, because they came naturally to you. Things about standing up and taking off your hat and opening doors –

Pickering: Oh, that was nothing.

Liza: Yes: things that shewed you thought and felt about me as if I were something better than a scullery-maid; though of course I know you would have been just the same to a scullery-maid if she had been let into the drawing room. You never took off your boots in the dining room when I was there.

Pickering: You mustn't mind that. Higgins takes off his boots all over the place.

Liza: I know. I am not blaming him. It is his way, isn't it? But it made such a difference to me that you didn't do it. You see, really and truly, apart from the things anyone can pick up (the dressing and the proper way of speaking, and so on), the difference between a lady and a flower girl is not how she behaves, but how she's treated. I shall always be a flower girl to Professor Higgins, because he always treats me as a flower girl, and always will; but I know I can be a lady to you, because you always treat me as a lady, and always will.

Mrs Higgins: Please don't grind your teeth, Henry.

Pickering: Well, this is really very nice of you, Miss Doolittle.

Liza: I should like you to call me Eliza, now, if you would.

Pickering: Thank you. Eliza, of course.

Liza: And I should like Professor Higgins to call me Miss Doolittle.

Higgins: I'll see you damned first.

Mrs Higgins: Henry! Henry!

Pickering: (*laughing*) Why don't you slang back at him? Don't stand it. It would do him a lot of good.

Liza: I can't. I could have done it once; but now I can't go back to it. You told me, you know, that when a child is brought to a foreign country, it picks up the language in a few weeks, and forgets its own. Well, I am a child in your country. I have forgotten my own language, and can speak nothing but yours. That's the real break-off with the corner of Tottenham Court Road.

Comparing the language

1 Compare Eliza's speech in the extracts. How successful has Shaw's attempt been to give an impression of Eliza's accent through:
   - his use of phonetic symbols
   - his spelling
2 'The difference between a lady and a flower girl is not how she behaves, but how she's treated.'

What lessons are there in this about how we should respond to other people's accents?

3 Look at Eliza's final speech. What are the possible gains and losses of trying to change your accent in this way (or, indeed, in any way)?

Phonetics

To represent the way Eliza speaks, Shaw writes:

   ahyee, bəyee, cəyee, dəyee

The odd-looking upside-down 'e' is called **schwa** and is one of the symbols of the phonetic alphabet.

   Dictionaries usually employ some form of phonetic alphabet to indicate how words are pronounced.

Received pronunciation

Eliza's 'ahyee, bəyee, cəyee, dəyee' is part of her class accent and also her regional accent, which we might call 'working-class London' or 'cockney'. The pronunciations given in dictionaries, however, are based upon the sounds of an accent called *received pronunciation* (known for convenience as RP). This accent is sometimes also known as 'BBC English', as, until recently, all BBC national announcers and news readers spoke in this accent.

Accent and region

Many television correspondents and presenters have become famous for their individual style of presentation and reporting.

How many main-channel news reporters and presenters can you name who speak with an accent other than received pronunciation?

A survey of accents

1 Conduct a survey of accents that you hear on television or radio programmes. You could do this over a few days (or however long it takes you to collect a reasonable sample). For the purposes of the research, confine yourself to:
   - national (rather than regional) channels
   - a maximum of five entries from any one programme
   - the categories of presenter or character listed A to F in the panel opposite

Categories:

A News presenters

B Weather reporters

C Special correspondents, e.g. 'our Finance correspondent'; 'our correspondent in Moscow', etc.

D Presenters of current affairs programmes, e.g. *Panorama* or *World in action*

E Characters in British-made situation comedies

F Members of Parliament and spokespersons of major organisations, e.g. Oxfam, trades unions, etc.

Contribution:

It is also useful to record whether a particular person's contribution is a major one. e.g. the main presenter or character, or a minor one, e.g. as a guest being interviewed or a minor character.

2 A convenient means of recording this information will be to put it on a database. This would give you the opportunity to add to it later or to select particular kinds of information for study.

. Alternatively, you could present your data on a chart like this:

Television/radio accent survey

Date	Name	Cat.	Programme	Accent	Appearances: Major Minor Contribution to the programme	
4 June	Ian McCaskill	B	Weather report	Scottish	✓	

3 When you have completed your survey, discuss your findings. Are there any patterns? For example,

- What is the proportion of non-RP speakers in each category? (Which categories have most of them? How do you account for this?)
- Are there categories in which non-RP speakers make as many 'major' contributions as RP speakers?
- Divide your speakers into 'serious' (e.g. news presenters) and 'non-serious' (e.g. comedy characters). Compare the proportion of RP to non-RP speakers.

4 If your statistics have raised some interesting issues, you might consider writing to the major television/radio channels, asking for a statement of their policy on the use of non-RP accents in particular categories of programmes.

For more on formal letter writing see Unit 5 in the Process of Writing module, pages 111-114.

5 Using your research and what you have learned from discussion, write a report of your findings, entitled 'Accent on British television and radio'.

First witness for the prosecution

'I am appalled by the sloppy English spoken these days by most television and radio presenters. Only last night one announcer declared that "*Twel'th Night* would be on in February". Not content with leaving sounds out, your news readers also put unwanted sounds in! It was some weeks before I realised that Laura Norder was not a female politician!'

(*A viewer*)

Second witness for the prosecution

'The other day, I had three applicants for one job. The first one called our company " 'Ills and 'Arris". The second talked about "comin' " to work and "arrivin' " on time. The third told me he played "foo'ball".'

(*From the Managing Director, Hills and Harris plc.*)

Third witness for the prosecution

'It's not fair or right that kids from Brixton are told it's OK to talk the way they do, when it's a monstrous depressant to their chances in life.'

(*Peter York, Marketing Consultant*)

Fourth witness for the prosecution

'We have to choose between the museum approach, which keeps these accents on in glass cases even though they are rotting the chances of the people who use them, or we recognise that the world would be a drearier but a fairer place if we got rid of them.'

(*Professor John Honey*)

Assignments

1 From what you have learned in this unit, what are your attitudes to accent?
The language users mentioned here are on trial for 'mugging the Queen's English' and, in particular, not pronouncing it 'correctly'.

2 In groups of 5, discuss the evidence of the first witness for the Prosecution and the first answering statement for the Defence.
Using your knowledge of accent, decide

24

– the case comes to court

First witness for the defence

'We always need to remind ourselves that speech came first, in the history of our species, and that we all learn to speak before we learn to write. To be worried about our pronunciation because it does not match the spelling is a strange reversal of priorities.'

(*Professor David Crystal*)

Second witness for the defence

'...the loss of h causes very little confusion, if any at all. It could therefore be claimed that accents without h are in a sense more "efficient" than those with...dropping your ts...is not an accurate description. The t is there – it is simply pronounced as a glottal stop...'

(*Dr Peter Trudgill*)

Third witness for the defence

'Teaching written Standard English is relatively unproblematic, but so much of speech is below the level of conscious control, that it is very hard to alter.'

(*The National Association for the Teaching of English, reporting on The National Curriculum Working Party on English*)

Fourth witness for the defence

'...the new National Curriculum contains no requirement to teach received pronunciation... the curriculum requires only that children be taught "to speak Standard English in an accent which is clear and comprehensible".'

(*Rosalind Sharpe, The Independent on Sunday*)

whose argument you most sympathise with.

Take a vote on whether you support the Prosecution or the Defence in this case.

Now do the same with the other three opposing pairs of witnesses.

3 Add up your group votes and compare them with the class as a whole to determine whether the defendants are guilty or innocent.

The way we speak: dialect

Dialect vocabulary

In the Middle Ages, as we have seen in Unit 1, there were several different dialects of English.

   John of Trevisa wrote about the problems that Northerners and Southerners had in understanding each other (see page 11); and it is not surprising when we consider what variations there were at that time even in common words.

This map charts the different words that people used for the pronoun 'she' in the Middle Ages:

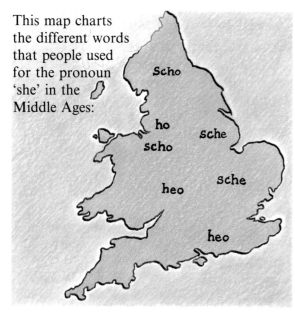

Perhaps it goes some way towards explaining the different dialect words for 'she' in Modern English.

Where does your dialect fit in on this map? What word does it have for 'she'?

Covered in fernytickles!

Do you have a local dialect word for 'freckles'?
It is quite possible that you will know them as...
   ferntickles fernytickles speckles frackens
   mirfles muffles summer moles
   brantickles...
In fact there are a large number of words in Standard English dialect which have regional alternatives.

1 Consider each of the following Standard English forms and some of their regional dialect variations. How many have you encountered before? Can you 'place' many of them in regions?
   Children: bairns weans childer
   Newt: ask eft asp esp asker swift evet ebbet
   Cow shed: byre shippon mistal cow house neat house skeeling beast house cow hovel cow lodge
   Funnel: tunnel tundish tunniger vunnel
   Infectious: smittin smittle catching catchy smittlin
   To make tea: mask mash brew wet soak
   Stream: burn beck brook
2 A particularly interesting one is 'left-handed'. Regional alternatives include:
   kervag corrie-flug cuddy-wifted marlborough...
   There are also a number of expressions ending ' -handed':
   pally- kippy- corrie- carr- cowie- gally- gawky- dollock- keggy- watty- keck- kack- scrammy- scutchy- squiver-
2 What do phrases such as 'kack-handed', 'gammy-handed', or 'gawky-handed' suggest about attitudes to left-handedness?
3 Use a dictionary to find the origin of the word 'sinister'. That casts interesting light on the subject of attitudes towards left and right.

Dialect grammar

The following extract is an example of Hampshire dialect.

Hearing cuckoos

I 'eard cuckoo 'smarnin'. I 'eard 'en. I 'eard 'en go 'Cuckoo. Cuckoo.' I were just thinkin' about gettin' out o' bed when I 'eard 'en, so I says to missus, 'Missus, can you 'ear cuckoo?' 'Er never answered I. 'Er were aslape. So I gives 'er a bit of a shake, careful like, and I says, 'Missus. Can yer year cuckoo?' She did open 'er eyes then and looked at I a bit agity like.

  'Wha' does say?'

  'I says, 'Can yer year cuckoo?'

  ' 'Ear cuckoo? No, I can't 'ear na cuckoo.'

  'Well, thee bide quiet and listen.'

  So we bade quite and then we 'ears 'en again: 'Cuckoo. Cuckoo.'

  'Dun't sound like cuckoo to me,' missus says.

  'Well, I don't know no other bird as do say "Cuckoo", dost thee?'

  She says, 'Oh, I don't know. I be goin' back to slape. Wakin' I up to year cuckoo! Thee get off up to milkin' else thee sh'll be late.'

  So I pulls on me trousers and I puts on me boots and I was just goin' on down past the boy's door when 'e 'ollers out, 'Fayther! Didst hear cuckoo?'

  I says, 'Ah.'

  'Well, you come on, on in 'ere and you can see 'en. ''E be sittin' in timber top by Miss 'Ayley's cottage.'

  I says, 'Well, I knew 'e wasn't fer away.'

  So I goes in wi' boy and we looks through winder and there 'e were, sittin' up on timber top up by Miss 'Ayley's cottage.

  I looks at 'en and I looks at 'en and I says, 'That bain't nah cuckoo, boy. That be pigeon!'

Standard English dialect

All of us, whether we realise it or not, are dialect speakers. And many of us speak more than one dialect.

The most widely known of all these varieties is Standard English dialect, the one that had its origin in the East Midlands dialect of Middle English. It is the one that foreign children learn in their schools and the one heard most frequently on television and radio. It is also the one that is almost invariably used in writing.

Why use Standard English dialect in writing?

Read each of the following pieces, A to D, which are written in a regional dialect.
1 Discuss each piece in pairs. How do you react to the fact that it is not in Standard English?
2 a) What exactly are the disadvantages of using a non-standard dialect in each case? For example,
 ● do the ideas come across less clearly?
 ● were there words which the writer needed but which could not be found in the regional dialect?
 ● do you take the passage less seriously because it is not in Standard English?
 b) Do any of the passages seem more appropriate in the non-standard dialect?

A When a language do cease to change, it is what us calls a dead language. Classical Latin be a dead language, for it have not changed for nearly two thousand year. I don't say nothing about legal Latin, though.

C **WEANS MUST BE CARRIED ON THE ESCALATOR**

B The Chancellor said she wouldn't take no responsibility for the current level of inflation. It was the oil crisis what done it, she said. In response to criticism of her junior minister's perform-ance, she reckoned he had done brilliant and said that him and her was to meet in the next couple of days.

Dear pen-pal,
You ask me about Sundays.
Usually I think I live in the poorest back-o-wall bush place. Yet maybe this Caribbean village here help to sharpen up Sunday happenings. So, I love Sundays. I not forgetting that dressing-up is a Sunday main-feature. And Sunday has best food. I like how it's different. Me and my big brother walk to church and no need saying we in our best clothes.

So it is possible to write in a non-standard dialect; but it is more appropriate at some times than at others. A well written piece in a non-standard dialect can be written with one or more of the following purposes in mind:
● to reflect something special and personal about the writer's background or character
● to suit the subject matter
● to make the reader sit up and take notice, as something different and fresh
● to have some of the liveliness of spoken English
● to seem less formal than Standard English
● to make the process of writing more interesting and varied for us as writers

Non-standard dialect can also be used to bring new life to an old story. This one was written by Lesley Alexander, a Year 8 pupil in Gosforth, Tyne and Wear.

The magpied piper of Newcastle-on-Tyne

Thor wes yence a toon caaled Newcastle-on-Tyne an' this toon wes full o' moggies. Thor wes moggies aal ower, moggies gobblin spuggies an' gliffin bairns, nickin tetties an' yowling aal neet. Soon the toon's folk wes really sick. They went to the Pollis an' yammered, 'Yees are aal fyuls. Thor ir moggies runnin aal ower. Howway, man, dee sommic.'

They hadn't been there lang when a fella appeared. The gaffer says 'Who are ye an' what de ye want?' 'Me name is Magpied Piper an' aa've come te help ye get rid o' the moggies.' 'An how are yee ganni de that?' asked the gaffer. 'Wi' me secret pipe full o' baccy.'

The weird fella had a black 'n white ganzie, dut, byuts an' troosers, just like the footy strip. 'Aal reet,' the gaffer says, 'We'll gi' ye a gan but meend, if ye divvent succeed, we'll poss ye in a posstub an' hoy ye doon a moudiewarp. But if ye de get rid o' the moggies we'll gi' ye a thoosand punds.'

The next day the Magpied Piper waalked through the lonnens blooin on his pipe full o' magic secret baccy. Soon the moggies come oot o' the hooses. They wes hacky wi' muck, an' there wes midgeys aal ower. Thor wes broon, black an' white moggies an' loads more different colours. Aal the folks followed the Magpied Piper until they come te the Tyne. An' aal the moggies fell ower the edge inte the hacky river.

Aaal the folks were yowling with fun an' doon the Bigg market the gaffer an' the Magpied Piper wes crackin. When the Magpied Piper said, 'Where's me thoosand punds?' 'You're not getting it!' 'If ye divvent giz me money aal nick aal your bairns.' 'Hadaway, man, ye wouldn't dare.' 'Ye just wait!!!!'

So the Magpied Piper put some more baccy inte his pipe an' went back inte the lonnens agyen. Soon aal the bairns came runnin an' followed the Magpied Piper. They wes gettin further an' further away from their hymes an' nearer an' nearer Tynemouth. They was gettin near Whitley Bay beach when they come te a fish an' chip shop.

The door oppened an' the Magpied Piper an' aal the bairns skipped in. The door closed ahint them an' they was never seen agyen.

Aal except from little Geordie who wes lame an' couldn't keep up wi' the wee bairns. When he got te the fish 'n chip shop aal the shutters was up, an' thor wes a big seyn in the winder saying,
'Nee chips left'
The moral o' this tale is:
If ye promise someone somic, divvent gan back on your word.'

Retelling a story in dialect

1 In order to see how cleverly Lesley has updated the original story, compare her version with a copy of Robert Browning's poem, *The pied piper of Hamlin*. With a partner discuss:
   ● the similarities between the two versions
   ● the changes that have been made
   For more on myths and legends see Unit 4 in the Forms of Narrative module in Book 4A.

2 If you are able to use your local dialect, try rewriting a well-known tale in the way that Lesley has.
   Notice how she has:
   ● used dialect vocabulary, e.g. 'dut', 'ganzie', 'gliffin'
   ● represented the accent, e.g. 'Thor wes yence'
   ● used the grammar of the dialect, e.g. 'The gaffer says'

3 If it is not possible to write in your local dialect, try the exercise in Standard English dialect.

The Queen's speech

Each year at the State opening of Parliament in November, the monarch reads out a statement prepared for her by the government of the day, which lists all the things that they propose to do in the coming year. It is known as 'The Queen's speech'.

As we might expect it is in Standard English dialect (see page 28 for more on this) and the accent known as received pronunciation (for more details see page 22). But when such a traditional and conventional speech is presented to us in a non-standard dialect, the effects on the reader or listener can be quite dramatic. We might be amused; we might be shocked; we are certainly shaken into seeing things in a new light.

Today sees the State Opening of Parliament, a glorious fusion of pomp and pomposity and the Government's opportunity to chart the way ahead. Rastafarian poet **Benjamin Zephaniah** (right) offers the monarch an alternative speech for the occasion

De Kings Speech

ME DEAR Larrds an Membas of de Dread House. I an I look forward wid great pleasure to receiving Spike Lee de King of Fine Arts an to being present at de Liberation Day celebrations in South Africa.

I government will stand fully by their obligations to de Natural African Togetherness Organisation (Nato) Alliance. They will sustain I an I contribution to de planets defence by pressing fe Western Civilisation (ASAP) an by increasing de effectiveness of our Anti-Poll tax forces.

I government will strive fe balanced an verifiable measures of thought freedom. They strongly oppose de Americans and de Russians proposals fe de 50 per cent reduction of strategic nuclear weapons, and dem talk bout balanced reductions leading to lower levels of conventional weapons. I government seh get rid a every one a dem, right now, dem too damn expensive mek we feed de masses.

I government is a little suspicious bout peace East and West up North when nobody nar deal wid de South, dem will tek measures to ensure dat alongside a United States of America an a United States of Europe there is a United States of Africa as agreed at de Congress of Marcus Garvey which will work alongside a United States of Asia to dismantle de barriers of trade, religion, sex, creed an class. I government will play a leading role in de development of a united non-warmongering alliance while safeguarding Broadwater Farm and other peace-loving communities. They will work fe de reforms of de Housing Bill, an mek house fe people.

They will not make chemical weapons an will therefore not need to control dem.

I government will sustain de fight against international hypocrisy an de trafficking of silly ideas.

They will stand by their pledges to de people of Palestine and East Timor while seeking more normal relations with Michael Jackson. They will fulfil their responsibilities to de people of Tibet and I and I will not co-operate wid de Chinese government until dem start freeing imprisoned an oppressed Kung Fu films which are much better dan de crap dat comes outta Hong Kong.

I an I will play an honest part in de United Nations an dat means sticking to all resolutions an not just ones dat suit dem. Dem will stick to de letters of de 'Commonwealth' an dat means meking common people wealthy.

I government will not arm crazy dictators who rule countries that we invented just because dem is we fren, because when dem is not we fren we have fe work bloody hard fe bullshit de people wid de help of de Gutter Press, I an I government would be unwilling to cooperate wid people in low places, anyway, how low can yu go?

Me dear Larrds an Membas of de Dread House I government will continue to pursue de policies of sound financial management, all speakers over 10 inches shall be non-taxable, status quo will go an Jah Shaka will be given lots a money so dat de breeda can dub de world in accordance wid de treaty of dance which was signed at de Riddim Convention in Trench Town, Jamaica.

I government will consult de Womanpower Services Commission wid a view to providing a comprehensive re-education of men.

There will be guaranteed places on training schemes for fallen high powered money loving, greedy belly, dibby dibby, one time yuppie, living duppy, pounds crazy city financiers in order to readjust dem into de real world an prepare dem fe de truth.

I government will introduce legislation to provide a wicked curriculum fe de schools dem.

Measures will be introduced to promote a well run International Health Service, available to all on request wid nice operating theatres so dat mummy an daddy can mek funny faces to each other in comfort when gay, joyful, cheerful guys like me pop out.

I government find it very odd to suggest dat water be privatised, why corrupt a natural system an confuse de clouds wid de idea dat dem a drop dom private parts.

A bill will be introduce to outlaw an mash down immigration controls. A bill will be introduce to pay wages fe housework. A bill will be introduce to give greater flexibility to yoga teachers.

A bill will be introduce to control all culture vultures and phase out de term 'world music' so people can respect all music fe what it is an not just as non-European music dat sounds really good wid French wine and bent knees.

A bill will be introduce to control Frank Bruno (when we find him). A bill will be introduce to abolish de vagrancy act an replace it wid a social conscience. A bill will be introduce to privatise de monarchy. A bill will be introduce to keep Ben company.

Other measures will be laid before you. Yu can touch dem if yu wash yu hands.

Me dear Larrds an Membas of de Dread House. I am outta here. Peace.

The Guardian 7 November 1990

Not the Queen's English

1 Discuss and make notes on your reactions to *De Kings speech*.
   a) Talk over any words or phrases that are at first sight difficult to understand.
   b) Pick a section of ten or twelve lines that is a good example of the dialect. Rewrite it in Standard English and then discuss how effective the new version is when compared with the original!
   c) List some of the examples of:
   - political references that you would expect to find in a traditional Queen's Speech, e.g. to East-West relations
   - references that you would not expect to find, e.g. to Michael Jackson!
   d) Now look at the language used.
   - Which expressions – quite apart from those which are dialect features – would you not expect to hear uttered by Her Majesty?
   - What effect do they have on you? Are you amused? Offended?
   e) Look through your responses to questions a) to d) and then summarise which parts of the speech were successful in:
   - amusing you
   - shocking, or at least surprising, you
   - making a serious point in an unusual but appropriate way
   In each case, how was the writer assisted by writing in non-standard dialect?
2 Using the notes that you have taken, write an appreciation of *De Kings speech* as a newspaper article. It might be helpful to use the five points a) to e) above as the basic paragraph structure of your piece.

Creoles

To understand more about the dialect features of *De Kings speech*, we need to look at the development of a particular kind of English.

Between the Seventeenth and Nineteenth centuries around four million black people were taken from Africa to the Caribbean by Europeans as slaves. This map shows how new Afro-Caribbean languages developed, known as **creoles**.

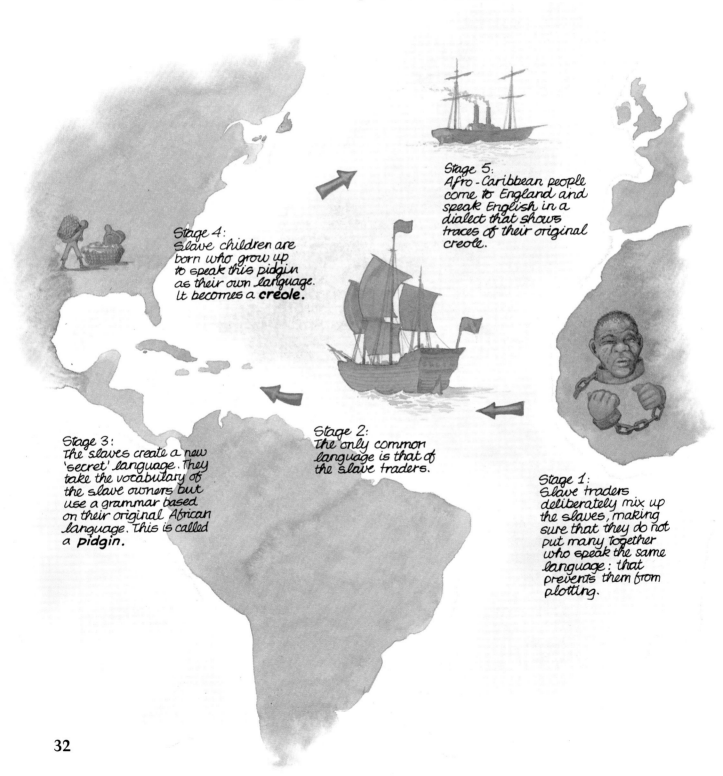

Stage 5:
Afro-Caribbean people come to England and speak English in a dialect that shows traces of their original creole.

Stage 4:
Slave children are born who grow up to speak this pidgin as their own language. It becomes a **creole**.

Stage 3:
The slaves create a new 'secret' language. They take the vocabulary of the slave owners but use a grammar based on their original African language. This is called a **pidgin**.

Stage 2:
The only common language is that of the slave traders.

Stage 1:
Slave traders deliberately mix up the slaves, making sure that they do not put many together who speak the same language: that prevents them from plotting.

Creoles are distinct languages with their own rules. They are not crude forms of 'broken' English or 'bad talk' and, as with all languages, have their own poetry.

Six o'clock feeling

You ever feel
dat 6 o'clock shadow falling
wrappin' you up
meking you stop
an tink
bout all dese tings
God doin
6 o'clock bee calling
All dem tree
tekking strange, strange shape
an stan up
sharp! sharp! gainst dat sky
You know dem 6 o'clock colour
pink an orange an blue an purple an black

dat 6 o'clock feeling
mekkin you feel like touchin
mekkin you feel so small
you could cry
or fall down pun you knee
and thank God
you could still
see He 6 o'clock sky

Kamal Singh

Looking at the dialect

Discuss the features of the language in this poem, comparing it with *De Kings speech*. Try writing some of it in Standard English dialect. What does this version lack?

Zephaniah's creole grammar

In *De Kings speech*, Benjamin Zephaniah occasionally uses dialect forms which derive from an original Caribbean creole language. Some people would call a dialect like this British Jamaican English.

See how many examples of the following features you can find in Zephaniah's article. Zephaniah's dialect tends to:

1 use the personal pronoun for the possessive pronoun, e.g. 'I book' for 'my book'
2 have plurals without final -s
3 use object pronouns, e.g. 'him', 'them' as subject pronouns, e.g. 'he', 'they'
4 use 'fe' where Standard English would use 'to' before an infinitive, e.g. 'fe go' – 'to go'
5 enjoy repetition
6 use 'dem' (which doesn't in this case mean 'them') to draw attention to the word before
7 use 'mek' to mean 'allow', 'let' or 'permit'

De Head's speech

Imagine that you are giving the Headteacher's annual report to the parents and governors at a school speech day, prize-giving or annual meeting. You decide that it might liven things up to give the speech in Zephaniah's dialect with all its Caribbean creole influences.

Write 'De Head's speech' inventing some new and unconventional aims for the coming school year.

Dialect in literature

Throughout the ages writers have tried to represent dialect in literature – some with more success than others. Extracts A to D are examples of dialect in literature from different periods and cultures. Read each of them through out loud and then look at the work on dialect that follows.

A: Henry V

It is a few days after the Battle of Agincourt in which Henry's army has defeated the French. Fluellen and Gower are two of Henry's captains. Fluellen is explaining to his comrade that he is wearing a leek in defiance of a soldier called Ancient (or Ensign) Pistol.

Gower: Nay, that's right; but why wear you your leek to-day? Saint Davy's day is past.

Fluellen: There is occasions and causes why and wherefore in all things: I will tell you, asse my friend, Captain Gower. The rascally, scauld, beggarly, lousy, pragging knave, Pistol, which you and yourself and all the world know to be no petter than a fellow, look you now, of no merits, he is come to me and prings me pread and salt yesterday, look you, and bid me eat my leek. It was in a place where I could not breed no contention with him; but I will be so bold as to wear it in my cap till I see him once again, and then I will tell him a little piece of my desires.

(*Enter* Pistol)

Gower: Why, here he comes, swelling like a turkey-cock.

Fluellen: 'Tis no matter for his swellings nor his turkey-cocks. God pless you, Aunchient Pistol! you scurvy, lousy knave, God pless you!

Pistol: Ha! art thou bedlam? dost thou thirst, base Trojan
To have me fold up Parca's fatal web?
Hence! I am qualmish at the smell of leek.

Fluellen: I peseech you heartily, scurvy lousy knave, at my desires and my requests and my petitions to eat, look you, this leek; because, look you, you do not love it, nor your affections and your appetites and your disgestions doo's not agree with it, I would desire you to eat it.

Pistol: Not for Cadwallader and all his goats.

Fluellen: There is one goat for you. (*Strikes him*) Will you be so good, scauld knave, as eat it?

Pistol: Base Trojan, thou shalt die.

(Act V Scene 1)

William Shakespeare

Note: the way in which the language not only shows the difference between dialects, but also the difference between characters. Compare Gower's language with Pistol's, for example. Why do you think Gower and Fluellen say 'you' but Pistol 'thou'? What link is there between this and his use of classical and legendary references (Cadwallader, Parca, Trojan)?

Look again at Fluellen's speeches. Given that Shakespeare has presented us in this play with an Englishman, an Irishman, a Scotsman and a Welshman, is it possible that he is perhaps deliberately exaggerating the features of language, in order to create a stereotype? (You might find it useful to read some of the speeches of the Irishman, Macmorris. Look, for example, at Act III Scene 2.)

B: Kes

The English teacher, Mr Farthing, has asked a boy called Anderson to tell the class something really interesting about himself.

'Well it was once when I was a kid. I was at Junior school, I think, or somewhere like that, and went down to Fowlers Pond, me and this other kid. Reggie Clay they called him, he didn't come to this school; he flitted and went away somewhere. Anyway it was Spring, tadpole time, and it's swarming with tadpoles down there in Spring. Edges of t'pond are all black with 'em, and me and this other kid started to catch 'em. It was easy, all you did, you just put your hands together and scooped a handful of water up and you'd got a handful of tadpoles. Anyway we were mucking about with 'em, picking 'em up and chucking 'em back and things, and we were on about taking some home, but we'd no jam jars. So this kid, Reggie, says, "Take thi wellingtons off and put some in there, they'll be all right 'til tha gets home." So I took 'em off and we put some water in 'em and then we started to put taddies in 'em. We kept ladling 'em in and I says to this kid, "Let's have a competition, thee have one welli' and I'll have t'other, and we'll see who can get most in!" So he started to fill one welli' and I started to fill t'other. We must have been at it hours, and they got thicker and thicker, until at t'end there was no water left in 'em, they were just jam packed wi'taddies.

'You ought to have seen 'em, all black and shiny, right up to t'top. When we'd finished we kept dipping us fingers into 'em and whipping 'em up at each other, all shouting and excited like. Then this kid says to me, "I bet tha daren't put one on." And I says, "I bet tha daren't."

So we said we'd put one on each. We wouldn't though, we kept reckoning to, then running away, so we tossed up and him who lost had to do it first. And I lost, oh, and you'd to take your socks off an' all. So I took my socks off, and I kept looking at this welli' full of taddies, and this kid kept saying, "Go on then, tha frightened, tha frightened." I was an' all. Anyway I shut my eyes and started to put my foot in. Oooo. It was just like putting your feet into live jelly. They were frozen. And when my foot went down, they all came over t'top of my wellington, and when I got my foot to t'bottom, I could fell 'em all squashing about between my toes.

'Anyway I'd done it, and I says to this kid, "Thee put thine on now." But he wouldn't, he was dead scared, so I put it on instead. I'd got used to it then, it was all right after a bit; it sent your legs all excited and tingling like. When I'd got 'em both on I started to walk up to this kid, waving my arms and making spook noises; and as I walked they all came squelching over t'tops again and ran down t'sides. This kid looked frightened to death, he kept looking down at my wellies so I tried to run at him and they all spurted up my legs. You ought to have seen him. He just screamed out and ran home roaring.

'It was a funny feeling though when he'd gone; all quiet, with nobody there, and up to t'knees in tadpoles.'

Barry Hines

Note: the differences between the sections where Anderson is telling the story to the class and the sections where he is reporting his own and Reggie Clay's actual speech.

C: A thief in the village

The narrator, a little boy, is describing his journey to church on Sundays.
Occasionally he meets a boy called Harness.

I see that troublesome boy who's much older than me, that Harness-'n'-Bigtoe.
He rushes up beside me and begins to walk with me. 'Harness' is called that because
his clothes are usually so much rags, that his body is as much exposed as a harness-
ed horse or mule. Then, also, he has big feet with large big toes.

I don't dislike everything about 'Harness' at all. Harness is the best boy cricketer
to watch batting, hitting sixes. Also, as a fielder, no ball passes his quick-quick long
limbs. But, Harness smokes. He swears. He teases girls badly. And, last Sunday,
Harness is the same one who made a puddle splash my clothes and caused me to
turn back and miss church. I decide I will say nothing to Harness. Absolutely
nothing!

Hear Harness to me, 'Bwoy. Dohn yu know yu frien'? I is yu frien'. Why yu
wastin' time goin' church? Eh, bwoy? Dohn yu know Satan-life much sweet-sweet
more dan sainty-sainty life. Yu can come wid we teday. Me an' Lanky an' Roadman
an' Duds an' Duke an' everybody curryin' a goat down a Levelland. We goin'
drink up rum an' t'ing an' get cool swimmin' in-a river. Come, bwoy. Com wid we.
Yu goin' come?'

I shake my head.   **Note:** as with the passage from *Kes*, the difference between the
narrator's language 'to the reader' and Harness's language 'to the boy'.

James Berry

D: Cold Comfort Farm

As both her parents have died, Flora Poste (addressed here as 'Robert Poste's child')
has decided to come and live with her relatives, the Starkadders, at the suitably
named Cold Comfort Farm. This is the scene at breakfast.

Adam shuffled forward into the light. His eyes were like slits of primitive flint in
their worn sockets. Flora wondered if he ever washed.

'There's porridge, Robert Poste's child.'

'Is there any bread and butter and some tea? I don't much care for porridge.
And have you a piece of clean newspaper I could just put on the corner of this table
(a half-sheet will be enough) to protect me from the porridge? It seems to have got
tossed about a bit this morning, doesn't it?'

'There's tea i' the jar, yonder, and bread and butter i' the crocket. Ye mun find
'em yourself, Robert Poste's child. I have my task to do and my watch to keep, and
I cannot run here and run there to fetch newspapers for a capsy wennet. Besides,
we've troubles enough at Cold Comfort wi'out bringing in sich a thing as a
clamourin' newspaper to upset us and fritten us.'

'Oh, have you? What troubles?' asked Flora, interestedly, as she busily made fresh
tea. It occurred to her that this might be a good opportunity to learn something
about the other members of the family. 'Haven't you enough money?'

For she knew that this is what is the matter with nearly everybody over twenty-
five.

'There's money enough i' the farm, Robert Poste's child, but 'tes all turned to
sourness and ruin. I tell ye' – here Adam advanced nearer to the interested Flora

and thrust his lined and wrinkled face, indelibly etched by the corrosive acids of his dim, monotonous years, almost into hers – 'there's a curse on Cold Comfort'.

'Indeed!' said Flora, withdrawing slightly. 'What sort of a curse? Is that why everything looked so gone to seed and what not?'

'There's no seeds, Robert Poste's child. That's what I'm tellin' ye. The seeds wither as they fall into the ground, and the earth will not nourish 'em. The cows are barren and the sows are farren and the King's Evil and the Queen's Bane and the Prince's Heritage ravages our crops. 'Cos why? 'Cos there's a curse on us, Robert Poste's child.'

'But, look here, couldn't something be done about it? I mean, surely Cousin Amos could get a man down from London or something – (This bread is really not at all bad, you know. Surely you don't bake it here.) – Or perhaps Cousin Amos could sell the farm and buy another one, without any curse on it, in Berkshire or Devonshire?'

Adam shook his head. A curious veil, like the withdrawing of intelligence from the eyes of a tortoise, flickered across his face.

'Nay. There have always been Starkadders at Cold Comfort. 'Tes impossible for any on us to dream o' leavin' here. There's reasons why we can't. Mrs Starkadder, she's sot on us stayin' here. 'Tes her life, 'tes the life in her veins.'

Stella Gibbons

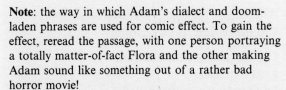

Note: the way in which Adam's dialect and doom-laden phrases are used for comic effect. To gain the effect, reread the passage, with one person portraying a totally matter-of-fact Flora and the other making Adam sound like something out of a rather bad horror movie!

Make a guess at what a 'capsy wennet' is? Check the meaning of parody and then look at Adam's dialect features again.

For more on parody see the Poetry module in Book 4A, page 114.

Looking at dialect features

1 Discuss the particular features that you are asked to 'Note' at the foot of each passage.
2 Write down and discuss the features of the dialect that the writer has attempted to represent, paying particular attention to those that have been marked.
3 Decide which dialect is being represented in each extract and how effectively the writing conveys the particular qualities of that dialect.

Assignment

Units 2 and 3 have contained many examples of the ways in which writers have attempted to write in a non-standard dialect.

Usually they do this only to represent the way certain characters speak, and the rest of the work is written in Standard English. Occasionally, though, and for a particular purpose, they write whole passages in a regional dialect.

Write a piece on 'The presentation of non-standard dialects in written English'. In planning this piece of writing:

- use the examples from Units 2 and 3 and any others you find in your own reading and research
- explore the different methods that each writer employs in order to represent the dialect
- consider the different effects that can be achieved (such as humour, interesting characterisation, sympathetic portrayal, realism, etc)
- decide which writers in your selection have been most – and which least – successful in using and representing dialect

Choosing words with care

A French lesson

j'ai fait = I made
un canard = a duck

Putting the two phrases together, 'j'ai fait un canard' plainly means 'I made a duck'
At least, that would be the **literal** meaning in each language.
But in both English and French there is a **figurative** meaning too.

In French it can mean:
'I played a bad note'
In English it can mean:
'I was out without scoring'

Other languages have phrases such as these, in which you cannot work out the meanings simply by understanding each individual word. These expressions are known as **idioms** and are special to a particular language or group of people. For example:

English: 'He's kicked the bucket.'
Spanish: 'He has stuck out his paw.'

English: 'Look before you leap.'
Arabic: 'Blow on the soup before drinking it.'

English: 'Once in a blue moon.'
Italian : 'Every death of a pope.'

Read the article opposite which shows that when someone is learning a foreign language, idioms can cause great confusion.

Working with idioms

The student in the article has enough problems with the idioms for 'put up' and 'put down'.
1 Discuss the possible meanings of these other 'puts' and illustrate each one by writing a sentence. For some there will be more than one possibility:

put back	put on	put away
put in	put into	put by
put off	put upon	put forward
put out	put under	put over
put across	put through	
put to	put about	

2 Write a conversation in which someone is having trouble with idioms.
a) If you are short of ideas, use a dictionary to find the range of idiomatic expressions involving the verbs:

do	lay	come	go	look
get	have	see	set	

b) Alternatively, base your conversation on the following 'take' idioms.

He takes after her mother.
I take it back.
She took down the details.
That took him down a peg or two.
I was completely taken in.
We take in lodgers.
My grandparents took in washing.
I took her into my confidence.
He took it into his head to leave.
I take off my hat to her.
He took himself off.
Everybody can take off that comedian.
He took on too much.
She took on the champion.
Don't take on so.
Allied planes took out five enemy aircraft.
I took my boy-friend out.
I took it out on him.
He took to humming a tune.
I really took to her.
It takes up a lot of time.
He took up with some criminals.

Could I say to the vet, 'Here is my cat, please have her sent up?'

Learning English as a second language

Part 597: Dealing with political pollsters.

Please help me. What do I say if I am stopped in the street by a man asking questions about elections? This was happening to me all the time during the general election.

You say: 'Put me down as a Don't Know'.

Put me down as a Don't Know. I see. What exactly does that mean?

It means you don't want any more questions.

I see. What does 'put me down' mean?

It means, write me down on paper.

But in lesson 413, you told me that 'put down' means to make a lot of fun of. Your sentence was 'Every comedian thinks it is funny to put down Val Doonican.'

Yes, well, it means that as well.

So maybe the man asking the questions will make fun of me?

No, no.

And in lesson 512, you said that 'put down' also means to have your favourite animal killed. Your sentence was: 'We are taking our cat to the vet for him to be put down.'

Did I? Well, yes, it means that too.

So I am afraid that the man asking the political questions will have me painlessly killed when I say 'Put me down as a Don't Know.'

No, no, he won't do that. I promise.

If 'put down' means to make fun of, I suppose 'put up' means to take seriously.

No, no. It means to accommodate for a few days. Here is another sentence for you: 'My mother has written to say she is coming to stay with us, so we will have to put her up for the weekend.'

That is a bit like a sentence I remember from lesson 87. 'I do my best to put up with your mother'.

Ah, yes, that's put up *with*.

What does 'put down with' mean?

Nothing.

Could I say 'Set me down as a Don't Know'?

No. 'Set down' means to let someone off a train at a railway station.

And 'set up' means to let them on the train at the railway station?

Mmm, not exactly. Actually, it means something the police do when all else fails. Here is another sentence for you. 'I spent three years in jail because the police set me up for the Croydon job'.

Would they do that?

Not if you'd really done the Croydon job. 'Set up,' by the way, also means to give someone lots of money. For example, my parents set me up as a teacher of English as a second language.

But the police would not give you lots of money for the Croydon job?

No, I think not.

Would it be possible to say to this man in the street: 'Send me down as a Don't Know'?

Well, not really. 'Send down' means to put someone in prison.

Oh, I see The police set you up first and then they send you down.

Yes. Well, not quite. The police set you up, but the judges send you down.

This is all done to make more jobs?

Yes, I think so.

Well, if 'send down' means to put you in prison, does 'send up' mean to get someone out of prison?

Not exactly. In fact, not at all. 'Send up' means to make a lot of fun of.

Ah, just like 'put down'. So the sentence from lesson 413 could also be: 'Every comedian thinks it is funny to send up Val Doonican'?

Very good, absolutely right. Spot on.

And I could also say to the man in the street: 'Send me up as a Don't Know'.

No.

And I could say to the vet: 'Here is my cat – please have her sent up'?

No.

English is very difficult to learn as a second language.

Believe me, English is very difficult to teach as a second language. It gets me down sometimes.

Get down? You mean, as in the phrase: 'Get down and boogie'?

Where did you learn to speak like that?

In a disco in the West End, where I also learn English as a second language.

Ah, no, that is American as a second language. Oh, just look at the time. I think that is enough for today's lesson. I must get off.

Get off with whom?

I will deal with that in our next lesson.

Miles Kington The Independent 26 June 1987

It colours what we say

A large number of idiomatic expressions in many languages involve colours.

French	faire chou blanc	to make white cabbage (to make a mess of something)
German	blau machen	to make blue (to take a holiday)
Urdu	daal maiyn koch kala hey	there is something black in the lentil curry (there is something suspicious going on)

Colour of English

With a partner discuss the following English colour idioms. In each case attempt to:
- define the meaning, giving an example if that seems helpful
- explain in what context or situation the expression might be read or heard
- find out the origin of the expression

Red
- in the red
- red-blooded
- red-letter day
- reds under the bed
- a red herring
- to see red
- red tape
- redbrick
- a red rag to a bull
- caught red-handed

Blue
- true blue
- blue chip
- blueprint
- blue blood
- blue ribbon
- feeling blue
- a hockey blue
- blue-collar worker
- blue-eyed boy
- singing the blues

And what about ...
- in the pink
- browned off
- an orangeman
- rose-tinted spectacles
- purple prose
- grey matter
- a yellow streak

Can you think of any others? Avoid expressions using black, white and green for the moment. We are coming to these.

The following illustration shows the first recorded (that is to say, written) uses of five green expressions through the ages.

And don't leave your greens

1 In pairs, write down all the expressions you know that include the words green/greens. Refer to a dictionary to check your green idioms and perhaps to find some more.

Some of these uses of green have plainly been around for a very long time. People must have talked about 'green grass' when discussing the conditions underfoot at the Battle of Hastings, and for a good while before that. Other uses, though, are comparatively recent developments.

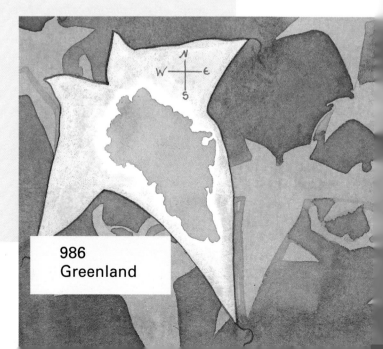

986
Greenland

40

1725
'eat your greens!'

1646
bowling green

1577
green bacon

1478
greenwood

2 Draw a simple time-chart and add some of
your own green expressions to it. One of the
large Oxford English Dictionaries in your
library will provide the dates of first recorded
uses but they may take some searching out.

Remember that a first recorded *written* use
means that a word or phrase was in the
spoken language for quite a while before that.

3 Which green phrases can only have arisen in
the Twentieth century? How do you know
this?

Words, society, and technology

It is perhaps stating the obvious to say 'green'
meaning 'an expanse of grass surrounded by
houses' could not have come into being before
villages evolved: a few dotted huts could not
have had 'a green'.

In the same way, the idea of governments discussing 'green' issues has arisen only because of
our concern with pollution, itself a side-effect of
developments in science and industry.

Words are living things. We must expect them
to take on new meanings to cope with the ways
in which society and technology themselves are
constantly changing.

Which other words that you know of have
taken on new meanings following a change in
society or technological development? To
begin with you might consider the world of
Information Technology and its new uses of
words such as 'format', 'access', 'file', 'menu',
'window', 'hack', etc.

41

It's here in black and white

One of the odd things about language is that the same word can have a pleasant or unpleasant ring to it depending on how and where it is used.

Before we move on to black and white, let's return for a moment to red and three of its uses.

- I am likely to look forward to a 'red-letter day'; it has a happy, positive sound.
- On the snooker table a 'red' could be a useful ball or otherwise, depending on the state of play, so I normally feel quite neutrally towards it.
- But I am likely to have a pretty negative and gloomy reaction to a bank statement that tells me I am 'in the red'.

Some words can cause us to react in a positive, neutral or negative way at different times. Now let's examine the word black. The following entries for black are from *The Oxford Study Dictionary*.

black *adj.* **1** of the very darkest colour, like coal or soot. **2** having a black skin. **3 Black** of or for black-skinned people; of their culture etc. **4** soiled with dirt. **5** dismal, sullen, hostile; *things look black*, not hopeful; *a black day*, disastrous. **6** evil, wicked. **7** not to be handled by trade-unionists while others are on strike, *declared the cargo black*. **-black** *n.* **1** black colour. **2** a black substance or material; black clothes. **3** the black ball in snooker etc. **4** the black men in chess etc.; the player using these. **5** the credit side of an account; *in the black*, having a credit balance. **6 Black** a black-skinned person. **-black** *v.* **1** to make black. **2** to polish with blacking. **3** to declare goods or work to be 'black'. **-blackly** *adv.*, **blackness** *n.* **black-beetle** *n.* a cockroach. **black box** an electronic device in an aircraft recording information about its flight. **black coffee** coffee without milk. **black comedy** comedy presenting a tragic theme or situation in comic terms. **black economy** an unofficial system of employment and paying people without observing legal requirements such as payment of income tax and National Insurance contributions. **black eye** an eye with the skin round it darkened by a bruise. **black hole** a region in outer space with a gravitational field so intense that no matter or radiation can escape from it. **black ice** hard thin transparent ice on roads. **black magic** magic involving the invocation of devils. **black mark** a mark of disapproval placed against a person's name. **black market** the illegal buying and selling of goods or currencies. **black marketeer** one who trades in the black market. **black out** to cover windows etc. so that no light can penetrate; to suffer temporary loss of consciousness or sight or memory. **black-out** *n.* a period of darkness when no light must be shown; the extinguishing of all lights; temporary loss of consciousness or sight or memory; prevention of the release of information. **black pudding** a large dark sausage containing blood, suet etc. **black sheep** a bad character in an otherwise well-behaved group. **black spot** a place where conditions are dangerous or difficult, one that has a bad record. **black tie** a man's black bow-tie worn with a dinner-jacket. **black widow** a poisonous spider found in tropical and subtropical regions. (The female of a North American species devours its mate.) **in a person's black books** having earned his or her disapproval. **in black and white** recorded in writing or print.

blackball *v.* to prevent (a person) from being elected as a member of a club by voting against him at a secret ballot.
blackberry *n.* **1** the bramble. **2** its small dark berry. **-blackberrying** *n.* picking blackberries.
blackbird *n.* a European songbird, the male of which is black.
blackboard *n.* a board usually coloured black, for writing on with chalk in front of a class in school etc.
blackcock *n.* a male black grouse.
Black Country the industrial area in the English Midlands.
Black Death an epidemic of plague in Europe during the 14th century.
blacken 1 to make or become black. **2** to say unpleasant things about, *blackened his character*.
blackfly *n.* a kind of insect infesting plants.
Black Friars Dominicans, so called from their black cloaks.
blackguard (**blag**-erd) *n.* a scoundrel. **blackguardly** *adv.*
blackhead *n.* a small hard lump blocking a pore in the skin.
blacking *n.* black polish for shoes.
blackish *adj.* rather black.
blacklead *n.* graphite.
blackleg *n.* a person who works while fellow workers are on strike. **-blackleg** *v.* (**blacklegged, blacklegging**) to act as a blackleg.
blacklist *n.* a list of persons who are disapproved of. **-blacklist** *v.* to put on a blacklist.
blackmail *v.* to demand payment or action from (a person) by threats especially of revealing a discreditable secret. **-blackmail** *n.* the crime of demanding payment in this way; the money itself. **-blackmailer** *n.*
Black Maria a secure van for taking prisoners to and from prison or into custody.
Black Power a militant movement supporting civil rights, political powers, etc., for Blacks.
Black Prince the name given in the 16th century to Edward Plantagenet (1330-76), eldest son of Edward III of England.
Black Sea a tideless sea between the USSR, Turkey, Bulgaria, and Romania.
blacksmith *n.* a smith who works in iron.
blackthorn a thorny shrub bearing white flowers and sloes.
blackwork *n.* a kind of embroidery done in black silk on fine linen.

Classifying the dictionary entries

1 In groups of 3 or 4, draw up a chart like the one below and place each example of the word's use into an appropriate column. To do this, you will need to discuss it and judge whether you would normally use the expression (or hear it used) in a context that arouses a positive, neutral or negative response.

2 Now conduct the same research for these dictionary entries for white, drawing up a similar chart.

Positive	Neutral	Negative
'in the black'	'of the very darkest colour'	'a black day'

white *adj.* **1** of the very lightest colour, like snow or common salt. **2 White** of the group of mankind having a light-coloured skin; of or for such persons. **3** pale in the face from illness or fear or other emotion. **-white** *n.* **1** white colour. **2** a white substance or material; white clothes. **3 White** a white person. **4** the white part of something (e.g. of the eyeball, round the iris). **5** the transparent substance round the yolk of an egg, turning white when cooked. **6** the white men in chess etc.; the player using these. **-whitely** *adj.* **whiteness** *n.* **white admiral** *see* **admiral. white ant** a termite. **white Christmas** one with snow. **white coffee** coffee with milk or cream. **white-collar worker** a worker who is not engaged in manual labour (e.g. an office worker). **white elephant** a useless possession. **white feather** a symbol of cowardice. **white flag** a symbol of surrender. **white frost** frost causing a white deposit on exposed surfaces. **white heat** the temperature at which heated metal looks white. **white hope** a person who is expected to attain fame. **white horses** white-crested waves on sea. **white-hot** *adj.* at white heat, hotter than red-hot. **White House** the official residence (in Washington) of the President of the USA. **white lie** a harmless lie (e.g. one told for the sake of politeness). **White Paper** a report issued by the government to give information on a subject. **white slave** a woman who is tricked and sent (usually abroad) into prostitution. **white slavery** this practice or state. **white tie** a man's white bow-tie worn with full evening dress. **white wine** amber or golden or pale yellow wine, not red or rose.

whitebait *n.*(*pl.* **whitebait**) a small silvery-white fish.

Whitehall *n.* the British Government. [from the name of a London street where there are many Government offices]

whiten *v.* to make or become white or whiter.

whitewash *n.* **1** a liquid containing quick-lime or powdered chalk used for painting walls, ceilings, etc. **2** a means of glossing over mistakes or faults. **3** a contest in which the losing side has failed to score. **whitewash.***v* **1** to paint with whitewash. **2** to clear the reputation of (a person etc.) by glossing over mistakes or faults.

whitewood *n.* a light-coloured wood, especially one prepared for staining etc.

Note: when a word or phrase is used in this negative way, we say that it is being used pejoratively; it has a **pejorative** meaning.

Analysing the data for black and white

1 Write the totals for black and for white separately at the bottom of each column of each chart.

2 Were there many phrases that caused a dispute, because people in your group reacted differently?

3 Did you find there were a much higher proportion of pejorative uses for black than for white? What explanations can you give for this?

4 In a dictionary for a foreign language that you are learning at school (or somewhere else), or for another language that you speak at home, look up the words for black and white. Is there a comparable number of pejorative uses in that language? Whether yes or no, what does that tell you about English?

A soul as black as coal

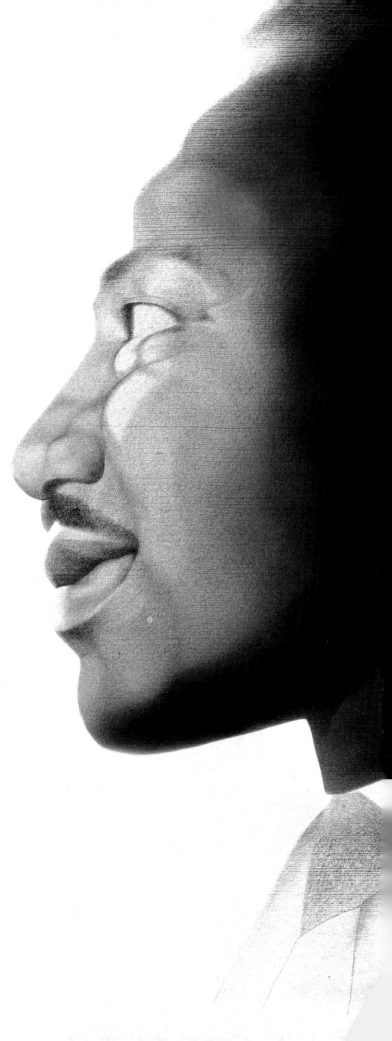

After the assassination of the black civil
rights leader, Martin Luther King, a Soviet
poet wrote a poem that begins:

> 'His skin was black
> but with the purest soul,
> white as the snow ...'

> *Yevtushenko*

A black poet composed this reply.

Such a white soul, they say,
that noble pastor had.
His skin so black, they say,
his skin so black in colour,
was on the inside snow,
a white lily,
fresh milk,
cotton.
Such innocence.
There wasn't one stain
on his impeccable interior.

(In short, a handsome find:
'The Black whose soul was white',
that curiosity.)

Still it might be said another way:
What a powerful black soul
that gentlest of pastors had.
What proud black passion
burned in his open heart.
What pure black thoughts
were nourished in his fertile brain.
What black love.
So colourlessly
given.

And why not,
why couldn't that heroic pastor
have a soul that's black?

Nicolás Guillén

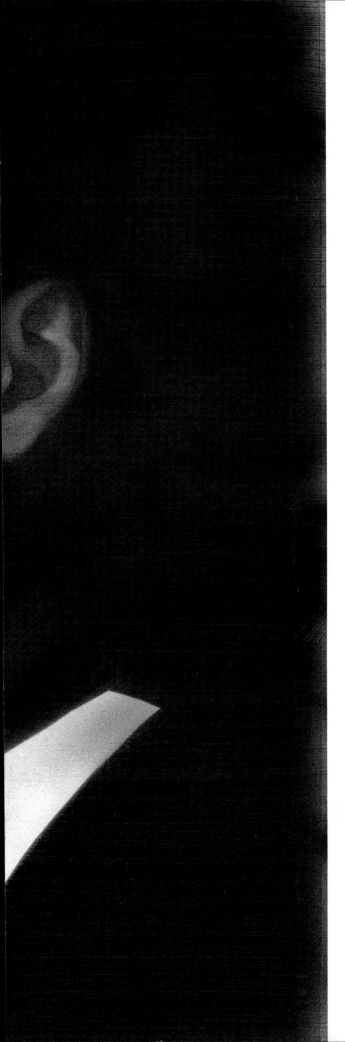

Comparing the messages

1 In the poem by Yevtushenko, what does the word 'but' imply?

2 In the first section of Guillén's poem, he refers to the traditional associations with whiteness: snow, lily, milk, cotton. Which shared qualities do we usually think of in connection with these?

 Similarly, what do we normally mean by a 'black soul' or 'black thoughts'?

3 Check the meanings of irony and paradox and comment on Guillén's phrase in the second stanza: '(In short ... curiosity)'.

4 'Colourlessly' normally implies 'uninterestingly', 'boringly'. What new meaning is Guillén suggesting here?

 How far, in fact, is the poet arguing that we should break away from traditional associations with 'colour' expressions?

5 a) In Guillén's poem, what are the main points that emerge about:
 ● Martin Luther King
 ● the English language
 b) What is the subject of the poem: Martin Luther King, the complexity of idioms or a combination of these things?

For more on Martin Luther King see Unit 4 in The Process of Writing module, pages 102-103.

Assignment

Using your black/white chart and the conclusions that you arrived at, together with the knowledge of colour expressions from other languages, produce one of the following pieces, entitled: 'It colours what you say'.
● an article for a young people's newspaper, such as *The Early Times*
● a full-colour poster
In either case you will need to consider the use of illustrations in colour. If you have access to graphic or illustrative software it might offer some interesting possibilities for this. If not, traditional forms of colouring will be as effective. For more on layout and presentation techniques used by newspapers and in advertising see Units 1 and 2 in the Non-literary Forms module, pages 122 and 136.

Spoken and written English

Spoken and written stories

Young children love to tell each other stories. And as soon as they are old enough, they begin to write these stories down.

Look at this transcript of part of a story, *Tom's spooky night*, told by Lucy, aged seven. By the time she came to make the recording from which this transcript was made, she had already told the story several times and so she was quite well-prepared. Next to the transcript on page 47 is Lucy's own written version of her story.

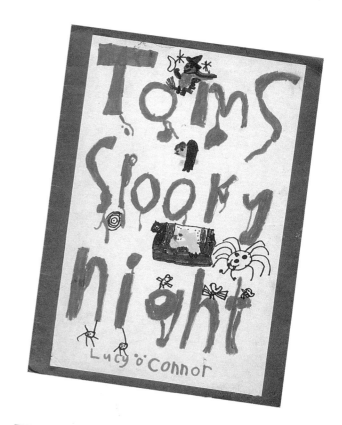

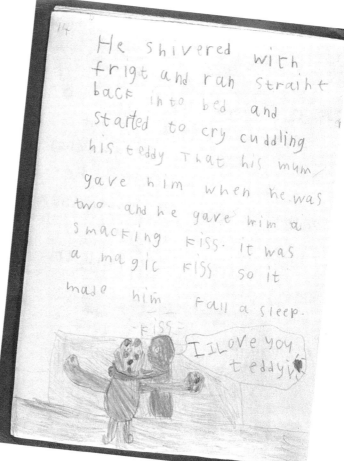

Tom's spooky night

Transcript of part of Lucy's spoken story

...he said m-mummy theres a monsters castle up there/dont be daft said toms mum theres no monsters castle up there/dont be a silly willy said his sister/dont be a dimwit said his brother/woof said his dog/cheep cheep said his pet budgie/eek eek said the mouse in the wall/oh shut up said tom and stamped upstairs in a mood/oh phoo i hate my parents said tom/just/ and screamed/just then his dad came up and said whats that noise get to bed/so tom brushed his teeth put on his pyjamas and combed his hair and got into bed/he went to bed feeling very frightened/he couldnt go to sl-sleep/so he kissed his teddy that his mum gave him when he was two/it was a magic kiss and he fell asleep...

Part of Lucy's written version of the story

... He said, 'M-M-Mummy, there's a m-monster's c-castle up there!'

'Don't be daft. There's no monster's castle around here,' said Tom's dad.

After tea, Tom went to bed feeling very frightened.

In the morning he had forgotten about it and he looked out of the window and there was the castle as fine as new. And he told his mum, but when she looked it had gone.

'Now look here, Tom, stop telling stories about monsters.'

'I'm not telling a story,' said Tom, 'I'm telling the truth.'

'Oh, don't be rubbish,' said his dad.

'Don't be a silly willy,' said his brother.

'Stop being a dimwit,' said his sister.

'Miaow,' said the cat.

'Woof!' said his dog.

'Cheep cheep,' said his pet budgie.

'Oh, shut up!' said Tom and stamped upstairs in a mood. 'Oh, phoo! I hate my parents!' And he screamed and screamed and screamed.

Just then Tom's dad came up and said, 'What was that noise? Get to bed.' So Tom brushed his teeth and washed his face and hands and combed his hair and put on his pyjamas and tried to get to sleep.

That night he was so frightened about the castle he looked out of the window. And there it was, standing there, still and dark. He shivered with fright and ran straight back into bed and started to cry, cuddling his teddy that his mum gave him when he was two, and he gave him a smacking kiss. It was a magic kiss, so it made him fall asleep.

Comparing the written and the spoken

1 What are the major similarities between the transcript and the written story?
2 What are the most interesting differences?
   a) Examine the phrases that Lucy has added, changed or left out. (Did she always make the right decisions, in your opinion?)
   b) Look particularly at the way in which she has changed the order of events as she recounts them.
   c) Note down some of the things that happen in speech which cannot happen in writing.
3 From reading published story books, and having them read to her, Lucy has come to understand – as all children do – that a written story is not going to look or sound the same as a spoken one written down. Using the work you have done in 2a) and 2b), try to pick out these features of spoken and written stories.

Now read this transcript of an adult describing a scene. He is not telling the story of something that actually happened to him; he is improvising. He has just read a passage from a play and is now putting himself in the place of one of the characters.

A soldier's story

Well... I... we'd camped there the day before and it ...well, you've got to imagine this really dark night, right? I mean, no moon – nothing. You had to strain your eyes just to put your boots on. Erm ...But there was this sound all the time, right? A kind of humming sound... Er... and it was the others, see. It was the French. I mean, they couldn't have been – I don't know – more than a few hundred yards away. I mean, when the light came up – you, know, at dawn – we could see 'em. Anyway you could hear this humming which was them talking and whispering and... and changing guard and things... and then about midnight the horses started neighing – terrible racket – and then you heard the first clank-clank, tap-tap – you know, the blacksmiths – the armourers – getting to work... (laughs) with their little hammers... and then the clocks started crowing, cos, well, we were surrounded by farms, see, yeh, and there was this village clock on the church or summink, I don't know, and I can remember hearing it go three and just sitting by the fire. Course, we didn't reckon on coming out alive, did we?

And then, about dawn, dawn time, he came round, like visiting, you know – Henry – cheering us up (laughs) like visiting people in hospital, more like. Give him his due, though, he didn't look frightened... I was.

(Based on *Henry V* Act IV Scene 1)

Taking a closer look

1 Mark a selection of the features in this speech that are usual in conversation, but inappropriate in writing.
   For example, look at:
   • long sequences linked only by 'and'
   • phrases special to speech ('I mean...')
   • repetitions
   • rephrasing
   • informal expressions
   • inexact or imprecise expressions
   • features such as sighing or laughter
   • pauses
   • er...
2 How many of these features are also found in Lucy's speech on page 47?
3 Compare these two speeches. List the features which seem to you to be typical in each case of a child's or an adult's speech. You will find not just differences in vocabulary, but also in syntax (the grammar or structure of the sentences).

An effective way of writing fresh, lively stories is to work from a spoken anecdote. This might be based on a real experience or an imagined one, such as the soldier's story on page 48.

The stages for converting a spoken story into a written one are as follows:

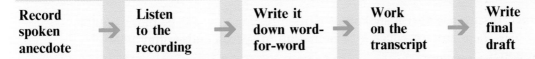

| Record spoken anecdote | → | Listen to the recording | → | Write it down word-for-word | → | Work on the transcript | → | Write final draft |

For example, working with an improvised speech the process might work as follows.

1 Record the improvised speech. As an example we will take the soldier's, but when you come to do this you will need to choose and record your own.

2 Listen carefully to the recording.

3 Write it down word-for-word without any punctuation (including capital letters).

> well i wed camped there the day before and it well
> youve got to imagine this really dark night right
> i mean no moon nothing you had to strain your eyes

Put dividing marks (/) where the speaker seems to have completed one thought and is about to begin another; put a dash (–) to indicate pauses.

> well – i – wed camped there the day before/and it –
> well youve got to imagine this really dark night right/
> i mean no moon – nothing/you had to strain your eyes

4 Begin work on the transcript. The aim is to turn it from a passage of spoken English that someone has written down into a piece of written English.

- Pick out all the features which are usual in spoken English but not appropriate in writing.

- Decide in each case whether to cut them out or rephrase them (by changing words, adding words or changing word order).

> ~~well i~~ wed camped there the day before/~~and it well~~
> youve got to imagine ~~this~~ really dark night ~~right/i mean~~
> no moon – nothing/you had to strain your eyes

(handwritten: a ... with)

- Punctuate the new piece of writing, using your break and pause marks as initial guides.

- Look at the draft so far. There might well be some reorganisation that needs to be done. For example, you might begin the story in a number of different ways:

    'We had camped the day before and were now...'
    'It was the darkest night I had known...'
    'Sitting there, listening to the village clock chiming
    three, my thoughts went back to...'

For more on drafting see Unit 2 in The Process of Writing module, pages 79-83.

5 Having 'worked' the drafts as far as you need to, write or type the final draft, in such a way as to suit the audience for which you intend it.

Speak and write

If we wish to communcate effectively, we need to be able to speak and write clearly. Look at each of these situations in which we might need to communicate.

Choosing a response

With a partner, discuss whether a spoken or written response would be more suitable in each case. Are there any for which a combination of speech and writing might be the best solution?

A   Giving directions to a stranger.
B   Keeping a record to refer back to later.
C   Getting important messages to people around the school.
D   Planning a debate or argument in detail.
E   Advertising a bike for sale.
F   Complaining about faulty goods.
G   Offering a detailed analysis of a piece of literature to a teacher or examiner.
H   Letting people know that the drinks machine is out of order.
I   Reshaping ideas after consulting reference books or other people.
J   Making arrangements with a friend to meet somewhere.
K   Giving confirmation that you will attend a job interview.
L   Wishing somebody Happy Birthday.
M   Letting someone know that you'll be home late.

Wordz and soundz

In many of the situations listed on the previous page, the best effect is gained by a combination of speech and writing, e.g. it might be most helpful to tell the stranger how to get to the bus station and then draw a clearly labelled sketch map.

Advertisers, too, have found that, if they hit upon the right words, they can have an impact both with the way their slogan or brand name *sounds* and with the way it *looks* in print. For example:

Can you think of further advertisements that have this dual effect – a catchy sound combined with an eye-catching spelling?

For more on the language of advertising, and particularly brand names and slogans, see Unit 2 in the Non-literary Forms module, page 141.

A question of spelling

Before people can create original brand names with catchy spellings, such as 'Kleeneze' for detergent, they have to be reasonably confident that they know what the conventional spelling is in the first place.

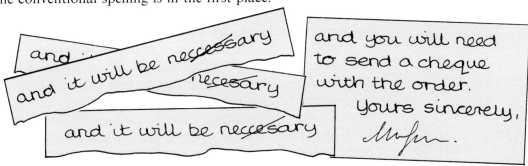

It is problems such as this that have given rise to endless arguments about the English spelling system. Most of these arguments are not new; and most centre upon the question: 'To reform or not to reform?'

Spelling 'reformers' through the ages have wanted to change the system so that words are spelt as they are pronounced.

Anti-reformers have argued that spelling is not a reflection of speech; and anyway, whose speech? The accent of Ulster or Guyana? And which sounds? For example, this century's pronunciations may be very different from those of the future.
It has been a long and hard-fought battle, and has continued for the last four centuries as pages 52 and 53 reveal.

To reform or not to reform

John Hart 1569
But in the modern and present maner of writing (as well of certaine other languages as of our English) there is such confusion and disorder, as it may be accounted rather a kinde of ciphring, or such a darke kinde of writing

W.R. Evans 1870
School teachers, school boards, and school inspectors come forward with their testimony, not in a few cases, but in hundreds, to the effect that teaching our anomalous system of spelling to the children of the poor is in most cases impracticable; and that when the task is in exceptional instances accomplished, it entails either the loss of much other instruction that might be imparted during school attendance, or the sacrifice to indigent parents of a child's possible earnings during a considerable period.

The Simplified Spelling Society 1948
We instinktivly shrink from any chaenj in whot iz familyar; and whot kan be mor familyar dhan dhe form ov wordz dhat we hav seen and riten mor tiemz dhan we kan posibly estimaet? We taek up a book printed in Amerika, and *honor* and *center* jar upon us every tiem we kum akros dhem; nae, eeven to see *forever* in plaes ov *for ever* atrakts our atenshon in an unplezant wae. But dheez ar iesolaeted kaesez; think ov dhe meny wurdz dhat wood hav to be chaenjd if eny real impruuvment wer to rezult. At dhe furst glaans a pasej in eny reformd speling looks 'kweer' or 'ugly'. Dhis objekshon iz aulwaez dhe furst to be maed; it iz purfektly natueral; it iz dhe hardest to remuuv. Indeed, its efekt iz not weekend until dhe nue speling iz noe longger nue, until it haz been seen ofen enuf to be familyar.

Dhe printerz braut about a surten ueniformity, on which Dr Johnson baest hiz dikshonary. Dhis to aul intents and purposez, iz stil our standard ov korekt speling.

It iz dhe printerz, and not dhe graet rieterz, huu hav deturmind our speling, widh dhe solitary eksepshon ov Dr Johnson; and, az we hav seen, he reguelariezd whot he found – he did not reform.

Jonathan Swift   1712
Another Cause which hath contributed not a little to the maim-
ing of our Language, is a foolish Opinion advanced of late
Years, that we ought to spell exactly as we speak; which beside
the obvious Inconvenience of utterly destroying our Etymology,
would be a thing we should never see an End of. Not only the
several Towns and Counties of England, have a different Way
of pronouncing; but even here in *London* they clip their Words
after one Manner about the Court, another in the City, and a
third in the Suburbs; and in a few Years, it is probable, will
all differ from themselves, as Fancy or Fashion shall direct: All
which reduced to Writing, would entirely confound Orthography.

Samuel Johnson   1755
Others ...have endeavoured to proportion the number of letters
to that of sounds, that every sound may have its own character,
and every character a single sound.

   But who can hope to prevail on nations to change their practice, and make all their old books useless? or what advantage
would a new orthography procure equivalent to the confusion
and perplexity of such an alteration?

Henry Bradley   1913
Many of the advocates of spelling reform are in the habit of
asserting, as if it were an axiom admitting of no dispute, that
the sole function of writing is to represent sounds.

   I assert that, so far as peoples of literary culture are concerned,
there never was a time when this formula would have correctly
expressed the facts; and that it would still remain false, even if
an accurately phonetic spelling had been in universal use for
hundreds of years.

Looking at the arguments

1 Read the passage printed in the Simplified
   Spelling Society's proposed system.
   a) How many of its 'rules' can you identify?
   b) Which advantages and disadvantages does
      it seem to have over our current system?
   c) How many 'rules' of our current spelling
      system can you write down?
2 Look again at the statements in the debate
   about Spelling reform.
   a) Summarise the main arguments for and
      against in note form.
   b) Hold a debate on this motion 'This House
      believes that the English spelling system is
      in need of reform'.

You may wish to take account of this
gentleman's views too.

Ways of speaking

The right speech in the right situation

It would be fair to say that the employee here has failed to appreciate that the language he might use with his family, his friends or his pet budgie is not appropriate for a conversation with his employer, especially when other work colleagues are present.

Getting it right

We are all capable of using the wrong kind of language on certain occasions. If we do so intentionally, sometimes the effect can be entertaining. Look at this list of situations:

- being interviewed for a job
- giving excuses to the Deputy Head
- asking a parent for a loan
- phoning the railway station
- telling a nursery story to a child
- giving directions
- meeting a long-lost relative
- talking to the cat (goldfish, dog, gerbil...)
- giving a report in assembly
- asking someone out for a date

1 a) In pairs, discuss what kind of speech might be appropriate in each case. For example, should you:
- use Standard English dialect
- change your accent
- be formal or informal
- include technical jargon
- be brief and to the point
- be personal
- be argumentative
- speak in a pre-planned, deliberate way
- be emotional
- lecture

b) How careful will you need to be in selecting vocabulary?

c) Which tone of voice will be suitable?

2 a) Select one situation from the list on page 54 and decide upon the appropriate manner of speech for it. Improvise a short conversation and tape record it.

b) Now improvise a second conversation in which the kind of speech chosen is totally inappropriate to the situation and record that. Try to make it humorous.

c) When you have completed your recordings, exchange the tape with another pair and listen to each other's. Discuss how appropriate the first recording was in each case; and what kinds of humorous effects were achieved in the second.

These activities have been about appropriate speech. For more on appropriate writing see Unit 1 in The Process of Writing module, page 73.

Getting the tone

How important was the effect of your **tone** of voice in the improvisations? It can make all the difference, as the following exercise will show.

1 With your partner, take it in turns to say the following phrase: 'I see you've finished, then' in these tones:
   - angrily
   - as though amused
   - wearily
   - as though pleased
   - gloomily
   - sarcastically
   - as if in some doubt

2 Pick another ordinary, neutral sentence. Decide on a tone and say the sentence to your partner. The object is to express the tone so effectively that your partner can guess it correctly. Try using different tones to those in the list above.

It's not just the words

After you have listened to other people's recordings from the 'Getting it right' activity, choose three to be performed in front of the class. It will help if each conversation can be videoed, as it can then be replayed, but this is not essential.

1 Make detailed notes as you watch the performances on two features which are essential for effective spoken communication: **facial expression** and **gesture**.

2 Try to record which expressions and which gestures accompanied particular phrases or sentences and noticeable changes in tone of voice. Discuss the contribution that these made to effective communication.

Dramatic gesture

The following photos are from a scrapbook about the great British actor, Sir John Gielgud.

A *The title role in Shakespeare's Richard II, 1937*

B *Vershinin in Chekov's Three Sisters, 1938*

C *John Worthing in Oscar Wilde's The Importance of Being Ernest, 1939*

D *The title role in Shakespeare's King Lear, 1940*

E *Raskolnikoff in Dostoyevsky's Crime and Punishment, 1946*

F *Leontes in Shakespeare's A Winter's Tale, 1951*

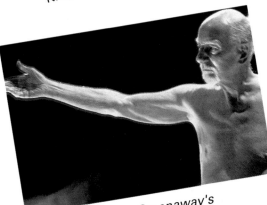

G *Prospero in Peter Greenaway's Prospero's Books, 1991*

Taking a closer look

Study the photographs which show Gielgud in a variety of dramatic roles.
1 How might you describe:
 ● the facial expression   ● the gesture
2 If you know the play in question (as you might in one or two cases with A, C, D and F try to find lines in the play that would seem to fit.

Language of approval and pleasure

There is one group of words in particular that is constantly changing, sometimes it seems from one week to the next: the expressions that we use to show our approval of something.

Journey's end is a play set in the Great War of 1914 to1918 and it was first produced in 1928.

Raleigh is an eighteen-year-old officer who has just arrived in the trenches and is learning about the rugby-playing background of an older officer, Osborne.

Journey's end

Raleigh: (*laughing*) Who did you play for?

Osborne: The Harlequins.

Raleigh: I say, really!

Osborne: I played for the English team on one great occasion.

Raleigh: What! For *England*!

Osborne: I was awfully lucky to get the chance. It's a long time ago now.

Raleigh: (*with awe*) Oh, but, good Lord! that must have been simply topping. Where did you play?

Osborne: Wing three.

Raleigh: I say, I – I never realised – you'd played for England?

Osborne: Tuppence to talk to me now! Anyhow, don't breeze it about.

Raleigh: Don't the others know?

Osborne: We never talk about Rugger.

Raleigh: They ought to know. It'd make them feel jolly bucked.

Osborne: (*laughing*) It doesn't make much difference out here!

Raleigh: It must be awfully thrilling, playing in front of a huge crowd – all shouting and cheering –

Osborne: You don't notice it when the game begins.

Raleigh: You're too taken up with the game?

Osborne: Yes.

Raleigh: I used to get wind up playing at school with only a few kids looking on.

Osborne: You feel it more when there are only a few. (*He has picked up a slip of paper from the table; suddenly he laughs.*) Look at this!

Raleigh: (*looking at it curiously*) What is it?

Osborne: Trotter's plan to make the time pass quickly. One hundred and forty-four little circles – one for each hour of six days. He's blacked in six already. He's six hours behind.

Raleigh: It's rather a good idea. I like Trotter.

Osborne: He's a good chap.

Raleigh: He makes things feel – natural.

Osborne: He's a genuine sort of chap.

Raleigh: That's it. He's genuine. (*There is a pause. He has been filling a new pipe. Osborne is puffing at his old one.*)

How topping – to have played for England!

Osborne: It was rather fun.

R. C. Sherriff

Surveying the language of approval

1 Pick out the expressions of approval that would not be used in the 1990s, such as 'simply topping'. (Are there some expressions that you would not use, but other kinds of people might?)

2 If you were Raleigh and Osborne having a similar conversation today, which expressions would you use in their place? Rewrite the scene as though it were taking place today.

3 Conduct some research amongst:
   ● older people
   ● people of your own age

   ● literature from other periods
   ● other cultures today
and collect as many examples as you can of words of approval (or approbation), such as Raleigh's 'topping' or words such as 'fab', 'wicked' and 'bad'.

   It might help to use a chart like the one below, or you could also record your findings on a database if there is one available to you.

4 Complete your research with a survey of the expressions that have been in use during the past year or two and the ones that are most fashionable at the moment.

Terms of approbation	Origin, if known	Decades of use
topping	from 'top', meaning 'best'	1910s and 1920s
fab	from fabulous	
wicked		

Discuss your findings:

1 Does it seem to you that the most recently 'dead' expressions have become even more laughable than the older ones?

2 In recent years, how have these expressions spread so quickly? And why do they go out of fashion so rapidly? Try to explore the following influences in particular:
   ● the popular music scene   ● television   ● non-European cultures

Local language

Your assignment is to research, write up and present a study of the language in your area.

Collecting information

This will involve researching and surveying:
- the accents and dialects of your area
- the current 'language events' of your area (in local theatre or music, for example)
- the language of your local radio and newspaper
- attitudes to language in the local community
- the language of your school
- your own language profile

Most of this cannot be researched by reading in the library. You will need to:
- tape record your parents, relatives and other people in the community (either on audio or video recorder) for examples of dialect, accent or other languages
- interview people in your community (again recording the interviews) to collect some attitudes to language
- conduct surveys using questionaires
- look at all available statistics (for example, to do with language groups in your areas)

Selecting and decision-making

From the mass of material that you collect, you will need to make decisions about what to use and how best to use it. A lot will depend upon how long your presentation is to be. You will need to:
- use only a few excerpts from recorded interviews
- present the findings of your surveys in ways that people will find visually interesting and easy to understand
- take great care over your use of statistics, so that they are not misleading

The presentation

An interesting presentation to the class might take a number of forms.
You might employ:
● charts and maps of the region (for example, of dialect features or languages spoken)
● the tape-recordings that you have made (of people's attitudes)
● a video (for example, of children using different dialects or languages in school)
● an overhead projector (for displaying the major 'headings' of your presentation)

The report

Your oral presentation can then form the basis of a written report.
As part of this written assignment, you might wish to:
● make transcripts of selected audio and video recordings
● produce explanatory notes to accompany your maps and diagrams
● summarise some of your arguments and explanations in a more concise form
You might find it helpful to consult The Process of Writing module for advice on
report-writing and techniques, pages 67-69; and the Non-literary Forms module
for advice on specialist writing and summarising, pages 162-163.

Module 2   The Process of Writing

Objectives

The material and activities included in this module aim to extend your skills in creative and analytical writing by:

◆ presenting a variety of written forms, produced for a wide range of purposes and giving you the opportunity to write in these
◆ encouraging you to introduce drafting, redrafting, revising and proof-reading as stages in your written work
◆ showing how written work can be organised to express meaning appropriately for different audiences

Why write?

What is the purpose of this piece of writing? You may decide that it is a message from one person to another living in the same house, or at least using the same refrigerator. You may be right, but you would also be right if you decided it was a poem. It was written by William Carlos Willams.

We use writing for all kinds of purposes, and it is usually very clear to us what the purpose of any given piece is, unlike the example given above. We can tell the purpose of a piece of writing by its means of expression.

For example, we do not expect to find shopping lists or telephone messages written in complete sentences and punctuated into the bargain...

Eggs
Bread
Lemonade
Cheese (6oz?)
Washing Powder
Coffee (filter)
Baked Beans
Toothpaste

Saturday tea
plain flour
pasta
low-fat spread
mushrooms
onions
tinned toms

Jill
Alison rang about 6:30.
What are you doing
this wk-end?
Sunday night —
cook a meal?
Ring her 237524

But we know a novel, newspaper article or report by their division into paragraphs or chapters and the fact that they are usually written in continuous prose.

At every corner there were men who called 'Taxi' at him as though he were a stranger, and all down the Paseo, at intervals of a few yards the pimps accosted him automatically without any real hope. 'Can I be of service, sir?' 'I know all the pretty girls.' 'You desire a beautiful woman.' 'Postcards?' 'You want to see a dirty movie?' They had been mere children when he first came to Havana, they had watched his car for a nickel, and though they had aged alongside him they had never got used to him. In their eyes he never became a resident; he remained a permanent tourist, and so they went pegging along – sooner or later, like all the others, they were certain that he would want to see Superman performing at the San Francisco brothel. At least, like the clown, they had the comfort of not learning from experience.

By the corner of Virdudes Dr Hasselbacher hailed him from the Wonder Bar. 'Mr Wormold, where are you off to in such a hurry?'

'An appointment.'

'There is always time for a Scotch.' It was obvious from the way he pronounced Scotch that Dr Hasselbacher had already had time for a great many.

'I'm late as it is.'

'There's no such thing as late in this city, Mr Wormold. And I have a present for you.'

Wormold turned in to the bar from the Paseo. He smiled unhappily at one of his own thoughts. 'Are your sympathies with the East or the West, Hasselbacher?'

'East or West of what? Oh, you mean *that*. A plague on both.'

'What present have you got for me?'

'I asked one of my patients to bring them from Miami,' Hasselbacher said. He took from his pocket two miniature bottles of whisky: one was Lord Calvert, the other Old Taylor. 'Have you got them?' he asked with anxiety.

Stores join 'green' fight

THE GOVERNMENT is using five supermarket chains to distribute five million copies of a leaflet which tells customers of all ages how to reduce environmental damage.

Yesterday, Michael Heseltine, Secretary of State for the Environment, went to a London store to launch the campaign. 'Governments cannot solve the problem of the environment alone,' he said. 'We have bottle banks and newspaper banks, but how many people use them?'

As well as advice on recycling, the leaflet – *Wake up to what you can do for the Environment* – recommends energy saving, green consumerism and using public transport.

We can also distinguish one type of prose from another by its tone, style or layout, all of which are signals to the purpose of the writing itself. Look at these examples and decide the purpose of each piece of text and where they might usually appear.

ACCADEMIA ITALIANA Images from Dante's Divine Comedy by Randy Klein. Metal beasts, collages, drawings and prints which illustrate the artist's personal view of a journey through Heaven and Hell. *Spazio Club Rooms, 24 Rutland Gate (091-245 3476) 6-28 Mar. Tues-Sat 10am-5.30, Wed to 8pm; free.*

CRAFTS COUNCIL Contemporary metal furniture. Avant-garde furniture designs by a group of innovative designers who distress, rust, crush and patinate metal into pieces which challenge the minimalist ascendancy with a new romanticism. *12 Waterloo Pl, (091-935 4871) Tue-Sat 10am-5pm, Sun 2pm-5pm; free.*

HAYWARD ROOMS Twilight of the Tsars. An exhibition which, through some 500 exhibits encompassing architecture, painting, sculpture, photography and the decorative, presents a picture of Russian culture during the reign of the last two Tsars. *Art Nouveau* is reflected in the work of architects Shektel and Fomin and Symbolism in that of painters Boris-Musatov, Roerich and Nesterov. Also included are Diaghilev's "World of Art" painters: Benois, Bakst and Somov and the artists of the "Blue Rose". *West Bank Centre, (091-921 0796) 7 Mar-19 May. Daily 10am-6pm, Tue & Wed to 8pm; £4, conc. £2.50, cat. £19.95.*

ROYAL ACADEMY OF ARTS Sir Christopher Wren and the Making of St Paul's. The evolution and construction of Wren's masterpiece, examined through his "Great Model", over 18 feet long, along with the original working drawings. *8 Mar-12 May. Daily 10am-6pm; £3, conc. £2, reduced admission with Buhrie Collection.*

ROYAL FESTIVAL HALL Prints, etchings and woodcuts by 15 printmakers. *Foyer Galleries, West Bank Centre, (091-210 4927) 9 Mar-1 Apr. 10am-10pm; free.*

Flyers stuck in a downward dive

FOR Fife Flyers the season is ending badly. Defeats at the hands of Durham Wasps and Ayr Raiders have guaranteed them a place in the end of season promotion/relegation play-offs to decide Heineken Premier Division status, and their last game next weekend is meaningless, writes Steve Pinder.

Flyers did themselves few favours against Wasps, who needed a win to secure the title. Three goals in 65 seconds ended doubts about the result; and with 10 minutes left Fife's Rick Fera picked up a penalty which left him free to contemplate a Sunday of inactivity, as well as an 11-4 Wasps victory.

With their leading scorer benched, Fife were 13-5. Fife, who reached Wembley last season, must now beware of opponents such as Slough Jets and Bracknell Bees, relative newcomers to the scene who may have the temerity to supplant them.

Humberside Seahawks could do likewise – they came within one point of clinching the First Division title with a 10-5 win at Medway Bears and a harder 7-4 home win over Romford Raiders.

Peterborough Pirates are the most improved team on the circuit. Their 10-6 Premier Division defeat of Murrayfield Racers was their first win over the Scots, and was also their sixth win in a row, a club record.

Collecting samples

1 We use a large number of writing types daily.
   a) Jot down all the things you have written in the last week, from birthday cards to Humanities essays.
   b) Next to each item say *why* you wrote it: were there any items you could not explain? If so, were they difficult to write?
   c) Compare your list with that of others and you'll be astonished at the variety.
   d) Decide how important you feel purpose is to your own writing.
2 Over the next few days collect as many samples of writing as you can. Your collection should include the kinds of writing you meet every day, such as the back of the breakfast cereal box, and anything more unusual you may encounter.

Sample analysis

1 a) With a partner or in a group sort your samples according to their purpose, using a chart like the one below.
   b) In the final column write in who the intended audience is for each piece.
2 In groups of 3 or 4, discuss your reasons for placing samples in particular categories.
3 Be prepared to explain to the whole class how the language and layout of the samples helped you to make your decisions.

Good luck with everything!
love, Amanda

to Graham
date 24-4-91
memo

You are invited to another 'night out' at Karen Scot's — 59 Kenton St, Oxford. Please bring a bottle plus a pudding to share as a buffet.
RSVP to Karen as soon as possible.
DATE: 23rd May
TIME: 7.30 pm to eat for 8pm

The War Poets: Background

The reason that such a tragically high number of war poets were killed is because they were mostly junior officers. Most poetry of the time came from the middle and upper classes; working-class writers like Rosenberg were very much the exception.

Plan	Inform	Explain	Hypothesise	Compare/ Contrast

Persuade	Entertain	Express attitudes	Express emotions	Describe imaginatively	Intended audience

Writing for yourself

In the sample analysis you have made you will have noticed two further things about writing:

- most types of writing are intended to be read by others, they assume an audience
- however, some types are intended for the eyes of the writer only

You will learn more about this first category later in this module, but before that we will take a closer look at the second.

Whether you use a personal organiser, a diary, or carry around slips of paper, you probably need to make notes to yourself from time to time even if it's only a shopping list. Writing can be an **aide memoire** – a reminder – and diaries are only one form of this.

Appointment diaries, year-planners, or even stick-on notes help you to organise your time and your life.

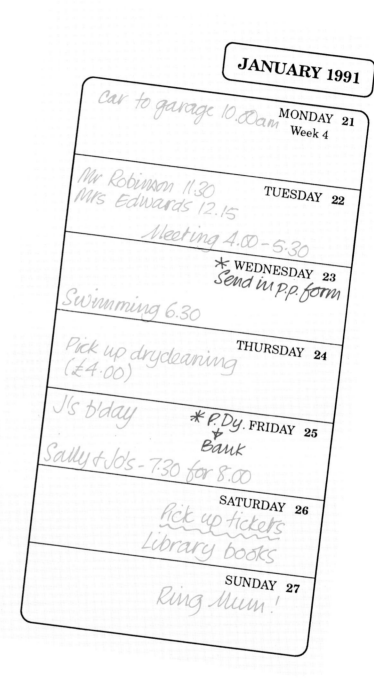

JANUARY 1991

Car to garage 10.00am   MONDAY 21
Week 4

Mr Robinson 11.30   TUESDAY 22
Mrs Edwards 12.15

Meeting 4.00 – 5.30

✱ WEDNESDAY 23
Send in P.P. form

Swimming 6.30

Pick up drycleaning   THURSDAY 24
(£4.00)

J's b'day   ✱ P.Dy. FRIDAY 25
↓
Bank

Sally & Jo's – 7.30 for 8.00

SATURDAY 26

Pick up tickets
Library books

SUNDAY 27

Ring Mum !

Decoding the diary

1 With a partner decide what the shorthand forms and messages in the diary example given above might mean to the writer.
2 What particular actions might the writer need to take on certain days to fulfil the notes they have made to themselves, e.g. what would they need to do earlier in the week to prepare for Friday?

Organising your thoughts

Writing can also be an effective way of organising your thoughts. There are no hard and fast rules for this type of writing as you can see from this diagram.

You could add to this diagram any type of writing whose intention is just to help you. Samuel Pepys wrote his diaries in a personal form of shorthand and Leonardo da Vinci recorded his observations in mirror writing! Both writers' aim was to keep their thoughts confidential. Of course, if you do use a form of coded diary you must be able to decode what you have written when you need it.

For more on diaries in code see the Forms of Narrative module in Book 4A, page 2.

Note-making

Making notes sounds easier than it is. The biggest pitfall is writing down too much.

Remember when taking notes:
- concentrate on key words
- record the overall sense of the writing
- ring or query (?) anything you don't understand

Read this article, then look at the work that follows it. It is addressed to teachers needing to deal with bullying in their classes.

The power and the glory

SCENARIO: Enter a third-year class. Cindy goes to sit. John pushes her aggressively out of the way. Teacher (overburdened by National Curriculum assessments): JOHN! See me afterwards!

THE dictionary defines *bully* as 'a person who uses strength or power to coerce others by fear'. *The bullied*, conversely, are the weak and the powerless. We all know the feeling; we have all been made to feel powerless by others, or have been influenced by circumstances which seem beyond our control. But it is not just Cindy who is a victim of bullying. So, paradoxically, are John and the teacher.

Bullying is a major educational concern. Abraham H. Maslow, the American psychologist, described a 'hierarchy of needs' common to all people, in the form of a pyramid. At the base was *survival,* then *security,* building through *belonging* and *prestige* to the apex of *self-fulfilment.* Bullying threatens the pyramid of learning at its very foundations – so we, as educators, need to stamp it out.

The bully exerts his, more commonly than her, power. We respond protectively to the bullied. John sees us afterwards; we exert our power over John. But what becomes of the powerless? Cindy may be protected in the classroom, but not necessarily out of it.

A teacher's intervention is likely to lose her esteem among her peers, making her even more of a victim. *Shaming* is a word children use.

We need to consider alternative strategies. The interaction between the bully and the bullied is clearly an exchange of power and esteem. The bully, stereotypically the low achiever with low self-esteem, gains (or thinks he or she gains) power and prestige through bullying; the bullied, conversely, loses self-esteem and becomes powerless.

Instead of taking control we need to find ways of *empowering* pupils – investing power where it needs to belong, to build the self-esteem of both the victim and the perpetrator.

Consider the power bases that exist in school: the culture of the teachers, and the sub-culture of the pupils, which are so often locked in mutual antipathy. We need to empower children, and one way is by building self-esteem.

As educators we need to ask ourselves fundamental questions. Do we really value childhood and adolescence, or merely perceive them as passing phases to adulthood? Are we truly 'pupil-centred'? Do we have high expectations for *all* our pupils? Is our approach success-oriented or based on criticism? Do we reward first and sanction last? Do we impose discipline or nurture self-discipline? By controlling classes through power and authority, do we actually provide a negative role-model? Or do we seek mutual esteem as their prime commodity of trading?

A second key to empowerment is sharing. The issues of bullying need to be put on the public agenda for discussion, not dealt with privately after the lesson. Children need to examine their own values and actions. Bullying, and the related issues of sexual harassment and racism, need to be built into our pastoral work. Most of all, children need to develop responsibility and need to be enabled to respond. They need to share their feelings and vulnerabilities with one another, and to learn to listen to each other. Teachers, too, need to learn to listen to children.

A third key to tackling bullying is equipping children with skills. They need to learn through example and practise the art of assertive (as opposed to aggressive) behaviour. Assertiveness training enables young people to deal more confidently with their peers and with adults.

If these suggestions are put into a practical classroom management strategy, a more useful dialogue may result:

Teacher (controlling): JOHN! Don't do that, it's bullying. *(Empowering)* Cindy, if he does that again, you must tell him to stop. If he does not stop, you must tell me. Allowing it to happen puts you down. *(Empowering)* John ...We treat everyone with respect in this school. If I don't treat you with the respect you deserve you must tell me. *(Separating*

the pupil from the mistake: positive reinforcement) I expect better of you, you're an intelligent and likeable young man. *(Empowering)* Cindy, have I done enough about this for the moment? Thank you. *(To class: sharing)* Let's stop for a moment, and talk about why this issue is so important to us all. Cindy, John...what are your feelings on the subject?

Education Guardian October 1990

Looking at the article

1 a) In a group of 3 or 4, discuss the article and then make notes under two headings: Fact and Opinion.

You could instead highlight the key words or topic sentences on your own copy using different colours, e.g. yellow for facts, orange for opinions, and go on to make your notes from this.

You could use another set of symbols to mark anything which is not clear to you.

b) When you have noted down the information, put the article away.

2 Try tabulating the information or presenting it as a spider diagram, flow-chart or in another diagramatic form. Add any ideas or questions of your own to your notes.

For more on the topic of bullying see the Media Scripts module in Book 4A, page 131.

Just one way of using notes

Usually notes are taken in class on subjects that you will want to return to later, perhaps for revision. But you can use them in a number of ways. For example, you could plan a debate on bullying with a motion like: 'Teacher intervention does not prevent bullying – it makes it worse', using the notes and research you have done on the article on pages 68-69.

1 In a group of 5 or 6, discuss the article, particularly anything of which you are unsure. What is your point of view? Note it down.

2 Compare your opinion with others in your group and decide who will propose and who will oppose the motion.

3 Using the notes you have made, prepare a short speech to deliver as part of the debate. If you are to propose or oppose the motion you may need to remind the audience of the starting point for discussion. Summarise the article's content briefly and add arguments of your own.

4 Transfer your prepared speech onto cue cards – these are notes which help you remember what to say. They should not be read! Memorise your speech and use them as another aide memoire. For more on summarising see the Non-literary Forms module, page 162.

If it is class debate you may not all be called upon to act as a speaker but with your argument summarised on cards you will be in a good position to ask questions in the debate.

For more on organising a debate see page 99 in Unit 4.

You are now ready to present your debate on the topic of bullying. For other possible debate topics see page 105.

A debate is only one way of presenting your opinions to others. With a group or a partner make a brief list of other forms, both oral and written, that you could use. If you prefer you could use one of these approaches to present your views on bullying. If you decide to present your argument in writing read through Unit 4 in this module, pages 96-99, before you begin.

On reflection

The types of writing you have examined so far all function as preparation for other work or as reminders. But there are forms in which the purpose of the writing is to look back on, to reflect, analyse or evaluate. If you keep a personal diary you will understand that this is sometimes not meant for public reading, and even if you do not keep your own diary you will know that it is considered taboo to read someone else's without permission.

However, diaries and journals are not always strictly confidential and are sometimes written with the intention of turning them into memoirs or autobiographies.

Sunday, 9 December — I spent the evening of Friday at Calvocoressi's with Ravel, the composer, and another man, also a musician, whose name I have already forgotten three times. Ravel played his own very difficult music pretty badly. A little man with very sloping shoulders indeed. In fact shoulders with a concave curve like this ⌣⌣. Dark; a little like a variety comedian at first, but producing, later, a considerable impression of dignity. Again the same opposition to Brahms. Again the same vivacious interest in English literature, and the same admiration for the wit of such French writers as Tristan Bernard.

Ravel and Calvo talked of the intrigues in which the new appointment of director of the Opera was involved. How a certain young woman there had great influence because she was 'protected' by Clemenceau, etc. etc., many names being similarly involved. It seemed strange to me, at the moment, to hear of that splendid and serious Radical, Clemenceau, spending time and substance on *petites femmes*.

Today I finished the second instalment of the *Statue*. I have now worked regularly in the mornings for a week, always finishing my creative stuff before lunch. Already the day is better portioned out. But I have still to put a little order into the afternoons. I haven't sufficient obstinacy of volition really to practise the piano, even for half an hour everyday. Nor to read Spencer every day. But I do all the other things that I appointed to myself.

Arnold Bennett

Looking at the language

1 Read through this diary and note down phrases that make it a public rather than a personal reflection.
2 Which details would be expressed differently in a personal diary?
3 Try rewriting one paragraph of this diary as Bennett's personal diary.

Reflective writing need not always be personal. You may be asked to keep a reading log when studying a novel or playscript. This is intended as a record of your thoughts on what you read and you would not be concerned if a friend or your teacher were to read it.

One particular form of writing which seems to be on the boundary between writing for yourself and for others is the 'Record of Achievement'. You may be familiar with these as 'reports', 'summaries' or 'certificates', but what they have in common is that you are asked to reflect on work you have completed and your attitude towards it.

Evaluating progress

The sheet below shows one student's assessment of her work on *The power and the glory*. Using a blank version of the same sheet write an analysis of the work you did in discussing and writing about the article.

The questions on the prompt sheet are intended to help you think about your achievement: do not feel that you have to answer all of them in turn.

Name: Shelley Amis **Group:** 4yz

Date: 24.9.91 **Activity:** The power and the glory

SPEAKING AND LISTENING
I enjoyed the group discussion because before we began to talk I wasn't sure about some of the article. When we all looked at it together it began to fall into place, like a jigsaw puzzle. Highlighting the text together helped with this. I'm normally a bit shy when I'm in front of others, so I felt self-conscious about my debate speech. I'd prefer to give it to a small group. Next time I would try to speak out more, because the people at the back couldn't hear it all, but they did give me a lot of support.

READING
I found the article a little difficult at first, but we made sense of it when we found the key words. I thought it was a bit one-sided but that made it easier to make notes and ask questions about it.

WRITING
When I came to make the table out I'd got too many notes so I had to cut them down; I think I tried to get too much information in. Once I'd made the diagram it was easy to summarise the article. My cue cards for the speech were cluttered, really. I was nervous about speaking so I wrote too much on them. Next time I'll try to use fewer cues and look at the cards less often.

EFFORT
I tried very hard at this. Speaking's not my favourite type of work, but I found out that you have to prepare for it in writing very carefully. If your notes have just the essentials then it's easier to speak. Too much writing makes you cheat and read it out. That's obvious to the audience, because you don't look at them.

TEACHER'S COMMENT

Communication counts

Much of the writing you do or read has as its purpose communication with other people; whether it is a note to explain an absence from school or a major work of fiction. As the reason for the communication will vary, so will its form and style of writing. These need to be appropriately matched to the message, otherwise the reader may be misled or become confused.

Dearest Pedagogue,
 I communicate with you by the means of epistle to impart to you the knowledge that my youngest offspring (the child you see before you, commonly addressed as Reginald Arthur Entwistle) has of late been striken with a bout of gripe. Please accept my humblest and most heartfelt apologies for the youngster's lack of attendance in the recent past, a period of some three days and nights. I implore you to inform me should there be any possible method of ensuring that the boy remains fully up-to-date with his programme of studies, as I will then personally oversee him in this labour.
 Most humbly and gratefully yours,
 E. J. Entwistle (Paternal guardian)

Looking at the language

- What is this piece of writing about?
- Is it written in an appropriate form?
- Does its style match its purpose?
- What is the effect of the language on the reader?

Rewrite the letter in an appropriate way. Add a short paragraph in which you explain why you think the original writing sounded odd.

In order to communicate effectively you need to bear in mind two things before you even begin to write:

The form, language and register you use in your writing should always be determined by the two questions above.

Assignment

The film brochure on the right has arrived on your doormat and you and a group of friends are keen to see one of the films. You are sure that others would be interested too and decide to set up a visit to the local Arts Centre one evening after school or one Sunday afternoon.

1 As a group, agree on which film you would like to see and note down its showing dates and times.
2 Decide when you will go. Consult diaries, timetables. Write a time plan for things you need to do in the lead up to the visit.
3 You will need to inform students, parents, teachers, and your headteacher of the plan, and possibly gain permission from several of these. What types of writing will be involved here?
4 How will you go about booking tickets? What will you need to do and write for this? Have you considered how you are to get to the Arts Centre? How long will it take? And will you need to arrange for transport?
5 How will you advertise your visit and sell the tickets? How will you collect the money and make other payments? Plan out the last minute arrangements and give those who are coming on the visit their final instructions and information.

Keep all your notes and paperwork and evaluate them at the end. How many different audiences and purposes did you write for? Record them on a new sample analysis chart, like the one on page 65.

Now you have seen what is involved, you could try organising a real visit to your local film club or cinema. Remember that you will be representatives of your school and that you must have permission from your headteacher before arranging the trip.

MAIN FEATURES

● *Friday 21 June to Wednesday 26 June* 8.30

HAMLET

US, 1990, 133 mins
Dir: Franco Zeffirelli. **With:** Mel Gibson, Glenn Close, Alan Bates, Ian Holm, Paul Scofield, Helena Bonham-Carter.

'Action Man' Mel Gibson may seem an unlikely choice for the title role, but his performance as the Prince of Denmark, tortured by self-doubt and indecision as he tries to unravel the intrigue behind his father's sudden death, has been widely and warmly praised. He certainly brings some much needed passion to the character in a traditional but surprisingly accessible reading of the play — a story of revenge and tragedy. Intelligently done, very well acted, and it looks good too. A meaty entertainment.
'The whole cast is distinguished . . . Zeffirelli has interpreted Shakespeare's masterpiece for popular rather than elitist consumption. It is, after all, a marvellous story.' (George Perry *The Observer*)
'Superior in every way to Olivier's 1948 version . . . a splendid film.' (Philip French *The Observer*)
'Tractable, pleasing and dosed with a handful of thrills . . . solid entertainment.' (Anthony Lane *Independent on Sunday*)

● *Friday 28 June to Wednesday 3 July* 6.30

THELMA AND LOUISE

US, 1991, 128 mins.
Dir: Ridley Scott. **With:** Susan Sarandon, Geena Davis, Harvey Keitel, Michael Madsen, Christopher McDonald, Stephen Tobolowsky, Brad Pitt, Timothy Carhart.

Susan Sarandon and Geena Davis star as two bored Southern girls who just wanna have fun. So Thelma, fed up with waiting all day for husband Dull Daryl to come home, and Louise, fed up with waiting tables in the local diner, pack up their troubles into an old T-Bird, set the motor running, and fly off down the highway for a girls' weekend away. But when they stop off for a drink at a roadside Honky Tonk, something happens — to tell you what would spoil it — and the women are on the run. The more trouble they get into, the more fun they have, and the more reckless they become. Like all road movies, *Thelma and Louise* is basically a journey of self discovery. En route, the women find their previously untapped skills and capacities (to their surprise and delight, hold-ups, car-chases and shoot-outs are second nature), strength in their shared fears and desires, and with every new day, new ways of looking at the world. The mood is definitely upbeat throughout; thrilling, exhilarating and at times extremely funny.
'I have to confess I loved it . . . we were all, it seems, born to run.' (Andrea Stuart, *City Limits*)
'Don't expect to believe it, just get ready for the big finish . . . in an indelible final image, it maintains the sense of reckless exhilaration to the end . . . a triumph. Despite some delectably funny scenes between the sexes, Scott's latest pic isn't about women *vs* men; it's about freedom. In that sense, and many others, it's a classic.' (*Variety*)

plus **CRIMES AND MISDEMEANORS** 8.30

US, 1990, 104 mins.
Dir: Woody Allen. **With:** Martin Landau, Woody Allen, Anjelica Huston, Alan Alda, Mia Farrow, Sam Waterston, Claire Bloom.

Woody Allen back on top form bringing fresh insight to familiar themes — life and love, good and evil, and of course, the movies. Martin Landau heads a magnificent cast as the wealthy doctor pondering the morality of murder when his brother offers to dispose of a troublesome mistress (Anjelica Huston, excellent), and Allen provides comic relief in pursuit of Mia Farrow.
'Intricate, grown-up and delicious . . . among his very best work.' (Angie Errigo, *Empire*)
'The best and most complete he's made for some time.' (Derek Malcolm, *The Guardian*)

● *Sunday 23 June* 5.30
CYRANO DE BERGERAC

Fr, 1990, subtitles, 135 mins.
Dir: Jean-Paul Rappeneau. **With:** Gerard Depardieu, Anne Brochet, Jacques Weber, Vincent Perez, Roland Bertin.

Surely *the* classic story of unrequited love, starring Gerard Depardieu as the swashbuckling poet who, convinced of his own ugliness, can only voice his passionate soul through love letters written on behalf of his true love's witless beau. Not till his dying breath does he openly declare his feelings to Roxanne, who realises too late the true object of her desires.
  'A truly splendid performance from Depardieu.' (Geoff Andrew, *Time Out*)
  'Spectacular . . . superb subtitles . . . elegant direction . . . a mesmeric, unforgetable piece of work.' (*Empire*)
  'Looks marvellous . . . Great stuff.' (Barry Norman, *Film 90*)
  'Does it really deserve so many plaudits? The answer must be an unqualified "yes".' (Derek Malcolm, *The Guardian*)

● *Sunday 30 June* 6.00
GREEN CARD

US, 1990, 107 mins.
Dir: Peter Weir. **With:** Gerard Depardieu, Andie MacDowell, Bebe Neuwirth.

A sophisticated topsy-turvy love story with Gerard Depardieu (charmingly oafish) and Andie MacDowell (suitably prim) as the ill-matched couple who enter into a marraige of convenience — he in order to secure the prized Green Card which foreigners need to work in the States, and she to get her green fingers on a gorgeous apartment cum conservatory which can only be let to married couples. Witty, tailor made for Depardieu and beautifully directed.
  'This gentle, bitter-sweet comedy is less wise-cracking than many, but it also has more depth and subtlety.' (*The Guardian*)
  'Weir likens this wholly delightful film to a "light meal". It's one to savour.' (Colette Maude, *Time Out*)

● *Sunday 7 July* 4.30
AN ANGEL AT MY TABLE

Aust/NZ, 1990, 158 mins.
Dir: Jane Campion. **With:** Kerry Fox, Alexia Keogh, Karen Ferguson.

Based on the autobiographical writings of one of New Zealand's foremost writers, Janet Frame, this charts her growth as a writer from childhood to painfully shy adulthood, and the power of her imagination to overcome the worst that life can throw. The story of someone who could never quite fit in, the film does not gloss over her regrets and bitterness, yet still manages to deal with her life in a celebratory and uplifting way. One of the most remarkable films of its year.
  'Simplicity is incredibly difficult in cinema, and the main reason why this is one of the very best films this year . . . there are fine and superbly well matched performances . . . They are extremely well directed too . . . a very special vision of a pretty special human being.' (Derek Malcolm, *The Guardian*)
  'Sensitive, imaginative and gutsy . . . a profoundly moving and strangely affirmative experience.' (Geoff Andrew, *Time Out*)

plus AWAKENINGS 6.30

US, 1990, 121 mins.
Dir: Penny Marshall. **With:** Robin Williams, Robert De Niro, John Heard, Julie Kavner, Penelope Ann Miller, Max Von Sydow.

Awakenings is based on the true story of shy young Dr Sachs' work with seemingly incurable catatonic patients. It focusses on the relationship between Sachs (in the guise of Dr Sayer, Robin Williams), and a patient afflicted since childhood, Leonard Lowe (De Niro), now in his 30s. The core of the drama lies in the effects on them both of the discovery and eventual failure of what seemed to be a miracle cure. Overly sentimental at times, but an extraordinary and utterly fascinating story nonetheless.
  'De Niro's acting offers a combination of research, intuition and sheer brilliance that is the highest his art has to offer.' (Iain Johnstone, *Sunday Times*)
  'Brave, powerful and effective' (Derek Malcolm, *The Guardian*)

● *Thursday 27 June* 7.00
AMERICAN FRIENDS

US/BR, 1990, 95 mins.
Dir: Tristram Powell. **With:** Michael Palin, Trini Alvarado, Connie Booth, Alfred Molina.

Inspired by the diaries of his great grandfather, Michael Palin wrote and stars in this quintessentially English tale of an Oxford don who meets a pair of American ladies on holiday in Switzerland, and finds himself torn between his desire to take over the college presidency (for which he must remain celebate) and the urge to run off with the lady Elinor.
  'The film has poise and equilibrium, a delightful restraint in its performances, and a peculiarly English sweetness of temper.' (Hugo Davenport, *Daily Telegraph*)

plus CELIA 9.00

Aust, 1988, 103 mins.
Dir: Ann Turner. **With:** Rebecca Smart, Nicholas Eadie, Victoria Langley, Maryanne Fahey.

Another outstanding debut from a notable young Australian director, this time Ann Turner. This affecting rites-of-passage drama charts one summer in the life of 9 year old Celia following the death of her grandmother and the arrival of new playmates. When her father puts a stop to their friendship, he offers a pet rabbit as a substitute, but even that is impounded by the authorities when rabies breaks out, and as Celia struggles to make sense of her losses, fantasy and reality blur with shocking consequences. Rather than the usual nostalgia trip, Turner offers a highly original tale of innocence corrupted.
  'Outstanding . . . Celia has the capacity to shock and make us think . . . the acting is consistently good.' (Philip French, *The Observer*)
  'Striking . . . Rebecca Smart gives one of the most truthful performances that can be imagined.' (Derek Malcolm, *The Guardian*)
  'Compassionate, stylish, humourous.' (*Empire*)

● *Thursday 4 July* 7.00
HIGHLANDER

Br, 1986, 116 mins.
Dir: Russell Mulcahy. **With:** Christopher Lambert, Roxanne Hart, Clancy Brown, Sean Connery.

Sean Connery and Christopher Lambert star as the sword-weilding time travellers hopping about through the ages from the Scottish Highlands in the Middle Ages to contemporary America, in pursuit of the evil villain. Some great effects.
  'Connery makes tosh dialogue sound like it was written by Noel Coward . . . Lots of energy, a frenzied pace, and a villain who sings Tom Waits while mowing down innocent pedestrians . . . a lot of utterly preposterous fun.' (Richard Rayner, *Time Out Film Guide*)

● *Thursday 11 July* 7.00
POSTCARDS FROM THE EDGE

US, 1990, 101 mins.
Dir: Mike Nichols. **With:** Meryl Streep, Shirley MacLaine, Dennis Quaid, Richard Dreyfuss.

Mike Nichols' Oscar nominated adaptation of the Carrie Fisher confessional. Meryl Streep and Shirley MacLaine star as Hollywood mother and daughter trying to resolve their relationship as one comes to terms with becoming a has-been and the other with her drug addiction.
  'Streep is a revelation, MacLaine superb . . . Small and gloriously hit and miss. Rob Reiner, Gene Hackman and Simon Callow all add extra class to Hollywood's best joke about itself in years.' (*Empire*)
  'Masses to enjoy.' (Anthony Lane, *Independent on Sunday*)

Planning and drafting

Getting started

Notes to yourself, a telephone message or diaries are all short and spontaneous. However, longer pieces of writing are always better for careful planning.

Writing without a clear idea of where you are going can be a waste of valuable time and effort. Yet it can be difficult to get started, so here are some tips and ideas.

1 Be clear about your **content**. Begin with your main idea and then branch out, jotting down essential points and associations. You could try doing this in the form of a spider diagram or brainstorm map.

For example, if you were to write a short article based on this statement: 'It is the Government's duty to ensure that no one has to suffer homelessness', the spider diagram of your first ideas might look something like the one shown opposite.

2 Drawing a spider diagram can also assist you with your **research**. Decide what information or evidence you need in advance and cut down on time spent on reading and research.

In the example given it may not be easy to obtain the figures, but you would know exactly what to look for in a library, or to ask for if you contacted Shelter or other organisations dealing with the problem of homelessness.

In the library use reference books, leaflets, magazines and newspapers. Look out for TV programmes on the topic. Real-life interviews and surveys can all become material for your written work.

When you have found the information you need, make clear notes, but never copy anything more than short quotations. Record your sources for rechecking at a later date and remember to acknowledge any quotations you use.

3 Be clear about your **purpose** and your **audience**. Who are you trying to persuade, inform, report to, entertain?

4 Be clear about your **form**. Will you be writing an article, an essay, a story, a letter, a poem?

5 Plan out the **structure** of your piece using these main sections.

> **Introduction**: introduce your topic and your purpose in a single sentence or a paragraph. Be clear. Engage your reader's interest.
>
> **Development**: divide your material into related sections. Paragraphs should show development of your argument. Try not to jump from idea to idea.
>
> **Conclusion**: draw together your ideas, reinforce them or round off. Avoid abrupt endings. Be positive.

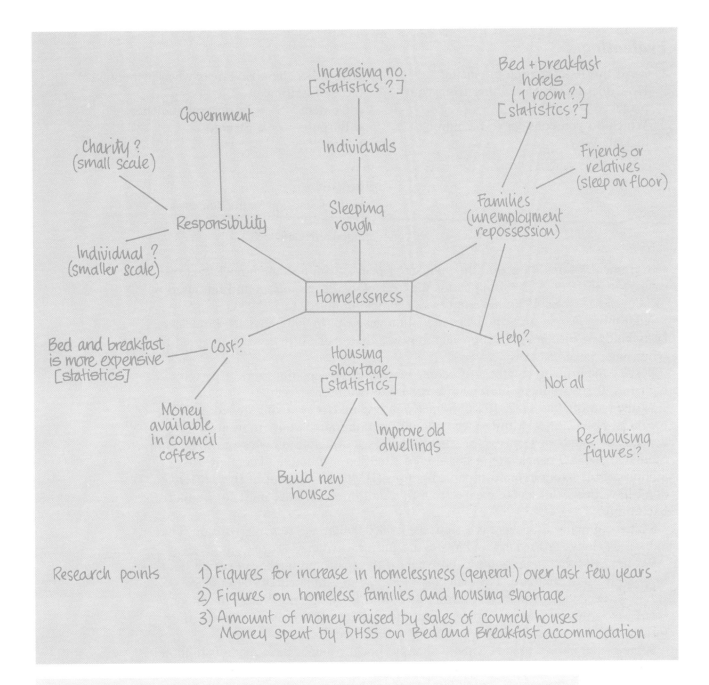

The spider diagram shows:

Homelessness (centre)

- Individuals
  - Sleeping rough
  - Increasing no. [statistics?]
  - Government
  - Charity? (small scale)
  - Responsibility
  - Individual? (smaller scale)

- Families (unemployment, repossession)
  - Bed + breakfast hotels (1 room?) [statistics?]
  - Friends or relatives (sleep on floor)

- Cost?
  - Bed and breakfast is more expensive [statistics]
  - Money available in council coffers

- Housing shortage [statistics]
  - Build new houses
  - Improve old dwellings

- Help?
  - Not all
  - Re-housing figures?

Research points

1) Figures for increase in homelessness (general) over last few years
2) Figures on homeless families and housing shortage
3) Amount of money raised by sales of council houses
   Money spent by DHSS on Bed and Breakfast accommodation

Making plans

Using the spider diagram for 'homelessness' decide upon and write out a linear plan for a short article on this subject. Follow the structure shown on page 76 like this:

Introduction   Increase in the number of people who are homeless

Development
{ Paragraph 1
2
3
4
5
6

Conclusion

Evaluating

1 Read this letter written by Shelter.
2 How does its structure differ from your plan?
3 Which do you consider to be more logical? Why?

Remember these key areas when planning a piece of writing:
- Content
- Purpose
- Research
- Form and audience
- Structure

Shelter
National Campaign for the Homeless
88 Old Street
London EC1 9HU

Government figures show that the number of people who become homeless is rising each year. In 1979, 57 200 households were recognised as homeless and rehoused by local authorities. By 1986 this number had almost doubled, to 103 000.

A lot more people suffer homelessness than get help. In 1985, 208 480 homeless households in Britain applied for help, but less than half of them were accepted for rehousing.

Besides the growing numbers of people who have to sleep outdoors, especially in big cities, there are many more with nowhere to call home.

At the end of June 1987, 10 870 homeless households were living in bed and breakfast hotels, often with the whole family in one room. Many thousands have to depend on friends or relatives for some floor space or a sofa on which to sleep – an estimated 300 000 people are in this sort of situation in London. There are 2.6 million people living in multi-occupied houses (HMOs). Four out of five HMOs don't have proper means of escape from fire, and one in ten are unfit for human habitation.

Shelter estimates that there is a shortage of 800 000 homes in Great Britain. Over 1 million dwellings in England and Wales are unfit to live in.

We need to build more homes, and we need to repair and improve existing housing to bring it up to standard. This will cost money – an estimated £45 000 million would be needed to remedy all housing defects in England and Wales. But money spent wisely now will avert a worse – and more expensive – housing crisis in the future.

Some of the money needed is there already. Local councils have made £8 billion from selling council houses, but they aren't allowed to spend it on building new homes. Some of the money that could be used is being wasted: it costs £10 900 a year to keep a family in bed and breakfast in London, when it would be cheaper in the long run to buy or build them a house to rent. The house would then be there for people to use in the future as well.

A housing problem of this size cannot be solved by individuals, or by charities. It needs organisation and commitment on a far larger scale. The Government are in a position to end homelessness should they choose to. They have the power to ensure that our taxes provide the housing that people need. Yet homelessness is still on the increase. For this reason, putting an end to homelessness and bad housing should not be left to choice. It should be a duty.

For more on homelessness, see the Media Scripts module in Book 4A, pages 144-153

Drafting, revising and editing

It would be a mistake to think that we can write exactly what we want to neatly and correctly first time around. Even professional writers cannot usually do this. They may write their first draft quickly, whilst their ideas are fresh, but subsequent revisions will be slower and more careful. In this section the writer, Christopher Rush, explains how he worked on part of a short story called *Tutti Frutti*.

The pen is mightier than the word!

The following extract from a short story is presented here in three stages: the original version from the first stages of draft composition (A); the second version showing the various revisions (B1); and the final published version (B2).

A

But what would happen, he wondered, if one night he were to come out into the garden and perhaps catch sight of her in her bedroom, standing with the curtains open and in the act of taking off her clothes? What if he were to see her absolutely naked? No, outraged by the very thought of it, he swung himself quickly over the fence. The cat hurried in behind him with his wet feet.

As soon as he was in bed he regretted his unworthy thoughts. After all she was a goddess. To hold her hand all day long would be enough and eventually to be allowed to kiss her on her chaste lips.

He fell into a wild web of dreams.

B1

But what would happen, he wondered, if one night he were to come
— should —
out into the garden and perhaps catch sight of her in her bedroom,
here   see   own   privately,
standing with the curtains open and in the act of taking off her clothes?
undrawn,
'Half-hidden, → should the very parts of which Ravished that N.P.
like a   Tutti Frutti was composed
mermaid in   back across   Shakespeare
seaweed' thought of it, he swung himself quickly over the fence. The cat hurried
at his feet,   dew-wet fur.
in behind him with his wet feet.
Once   vision of a naked Tutti Frutti.
As soon as he was in bed he regretted his unworthy thoughts. After
S
all she was a goddess. To hold her hand all day long would be enough.
at the end of the day ———— remove her spectacles alone and
A and eventually to be allowed to kiss her on her chaste lips. granted a kiss.
// On those chaste lips.
He fell into a wild web of dreams. spun himself

79

But what if one night he should come out here and see her in her own bedroom, privately, the curtains undrawn, taking off her clothes?

Half-hidden, like a mermaid in seaweed.

What if he should see the very parts of which Tutti Frutti was composed?

No.

Ravished by that thought, he swung himself back across the fence. Shakespeare hurried in at his feet, with dew-wet fur.

Once in bed he regretted his vision of a naked Tutti Frutti. She was a goddess. To hold her hand all day long would be enough. And at the end of the day, to remove her spectacles alone, and be granted a kiss.

On those chaste lips.

He spun himself into a wild web of dreams.

I have chosen this passage partly because it is a fairly straightforward piece of prose in which there is very little action and which is not particularly heavy on description. Yet, even this simple piece of writing has been subjected to a number of revisions which have resulted in improvements of one kind or another. Let us look at the principal changes.

Before doing so it is useful to point out that the main character in the story is a teenage boy of the 1950s who has fallen in love with the girl next door, a girl with highly religious and protective parents. At this point in the story it is past midnight and he is standing in her back garden, which is adjacent to his own.

(1) The first sentence originally consisted of 40 words. In the B version it has been reduced to 25 and there are other examples in the passage of this kind of pruning. Can you spot these? I could just as easily have *expanded* my first draft. Instead I chose to reduce the wordage. Why? The effect is clearly to tighten up the sentence and in this newly achieved tautness of idea and expression there is a distinct heightening of tension, echoing the boy's nervousness, his emotional expectations. Read the two versions aloud and you will hear the difference.

(2) Still in the same sentence, look at the increased number of commas after 'bedroom' in the B version. Again this dispels the more relaxed and pedestrian tone of the A version. The commas introduce significant pauses equivalent to the boy's held breath. The overall effect is more suspenseful and atmospheric.

(3) The rather prosaic 'he wondered' is removed so that the sentence is taken away almost entirely from me, the author, and placed inside the boy's own head. *Almost* entirely. The retention of the 3rd person, 'he', is the one wisp of authorial presence in the sentence.

(4) A quotation is introduced: 'Half-hidden, like a mermaid in seaweed'. Why? The boy's head is stuffed full of the literature he has been studying at school. It has fired his imagination and he is at the stage where he is thinking in quotations. There is more to it than that, however. The line is taken from a poem by John Keats, *The eve of St Agnes*, in which a young lover called Porphyro watches the girl he loves undress. He has crept into her room and hidden himself and at the conclusion of the poem they elope together into the night. So: the allusion is both appropriate and at the same time adds to the picture of the boy as an over-romantic teenager, identifying himself too readily with characters and situations in literature. The quotation therefore glances with gentle irony at his fantasy role but also softens his preoccupation with the girl's undressing, saves it from crudity and raises it above the level of mere voyeurism.

(5) Now look at the rephrasing of the sentence immediately following the quotation. What do you think it gains in the rewriting? In other words, why did I change it?

(6) It is amazing what can be achieved by the simplest of typographical changes: the appearance of a word on the printed page, seen in relation to other words. Consider the increased emphasis gained in the B version and the effect created by the 'empty line' that follows, with its impressions of silence and speculation. The same technique may be seen in some of Shakespeare's soliloquies, which is just one of the places I learned it from! It is not dissimilar to the effect of a sudden bar of silence in a piece of dramatic music.

(7)   'Ravished' is entirely different in meaning. Why is it better than 'outraged'?

(8)   The cat is given his name in the B version. Can you see why? 'At his feet' is also more cat-like than 'behind him', as is 'dew-wet fur'. 'Wet feet' was not sufficiently feline for me the second time around!

(9)   'Unworthy thoughts' is an abstraction. 'A naked Tutti Frutti' is more startlingly real; almost absurdly life-like.

(10)   Compare the A version's 'eventually' with the B version's 'at the end of the day'. The latter continues the idea of the long lovers' day and the ideal courting introduced by the previous sentence.

(11)   The notion of the boy's removing her spectacles is brought in to add a touch of adolescent idealism and absurdity.

(12)   'On those chaste lips' is taken off the end of its sentence and placed in a line on its own for the same reason as in point (6) above. Note that the four words do not grammatically constitute a sentence. The effect of the compression and isolation of the phrase is to focus our attention even more sharply on the girl's lips, his thoughts of kissing her and his general view of her as a creature set apart.

Christopher Rush

Group discussion

When you have read through the different versions and the writer's comments, discuss the following questions in a group of 3 or 4.

1   Read the versions of sentence 1 aloud. Can you hear the difference? What, apart from shortening the sentence, causes this? Does it add anything to our understanding of the main character?

2   Why do you think the quotation has been introduced to version B? Look it up in Keats' poem, *The eve of St Agnes*. What does it add to our knowledge of the boy's thoughts and feelings towards Tutti Frutti?

3   Notice the layout of the section immediately following the quotation. Does the spacing on the page make a difference to reading it aloud? Which words now carry the emphasis and why?

4   What differences are there in the portrayal of the cat between versions A and B? Can you explain them?

5   What does the introduction of Tutti Frutti's spectacles add to the picture of the boy's wooing of her?

6   In the final line, why has 'fell' been replaced by the more lyrical 'spun himself'?

Report back your conclusions to the class, and as you begin your next piece of writing and redrafting, bear these techniques used by Christopher Rush in mind.

Assignment

1   On your own, spend ten minutes brainstorming one of these ideas for a short story. Use a spider diagram to record your thoughts.
   - The generation gap
   - The time bomb
   - Strangers on a train
   - A lucky break
   - Memories
   - Exile

2   Spend the next ten minutes discarding any ideas you don't want to use and preparing a linear plan, using the guidelines for planning on pages 76-77 and omitting the research section. Hints for short story writing can also

be found in the Forms of Narrative module in Book 4A, page 47.

3   Write the first draft of your story, setting yourself a time limit (say twenty minutes) so that you don't write too much at this stage. You must, however, get to the end of your story in the set time.

4   Working with a partner follow the guidelines for redrafting, particularly points 2 and 7, for each of your short stories. Take as long as you like over this, but aim to each produce a new draft.

Guidelines for drafting

You may not always be asked to redraft your work, but when you are it is worth spending more time on it than you did on your original piece.

It's important to note that redrafting is not the same as **proof-reading.** (For more on this see page 83.). **Redrafting** is about making deliberate changes to what you have written until it says exactly what you want it to, in exactly the way that you want. Do not be afraid to highlight or write on your original draft in different ink. It may look messy to you at first, but this is not too important at this stage.

Redrafting is often easier to do with the help of another person. By reading or showing your work to one another, work through the questions below with a partner, making notes as you go along.

1 Is there anything which is not clear or even confusing in this piece? How could it be made clearer? Try changing the word or sentence order to begin with.

2 Is there any part of this piece which could be removed without losing the sense of the writing? Is there anything missing? Does the reader need more information, explanation or description?

3 Is the beginning suitable? What about the end? Is the reader properly introduced to the content? Is the reader left in mid-air? Do the paragraphs lead on well from one another?

4 Is the language appropriate for the intended audience? Are there any phrases or words which do not seem appropriate? Can you suggest helpful changes or substitutes?

5 Has the writer fulfilled the task, or answered the question? Is the writing enjoyable/ interesting? Can you help your drafting partner with this?

6 Is the length of the piece appropriate for the purpose? What could be done to adjust it if necessary?

- One person's suggestions are useful but may not be enough to solve all problems.
- Get a second opinion from another friend, a teacher or a parent if you wish.
- Look again at your own writing.

Producing a revised version takes time, but is worth it in the end. If you have access to a word-processor redrafting is a very easy process indeed. It is a good idea, however, to save your original redraft too, just in case you change your mind about things on your third or fourth draft!

Proof-reading

Proof-reading should always be the final stage of your finished piece of work.
It should be the last check for accuracy, and again, it is useful to work with your
drafting partner, checking with and for one another, as it is often difficult to spot all
the errors for yourself.

Basic proof-reading steps

❶ Check for spelling mistakes. Query anything
you are not sure about. Use a dictionary, a
thesaurus, a spell-check program or a human
being to make certain.

❷ Check punctuation. It should make the
writing clear, so if anything is confusing,
query it. Check full stops, capitals, question
marks, speech marks, etc.

❸ Check paragraphing. These help the reader
because they are easier on the eye than
continous text and divide the writing into
convenient parts each dealing with a different
point about the topic. If there are no paragraphs, think about where they should go!

❹ Check the layout. If you have used headings,
are they consistent? Does the writing look
neat on the page?

Writers and publishers use a special set of
symbols to help with proof-reading. A selection
of these showing the marks to be made in the
margin and on the text itself is given here.

Try researching a more complete list of these
or create a class-system of symbols, so that
anyone in your class could be your proof-reading
partner and you would still understand the
corrections made to your work.

When you are happy with using the symbols,
proof-read your stories before producing a final
version.

Instruction to Printer	Textual mark	Marginal mark
		New matter followed by $\wedge$
Insert in text the matter indicated in the margin	Stroke through character(s) to be deleted	ठा
Delete	___ under character(s) to be set or changed	⊔⊔
Set in or change to italic type	Encircle character(s) to be changed	⊔⌐
Change italic to roman type	≡≡≡ under character(s) to be set or changed	≡
Set in or change to capital letter(s)	Encircle character(s) to be changed	≢
Change capital letter(s) to lower-case letter(s)	∿∿ under character(s) to be changed	∿∿
Set in or change to bold type		
Insert full point or decimal point	$\wedge$ where required	⊙
Insert colon, semi-colon, comma, etc.	$\wedge$ where required	⊙/;/·/:/‹›/[‹]/‹›
Rearrange to make a new paragraph here	⌐ before first word of new paragraph	⌐
Run on (no new paragraph)	⌐ between paragraphs	⌐
Transpose characters or words	⊔⌐ between characters or words to be transposed, numbered where necessary	⊔⌐
Insert space between words	Y between words	↑
Reduce space between characters		between characters	⌃
Reduce space between words	⊤ between words	

83

Writing for information

Travel information

In a group of 3, examine the pieces of travel writing on these pages. It may help if you each read one piece and then report back with your comments to your group.

Group analysis

1 For each piece try to establish:
   ● the purpose of the piece
   ● its intended audience
   ● the facts (as opposed to opinions or story elements) and list them
2 Which piece carries the most useful information for prospective travellers to the places described?
3 Which piece requires the most accurate information? Why?
4 Which piece did you most enjoy reading?

Travels in West Africa

July 22nd, 1895 – Left Kangwe. The four Ajumba[1] did not turn up early in the morning as had been arranged, but arrived about eight, in pouring rain, so decided to wait until two o'clock, which will give us time to reach their town of Arevooma before nightfall, and may perhaps give us a chance of arriving there dry. At two we start. We go down river on the Kangwe side of Lembarene Island, make a pause in front of the Igalwa slave town, which is on the Island and nearly opposite the Fan town of Fula on the mainland bank, our motive being to get stores of yam and plantain – and magnificent specimens of both we get – and then, when our canoe is laden with them to an extent that would get us into trouble under the Act if it ran here, off we go again. Every canoe we meet shouts us a greeting, and asks where we are going, and we say 'Rembwé' – and they say 'What! Rembwé!' – and we say 'Yes, Rembwé,' and paddle on. I lay among the luggage for about an hour, not taking much interest in the Rembwé or anything else, save my own headache; but this soon lifted, and I was able to take notice, just before we reached the Ajumba's town, called Arevooma. The sandbanks stretch across the river here nearly awash, so all our cargo of yams has to be thrown overboard on to the sand, from which they can be collected by being waded out to. The canoe, thus lightened, is able to go on a little further, but we are soon hard and fast again, and the crew have to jump out and shove her off about once every five minutes, and then to look lively about jumping back into her again, as she shoots over the cliffs of the sandbanks.

Mary H. Kingsley

[1] These four Ajumba had been engaged, through the instrumentality of M. Jacot, to accompany me to the Rembwé River. The Ajumba are one of the noble tribes and are the parent stem of the M'pongwe; their district is the western side of Lake Ayzingo.

Of all the towns in all the world

ROMANTICS may find it hard to accept, but the only Rick's Bar in Casablanca is in the international Hyatt Regency Hotel. Huge stills from *Casablanca* look at you from every wall, but the piano is in the jazz bar next door. So much for atmosphere.

On the north-eastern side of the city, just a few yards away from the European-style cafés, modern streets and luxurious air-conditioned hotels, lies the old Casablanca. Pass through the arched gate of the *medina* and you will find yourself in the *souk*.

The first thing to hit you is the smell. On the stone-paved lanes are small sacks – upright with their top edges rolled down – filled with herbs, spices, nuts (especially almonds, which Moroccans put in almost every dish along with roasted peanuts), sunflower and pumpkin seeds, and other strange, aromatic substances. In the alleys of the old market, things may appear cheap – but you are expected to haggle. You'll spoil the stall holder's day if you don't.

In the oldest part of the *souk*, close to the harbour, are the single-sex public baths. Here, men can enjoy the skills of an old-fashioned barber and a heavy-handed masseur. The women's baths also serve as a beauty parlour: treatments include hair dyeing, massage, manicures and pedicures, as well as a full artistic make-up for the face and body – beautiful designs in henna printed on wrists, ankles and palms that will last for more than a week.

To quench the thirst generated by a hot, steamy bath, look out for the juice sellers, called *gerabs* (which means water carriers) on the corners of the *zenqas* (tiny, narrow alleys). They serve fresh orange juice from specially-treated goatskins slung around their waists.

Only six hotels remain within the walls of the old *souk*. They have no running water, just a tap in the middle of the courtyard. No one can recall a foreign visitor ever staying, only Moroccans bringing rugs from Agadir or handicraft from Marrakesh to be sold in the stalls and bazaars of Casablanca. If you buy from the shops on the fashionable Boulevard Mohamed El-Hansali, you can expect to pay double or even treble the price you would in the *medina* a few feet away – at a store which will often be run by the same shopkeeper.

To escape the pedlars, jump on a bus and go to the Atlantic coast, La Corniche. The area known as Ain-Diab is where the wealthy live, but along La Corniche lie daytime cafés and the sleazy bars, nightclubs, discos and cabarets that form the red-light district. Officially, Aids doesn't exist in Morocco.

For the equivalent of £2.50 you can take a taxi back to the centre of Casablanca to Houbous – a huge area of little shops selling all kinds of Moroccan artefacts. In the afternoon, the cafés in the Houbous are popular with students. Close by you can spot the secret police keeping a watchful eye on them, since universities are considered places of dissent against King Hassan. Both police and students enjoy a variety of drinks. Fresh green-leaf tea with plenty of fresh mint is the most popular – but ask them to leave the sugar out...

...Near the old harbour, there are a few fish restaurants serving the freshest fish – caught before your eyes. Finish up here and enjoy a meal, accompanied by one of the good local wines. Red Toulal would be my recommendation.

GETTING THERE:
Gibraltar Airways (through agents British Airways) and Royal Air Maroc offer Apex returns from £194, flying direct. Flights from budget travel agents start at £159.

In Patagonia

I left the boneyard of La Plata, reeling under the blows of Linnaean Latin, and hurried back to Buenos Aires, to the Patagonia station, to catch the night bus south.

The bus was passing through low hilly country when I woke. The sky was grey and patches of mist hung in the valleys. The wheatfields were turning from green to yellow and in the pastures black cattle were grazing. We kept crossing streams with willows and pampas grass. The houses of the estancias shrank behind screens of poplar and eucalyptus. Some of the houses had pantile roofs, but most were of metal sheet, painted red. The tallest eucalyptus trees had their tops blown out.

At half past nine the bus stopped at the small town where I hoped to find Bill Philips. His grandfather was a pioneer in Patagonia and he still had cousins there. The town was a grid of one-storey brick houses and shops with an overhanging cornice. In the square was a municipal garden and a bronze bust of General San Martin, the Liberator. The streets around the garden were asphalted but the wind blew in sideways and coated the flowers and the bronze with white dust.

Two farmers had parked their pick-ups outside the bar and were drinking *vino rosado*. An old man huddled over his maté kettle. Behind the bar were pictures of Isabelita and Juan Peron, he wearing a blue and white sash and looking old and degenerate; another of Evita and Juan, much younger then and more dangerous; and a third of General Rosas, with sideburns and a downcurved mouth. The iconography of Peronism is extremely complicated.

An old woman gave me a leathery sandwich and coffee. Naturally, she said, I could leave my bag while I tried to find Señor Philips.

'It is far to Señor Philips. He lives up in the sierra.'
'How far?'

Bruce Chatwin

Each writer is describing a place that they have visited. They all provide the reader with information about their visit, yet their styles are very different indeed. In each case the style of writing is linked closely to the purpose of the piece. Mary Kingsley records details of her minutest activities, Adel Darwish describes locations, hotels and facilities, whilst Bruce Chatwin's travels take the form of a narrative. The styles also reflect the audiences for whom the pieces are intended. Mary Kingsley for herself and for an audience unlikely to follow in her footsteps, Darwish for a newspaper whose readers are likely to have more adventurous tastes in holidays and Chatwin as a memoir of his travels and his reflections upon them.

You will have noted these differences in purpose and audience in your discussion. What they tell us is that writing to give information takes more than one form and will be as matter of fact or as lively as the form and the language the writer chooses.

For more on travel writing see Unit 3 in the Forms of Narrative module in Book 4A.

Information leaflets

Leaflets and brochures for tourists can be found readily in every town and city in Britain. Their aim is not only to provide basic information on location and services but also to attract visitors to certain places of interest and to advertise these places. Look at the following leaflet for tourists visiting Oxford.

OXFORD'S LIVELIEST ATTRACTION

Discover 800 years of Oxford University history in a ride through time.

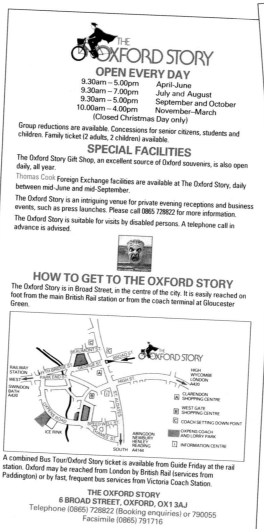

THE OXFORD STORY

OPEN EVERY DAY

9.30am – 5.00pm	April-June
9.30am – 7.00pm	July and August
9.30am – 5.00pm	September and October
10.00am – 4.00pm	November–March

(Closed Christmas Day only)

Group reductions are available. Concessions for senior citizens, students and children. Family ticket (2 adults, 2 children) available.

SPECIAL FACILITIES

The Oxford Story Gift Shop, an excellent source of Oxford souvenirs, is also open daily, all year.

Thomas Cook Foreign Exchange facilities are available at The Oxford Story, daily between mid-June and mid-September.

The Oxford Story is an intriguing venue for private evening receptions and business events, such as press launches. Please call 0865 728822 for more information.

The Oxford Story is suitable for visits by disabled persons. A telephone call in advance is advised.

HOW TO GET TO THE OXFORD STORY

The Oxford Story is in Broad Street, in the centre of the city. It is easily reached on foot from the main British Rail station or from the coach terminal at Gloucester Green.

A combined Bus Tour/Oxford Story ticket is available from Guide Friday at the rail station. Oxford may be reached from London by British Rail (services from Paddington) or by fast, frequent bus services from Victoria Coach Station.

THE OXFORD STORY
6 BROAD STREET, OXFORD, OX1 3AJ
Telephone (0865) 728822 (Booking enquiries) or 790055
Facsimile (0865) 791716

Heritage
Bringing the past to life

THE OXFORD STORY

The Oxford Story is a revealing introduction to one of the world's greatest universities. How do students live? Why has Oxford produced 24 Prime Ministers? What are the origins of the University?

Come to the Oxford Story and find out. Take your seat at a Medieval scholar's desk for a ride through Oxford University's 800 year history. The sights, sounds and even smells of former times are superbly recreated, as you meet the learned men, writers, monarchs, academics and even eccentrics who all have a role in the Oxford Story.

You will discover how student life has changed over the years; from the cold and gloom of a Medieval lecture hall to the privileged world of Edwardian Oxford. There is also a look at student life today, from midnight essay crisis to graduation.

The Oxford Story is the perfect start to a day in Oxford, with an informed and witty insight into the romantic past of the colleges and buildings which surround it, in Broad Street, in the heart of the city.

The Oxford Story is open every day. Allow 1 hour for your visit.

What do you think?

1 How useful is the information given in the Oxford Story leaflet? List the types of information offered, e.g. opening hours, images of Oxford.
2 If you were planning a visit to the Oxford Story, what other information would you need?

87

Hundreds of leaflets like this jostle for competition in every Tourist Information Office. Unless they are bright and attractive they do not stand out. Just as importantly, if the information within them is anything other than clear, concise and easy to use, they will be discarded.

Writing your own

1 Collect or send off for some sample leaflets and spend time comparing them. Using your selection compile a set of guidelines for the essential things to be included in an informative leaflet.

2 Choose a local place of interest. It can be your area's major attraction or a lesser known place which tourists might like to visit. Using the Oxford Story leaflet and your own guidelines to help you, plan a leaflet to attract and assist tourists.
   - Think hard about your target audience.
   - Consider volume of information – keep the length of your writing appropriate to its purpose. Be concise.
   - Read the section on layout in the Non-literary Forms module (pages 150-153)

before you mock-up a final leaflet with text and diagrams. Publish it in any way available to you. Before you begin refer to the planning and drafting unit in this module, pages 76-83.

3 Show your leaflet to others in your group. Would they visit the place you have chosen? Would they know what to find there? Or how to find it?

4 Your leaflet could become part of a coursework assignment if you combined it with a written analysis of the features of some commercially produced leaflets in your collection. You might also include an assessment of how you incorporated these features in your own leaflet.

Step-by-step instructions

Often we find ourselves in need of information or instruction to carry out even simple tasks because they are unfamiliar to us, for example, wiring a plug, giving first aid. At this point we turn to leaflets or manuals where instructions can be found, usually in simple steps and often accompanied by diagrams. Look at the following illustrations which show the jumbled instructions for wiring a plug.

Step-by-step instructions for wiring a plug

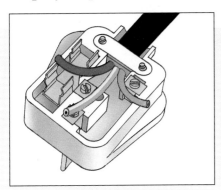

Carefully cut away 50mm (2in) of flex outer sheath. Fasten sheath firmly under clamp. Cut coloured cores so that they reach approx. 13mm (1/2in) beyond terminal.

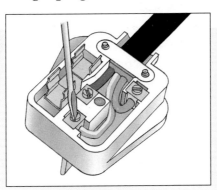

Tighten screws firmly. Fit correct fuse. Check coloured cores are connected to correct terminals. Make sure all is secure. Refit cover.

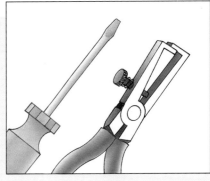

Wiring a plug is quite straightforward. All you need is a small screwdriver and something to cut the wires to length and to strip away unwanted insulation – a proper wire stripper and cutter is best.

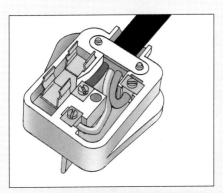

Twist strands of wire of each core together and fit into the hole near the top of the pillar terminal or loop once clockwise round clamp terminals. Check that there are no stray 'whiskers' of bare wire.

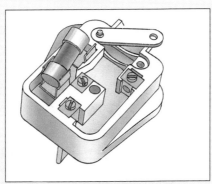

Unscrew plug top. Remove fuse (carefully lever with screwdriver if necessary). Loosen one flex clamp retaining screw; remove other where applicable.

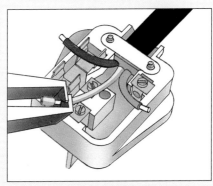

Carefully strip enough insulation to expose about 6mm (1/4in) of wire for screwhole (pillar) terminals about 13mm (1/2in) for clamp type ones, being very careful not to damage the fine strands of wire inside. Loosen screws in pillar terminals or remove screw-nuts and any washers from clamp terminals.

Working it out

1 Place the instructions for fitting a plug in the correct order.
2 How did you work out the order?
3 What clues do the pictures give you? What clues does the text give you?
4 Would you be able to follow these instructions:
   a) without the pictures
   b) without the words

The language and layout of instruction is often very specialised. Read through 'What to do if fire breaks out', paying particular attention to the labelled features.

WHAT TO DO IF FIRE BREAKS OUT

Remember that smoke can kill as well as flames.

If there is smoke, or whenever the fire is too big to tackle quickly and safely:

> Get everyone out of the house at *once*
> Shut all doors behind you
> Call the Fire Brigade

Coloured panel emphasises importance of these points

If you are trapped in a room:
- Keep the door shut.
- Put a blanket or carpet at the bottom of the door.
- Go to the window and call for help.

Each point is flagged or signposted

If the fire is small enough to tackle safely shut the door and then:

Chip pan fires:
- Switch off the heat.
- Smother the pan with a large lid or damp cloth.
- Don't move the pan or throw water on it.

All these verb phrases are in the imperative mood. They direct you towards an action, or instruct you what to do

Electrical fires:
- Switch off at the socket and unplug.
- Never use water while the power is on.
- Use a dry powder extinguisher to put out the fire.

Oil heater fires:
- If you have a water fire extinguisher and know how to use it stand at least six feet away and direct into the fire, concentrating on cooling the heater.
- Otherwise, play safe and follow the evacuation procedure set out above.

Sub headings indicate different types of fire emergency

Other small fires:
- Smother the flames with a rug, blanket or fire blanket.

Clothing on fire:
- Lay the person down at once and roll them on the floor.

Writing in the imperative

1 Invite someone who is proficient in first-aid to demonstrate how to do one of the following things:
- use a triangular bandage
- strap someone's foot
- prevent someone from choking

Make notes on each stage of the process and then write clear instructions for the activity. Check that your information appears in the correct order and include diagrams to help explain the process.
For more on note-taking, see page 68 in this module and Unit 3 in the Non-literary Forms module

2 a) Write the rules and instructions for playing a well-known card or board game. Test your attempts on other members of the class. They are to be your 'audience'.
Have you explained it clearly and logically? Can they play the game by following your instructions?

b) Redraft your work where necessary, giving particular attention to the level and appropriateness of the language you are using for your intended audience. For example, chess rules are essentially the same whoever the players are, but in this case you would have to think of the best way to phrase them for a teenage audience.

3 Take this last suggestion a stage further and invent your own board game. It could be based perhaps on the events of a novel or fantasy story you have read or on a journey from a travel book.
Think about the main features of the game, devise the rules and then try writing them in the imperative. Ask other members of your group to read them through. Do they make sense?

Read the following article in which the writer talks about mountain biking.

Fit for the finish

Can you imagine biking over rough countryside for two and a half hours, and about 13 miles per hour with no respite, your heart rate averaging 180 and peaking at 195? Professional moutain bikers can tolerate this intensity of exercise week after week. In terms of exertion, a pro mountain bike race ranks with running a top-level marathon.

In laboratory tests these masters of mud have shown themselves to be on a physiological par with élite endurance athletes. They have a higher exercise endurance capacity, and can operate at a higher percentage of that capacity for longer. They are born with that ability and train by riding up to 450 miles a week.

Yet, however awesome the ability of the élite, MTB racing is accessible to anyone who takes up the challenge. The fun and novice categories are full of weekend bikers who have neither the talent or training time to mix it with the stars.

The typical novice race distance will be about 12 miles, which the best fun riders will cover in around an hour. Most novice riders would find little difficulty doing that, but the fitter you are the easier you'll find it. Fitness for this type of race could be developed in a few weeks. Intense mountain biking off road is very stressful on the body, therefore pros train predominantly on road bikes or with mountain bikes on the road. But don't worry: for the informal racer, three or four MTB rides a week will be OK.

If you do other exercise such as going to a gym, concentrate on developing leg muscle endurance. Also important are a strong back, toned abdominals, and flexible hamstrings.

To increase your cardiovascular fitness try swimming or running, and best of all is muscle-conditioning low-impact aerobics.

The main source of pain is hill climbing, therefore hills should play a part in your preparation. It is tempting to go all out for the top, but the top of the climb may still be five miles from the finish, which will be a slow painful five miles if you've put all your energy into reaching the top of the hill. So pace yourself, ride well within your limits, then ride hard over the top of the hill and keep going for a couple of hundred yards. The real strain of an uphill climb is the concentrated effort. It's best to stay in the saddle when climbing rather than standing up on the pedals, which will quickly tire you out.

While training you should concentrate on pedalling speed, trying to maintain about 90 revs a minute. Although this will feel uncomfortable at first, persevere because it is more effective than trying to push a big gear more slowly. It also reduces the risk of knee injury and improves fitness by increasing blood flow and breathing rate.

Use your gears to help maintain this rate as the terrrain changes. There are times when pedalling quickly will affect bike control, and sometimes you will need to push harder to aid balance or acceleration away. Selecting a higher gear will do the trick.

Dave Smith

Presenting a hobby

1 Did you find this article easy to understand? Which technical terms do you feel need more explanation?
2 Explain your favourite pastime to your group or class. Spend five minutes planning the key points you want to make in your presentation. Remember, your audience will need to have any technical terms clarified.

For more on themes in specialist writing see Unit 4 of the Non-literary Forms module.

Spoken and written instructions

1 a) How does giving instructions orally differ from writing them down?
   b) How do we get across any visual ideas in each case?
   c) What differences are there in the vocabulary we use in each case?
2 Discuss these ideas as a class and produce two sets of guidelines for other students to use:
   ● A guide to making presentations
   ● How to write clearly and informatively

Assignment

Topical 'magazine' programmes for teenagers are extremely popular and are often shown in the early evening. They combine music and video clips with information on fashion, stars and contemporary issues. For younger children programmes like *Newsround* are also packed with up-to-the-minute information but in a much more journalistic format, and one which seeks to treat its audience as young adults. Before you begin the work in this section it would be useful to watch an edition of at least one of these programmes or to discuss them with those who have.

Consider how you might be able to combine the up-to-date journalism of *Newsround* with the more general topics of interest provided in teenage magazine programmes.

The Newsround team

1 You are going to design a 15 to 20 minute episode of *News Round-up*. Your audience will be between 8 and 12 years old.
   In groups of 5 or 6 work through these stages.
   - Brainstorm ideas for items to appear in the programme. Plan your content carefully. How much time will you allocate to each item?
   - Make each member of your group responsible for the research and writing of at least one item. One of you should also take the role of presenter and write the link passages.
   - Be inventive and include video clips, maps, graphs, diagrams, demonstrations, interviews, etc.
   - Storyboard the programme carefully and don't forget the lead in and out with music, etc.
   - Finally, if you are able to, video-tape your programme and show it to a young audience.
2 a) If you prefer you could present this as a radio programme, but then you would not be able to rely on visual effects.
   b) Alternatively, your ideas could be presented as a magazine or even entries for a children's encyclopaedia.

Presenters of DEF II

When your *News Round-up* is complete, write a report on it. Include the following sections.
- A description of how you went about it. How did you decide what to include? Who made the decisions about which group members should work on which parts, etc?
- An analysis of the programme saying whether or not you succeeded in what you originally set out to do? What were the difficulties? How did you overcome them?
- What was your own personal input?
- If you were to do another edition of the programme what would you change?

Argumentative and persuasive writing

Presenting an argument

You will often be asked to present your opinion in writing on a difficult or sensitive issue. When dealing with topics of this sort it is important to be clear about the differences between fact and opinion, and between opposing points of view. Unless you are clear about these things your writing may be in danger of appearing biased or unconsidered.

Hunting – fact or opinion?

When considering an issue, such as abortion, euthanasia or field sports, where many people get carried away by the strength of their opinions, it is vital to distinguish fact from opinion in what you read, see or hear.

Support or sabotage?

Cruel and out of date, or a great British tradition? Here a hunt saboteur and a hunt supporter put their opposing cases.

Andrew Thompson has been an active hunt saboteur for eight years.

'I became instantly opposed to hunting after I stumbled across a pack of foxhounds when I was out walking in the countryside. I saw the fox which had just been killed. I was horrified. I thought: this is wrong.

'A few years later I met a group of people in my home area, Derbyshire, who were hunt saboteurs. They tried to protect foxes against hunters. I decided to join them.

'Since then I've gone on regular 'sabs', as we call an outing, to disrupt a hunt. It can be quite scary. Some hunters are quite friendly towards us. But others get aggressive and you can get beaten up quite badly. Once a group of hunt supporters who disagreed with us started hitting us with sticks. Some saboteurs get their cars smashed and bricks thrown through their windows.

'I put myself at risk because I strongly believe that hunting is cruel, not only for the fox but also the dogs. The hounds are kept in cruel conditions. They are starved for two days before hunting and during the summer months they are whipped to

Robin Mackenzie is a farmer and a former joint master of the Vine and Craven hunt which covers land from Basingstoke, Hampshire, to Swindon, Wiltshire.

'I was born in south London so I have no background in hunting. In fact, when I was an undergraduate I was rather critical of it. But then I attended my first hunt and I enjoyed it immensely.

'It gave me an opportunity to ride horses across natural countryside. It is a great thrill following a fox because you never know where it is going to take you next. I love the challenge.

'I also enjoy the pomp and ceremony, which is important because it is part of the tradition of hunting. I wear a scarlet coat as an ex-master. Everybody must be tidily dressed so that they are a credit to the hunt.

'Thirty years ago hunting was quite an upper-class affair. But that is no longer the case. Today we have a complete cross-section of people in our hunt. On Saturdays we get up to 100 people on horseback, and twice that number following on foot or by car. They come from all walks of life.

'Hunting is not cruel. We don't train the hounds by whipping them, but by looking after them extremely well. They are all fit and healthy – they have to be to keep up with the fox.

'If a fox is caught, it is killed instantly by the lead hound who breaks its neck. It is a humane way of make them obey orders. The fox is chased and chased until its heart is fit to burst, and then it is ripped apart by the hounds.

'People try to defend hunting by saying it is a great British tradition. But so was slavery – and that was banned. I cannot see how killing a defenceless animal adds to our culture. It is not what most people want in this country.

'Being a hunt saboteur is not fun. Most of the time it is boring, waiting for the hunt to turn up. But it is very fulfilling because at the end of the day you know you saved animals' lives.'

(Andrew Thompson is not his real name.)

controlling the numbers of foxes, and as a farmer I know how important that is. If hunting was banned, it would be bad news for foxes because farmers would use less humane ways of killing them such as shooting or gassing.

'These days I try and go hunting once or twice a week. I have come across hunt saboteurs, but I just ignore them. I understand they oppose hunting, and I believe they have the right to say so. But I wonder sometimes why they claim to be concerned about animal welfare. They frighten the horses and one group put nails under their hooves. That's not animal welfare, is it?

'Hunting is a tradition that goes back centuries and gives enjoyment in the countryside to thousands of people. I see nothing wrong with it, and no reason why it should stop.'

Hue and cry

The deepening row over the hunting of deer and foxes has caused a split in the National Trust which, with more than two million members, is Britain's largest charitable membership organisation.

Members last month voted to ban deer-hunting on land which belongs to the Trust. However, the sport will continue for at least three years while a working party considers the implications of a ban. At the same meeting, a motion calling for a ban on fox-hunting was narrowly defeated.

The vote signals a growing controversy within the National Trust. Some members believe that hunting benefits the countryside because it helps preserve hedges, woods and copses in which foxes and deer live. Others argue that hunting is cruel and barbaric and cannot be justified in modern Britain.

But the arguments are not confined to members of the National Trust. The pros and cons of these types of sport continue to be part of a fierce national debate. The two sides even use different words to express their points of view: supporters of sports which involve the death of animals call them 'field' or 'country' sports, while opponents call them 'blood' or 'cruel' sports.

In Britain about five and a half million people legally take part in sports which involve hunting a variety of animals. Of these, fishing is the most popular, followed by fox-hunting and bird-shooting. There are also a number of illegal sports which involve animals, such as dog-fighting and badger-baiting.

Fox-hunting has aroused the most vocal and active opposition. Some groups of people, called hunt saboteurs, disrupt the sport by laying false scents over the routes that hunts take or by attempting to distract the hounds. But fox-hunters deny that the sport is cruel. Brian Toon, spokesman of the Masters of Foxhounds Association, says: 'Nobody loves foxes more than the people who hunt them.'

95

Uncertain future for the hunters

Hunting is alive and well but its future may be in doubt because of growing opposition to it within conservation groups.

Humans have hunted wild animals for thousands of years. At first they did so in order to survive. But even when people began to grow crops and keep domestic cattle and food was more plentiful, they continued to hunt – for pleasure.

The Romans, Saxons and Normans pursued hare, deer and wild boar for enjoyment. Gradually, fox-hunting became the most popular form of hunting in Britain. Many of the largest packs of foxhounds date from the mid-Eighteenth century, when dogs were trained to hunt by scent.

Today there are 194 registered fox-hunts in England, Scotland and Wales. Hunts operate over almost all of Britain's land area, with the exception of pockets of Scotland, Lancashire and the Pennines. There are also hunts in Northern Ireland and several in the Irish Republic, including two otter hunts.

Otter-hunting stopped in Britain over 10 years ago. But in addition to foxes, hares are still hunted either on foot or on horseback. There are also four packs of staghounds, which hunt wild herds of red deer.

Hunting shows no sign of dying out. But its future looks more precarious than ever because of a vocal and growing movement which argues that the sport is cruel and should be banned.

This anti-hunting movement is becoming increasingly prominent within conservation groups. For instance, hunting has become a major issue of debate within the National Trust, Britain's biggest private landowner and conservation organisation. Hunters have the right to cross a third of the Trust's property, although the Trust says that in practice they cover a much smaller area.

At the Trust's annual meeting last month members voted for a ban on deer-hunting on its land, although they will have to wait for a final decision on this. The Trust is conducting an inquiry which will look at the implications of banning red-deer hunting in the Quantocks and Exmoor and the effectiveness of other methods of controlling the size of herds. The inquiry will take at least another three years.

At the same meeting, a motion was proposed to ban fox-hunting on National Trust land. The motion said that 'the Trust should be at the forefront of the work protecting and conserving wild animals on their land, not allowing animals to be killed for fun.' It was narrowly defeated.

It later emerged that Dame Jennifer Jenkins, who chaired the Trust last year, had used an

Looking at the arguments

1 First, read the two statements in *Support or sabotage?* carefully. As you read, list or highlight the facts and opinions that emerge from each statement. If you are using highlighters, facts should be in one colour and opinions in another.
2 How do these two pieces differ in tone from the articles *Hue and cry* and *Uncertain future for the hunters*?
3 Why is there this difference and what does it tell us about each piece's purpose?

For or against?

1 a) Read the two articles again and compile lists under these headings:
   - Arguments for hunting
   - Arguments against hunting

b) Add to your lists any ideas that have come from the two statements in *Support or sabotage?* or from your own reading. Information from libraries or newspapers could form part of this research and you could interview someone who participates in hunting or an anti-hunt organisation.

2 When your lists are complete you should be in a position to decide which side of the argument you will support. Pair off with someone who has an opposing point of view to your own and take two minutes each to put your cases to one another. Let your partner have their say and remember that there are grey areas and that each person is entitled to their own opinion, however strongly you feel your views are justified.

undisclosed number of proxy votes in favour of allowing hunting to continue in line with the Trust council's recommendation. The ballot forms had been signed but left blank by Trust members. Anti-hunting activists claimed the members had been confused by the complicated ballot paper.

Dame Jennifer believes that the right to hunt is a moral issue which only Parliament can resolve. But within Parliament, the political parties cannot agree. The Conservative party has no plans to change the present laws on hunting. Labour, on the other hand, has long been opposed to it.

Newspaper reports last month suggested that the party was preparing plans to ban the hunting of foxes, deer and hares with hounds. According to the reports, Labour would also strengthen laws against badger-baiting and control the use of terrier dogs in the countryside, but would allow the shooting of game birds and fishing.

Such a ban would receive the enthusiastic support of groups such as the League Against Cruel Sports. The league says hunting is a barbaric hangover from the days when bear-baiting and cock-fighting were common forms of entertainment. The league estimates that one in three hunts ends in the death of a fox and that about 13,000 are killed every year in Britain.

Opponents of hunting say there is no need to use foxes as targets. They point to recent scientific research from Aberdeen University which suggests that if hunting were suspended, the number of animals would not rise dramatically. They also point to a recent Gallup poll which showed that 83 per cent of the general public opposes blood sports.

The Hunt Saboteurs Association says that the sport can be organised with no harm to animals by dragging a bag along a pre-arranged course. The bag lays a scent for the dogs to follow. There are already 11 registered 'drag-hunts' in Britain and the Channel Islands, some of which are well established. The Cambridge pack dates from 1855.

But supporters of hunting say that removing the fox would spoil the sport. They argue that the excitement of hunting lies in the challenge of being led wherever the fox runs.

The British Field Sports Society claims that only one in 10 fox-hunts ends in a kill. It argues that foxes need to be controlled because they are pests which are a threat to lambs and other farm animals, as well as wild species of nesting birds. A ban would cause environmental damage as fox numbers rise, and lead to the loss of many jobs as full-time hunt staff would have to be made redundant.

Hunting is not purely confined to the British Isles. There are also well-established packs of hounds in America and Canada, India, Australia, New Zealand, Kenya and South Africa.

There are a number of popular European hunts, such as the Bavarian Bloodhounds in Germany, which began in 1888, and the French Equipage de Vens et Venaille formed in the early Eighteenth century.

A variety of blood sports are practised around the world. Perhaps most famous of these is bull-fighting in Spain, enjoyed by thousands of Spaniards and tourists. But there is opposition here as well. Tossa de Mar, on the Costa Brava, last year became the first village to ban bull-fighting. The local mayor replaced it with an annual festival dedicated to animal rights.

Education Guardian 15 January 1991

You may find that you can't decide which side you agree with. Don't worry – you can still present both sides of the argument and state your feelings in full at the conclusion of your written work.

Help! I'm not sure

For writing

1 Plan a piece of writing entitled:
   'Field sport or blood sport – which title does fox-hunting deserve?'
This piece of writing need not be a formal 'essay'

– you can choose any form you wish to argue your point of view. But if you do choose to write in essay form, the next section offers some useful advice in 'Two ways to outline arguments clearly'.

Before you begin, turn back and revise the section in Unit 2 on planning, pages 76-77. You will see that you have already carried out much of the research into content and ideas. The development section of this essay needs to include arguments on both sides of fox-hunting and you need to be clear on these before you start. Whatever you do, do not ignore the view of the opposition. Put a clear case against it and your own case will be strengthened.

Two ways to outline arguments clearly

Let's suppose you support fox-hunting.

1 You could:
  - begin by outlining all the arguments *against* fox-hunting in a few paragraphs
  - continue by giving the case *for* fox-hunting and explain how these ideas cancel out those given earlier

2 You could:
  - work on the 'set them up and knock them down' principle. In this you provide an argument against the sport and, in the same paragraph, give the opposite view, stating clearly why you believe the latter case to be stronger.
  (N.B. If you are not certain which side you are on this becomes difficult and it would be better to use 1.)

These are not the only techniques you could use, for instance relevant facts, statistics and quotations can play an important role in supporting your argument.

Before you start your first draft, consider your tone. When you have really strong feelings about an issue it is easy to get carried way by anger or sentimentality. Try to set out your views calmly, and support them with evidence and clear reasoning.

The conclusion of your writing is the place to recap on your main argument and, most importantly here, to give your final answer to the question posed: 'Which title does fox-hunting deserve?'. Try to come up with a strong finish.

The language of argument

Can you add to the boxes on this page using your own ideas.
Look back at the articles on hunting for some more examples.

Introducing arguments with which you disagree...
'Several people think...'
'Many believe that...'
'It is often (sometimes) said...'
'There is a train of thought which runs...'

Giving your opinion...
'It is my belief...'
'I disagree...'
'This argument does not convince everyone...'

Useful linking phrases...
However...
Nevertheless...
This may be true, but...
In spite of this...

For more on linking language see Unit 3 in the Non-literary Forms module, pages 160-161.

Beware!
'It is a well known fact...' – Is it? Or is it just your opinion?
'Almost everyone knows...' – Do they? Are you generalising?
'This is nonsense...' – Take care not to be dismissive of others' beliefs.

Playing devil's advocate

Once you have your first draft, one way a drafting partner can help you with revisions is to play devil's advocate. (See drafting partnerships on page 82 in Unit 2.) If they agree with your viewpoint they should try to argue from the opposite point of view. This will help you to strengthen and clarify the evidence supporting your opinions. Doing it this way, you must convince them that your views are right. Of course, if they disagree with you it's plain sailing.

Debating the issue

Most people only ever hear of debates as part of the work of Parliament. However, debates are an exciting way of discussing almost any issue, whether in class or at a public meeting. In this section you will find a brief summary of the procedure for conducting a debate. When you have read this through, the floor is yours for a debate on hunting.

For the debate you will need:
A **motion**: 'This House believes that...' followed by the topic you will argue, in this case '...bloodsports have no place in a civilized society'
A **Chair**: known in Parliament as the Speaker, this person directs the debate and decides who will speak
A **Proposer** of the motion and **seconders**
An **Opposer** of the motion and **seconders**
} These are the speakers who begin the debate.

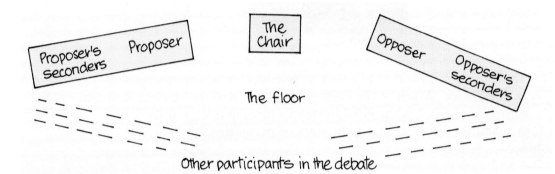

The Chair opens the debate and each of the main speakers mentioned above take their turn to speak. The motion is then declared 'open to the floor' and the Chair takes questions from other speakers. The Proposer and Opposer are then asked to 'sum up' and the motion is put to the vote. Those in favour and those against are asked to raise their hands and the votes are counted. The motion is then either declared 'carried' or 'defeated' by the Chair.

Writing debate speeches

Even if you are not one of the main speakers in a debate, it can help to have your speech written down. Speech writing needs just as much care as any other type (and just as much research if you are the Proposer or Opposer of a motion). You will find guidelines for writing speeches in the 'Just one way of using notes' section on page 70.

1 Using the piece of writing you have already completed on hunting, write a debate speech of 2 to 5 minutes in length. With a partner compare your speeches with the original pieces on hunting.
2 Discuss the differences between spoken and written language in these pieces. Has rewriting your view as a speech changed the structure or content of your argument in any way?

Talking others round

Most of the persuading we do is never written down at all. It might be as simple as asking your next-door neighbour to lend you a lawn-mower, or as subtle as talking someone into spending their savings on a time-share apartment in Spain. As a consumer you might buy two tins of green shoe polish when you only need one because they are on offer at two for the price of one. Or order a subscription to a magazine because there's a free gift up for grabs. Either way, most of us are regularly persuaded or bribed, depending on how you look at it, in our everyday lives.

Persuasion is the art of getting others to do or believe what you want them to. and it can be a fine art too. Much of the persuasive talk or writing we meet is in the form of advertising (see Unit 2 in the Non-literary Forms module), but there are also other forms, and the language and techniques of persuasion can be very specialised indeed.

Trying it out for yourself

Role play these activities or invent some of your own.

- Persuade a brother, sister or best friend to let you borrow their new leather jacket, their mountain bike, or some other treasured possession.
- Talk a parent into letting you stay out late for a party or dance.
- Persuade your Saturday job boss that you deserve a rise!

If you have a tape recorder or video camera available to you, record these improvisations. Play them back and make a transcript. (For more on transcripts see the Knowledge about Language module, pages 46–49.) Analyse the vocabulary and persuasive phrases that you used instinctively.

You were probably very polite and used words like 'please' and 'grateful' a number of times. It's quite likely that you speculated a little, e.g. 'I wonder if...' and used modal verbs, such as 'might' and 'may'.

Did you have to resort to stronger forms of persuasion, e.g. bribery, intimidation, threat, blackmail? It will, of course, depend on how subtle you were, but the more subtle your language, the less 'aggressive' your techniques will need to be.

The art of persuasion

All of the role plays on page 100 aim to obtain concrete things. Subtlety of language is even more important when you are trying to persuade someone to adopt your way of thinking. The following section looks at how one of the masters of the English language employs persuasion.

William Shakespeare's play, *Julius Caesar*, tells how Caesar, a Roman statesman is assassinated by other senators who feel that he is too powerful and a threat to their own political careers. The assassins (Brutus is one of these) claim that they have acted for the good of the State, but Mark Antony, who has his own political ambitions, sees through their wiles and persuades the assembled people that what they have been told about Caesar is not the case. Here is his speech to them.

Friends, Romans, countrymen, lend me your ears.
I come to bury Caesar, not to praise him.
The evil that men do lives after them;
The good is oft interred with their bones,
So let it be with Caesar. The noble Brutus
Hath told you Caesar was ambitious.
If it were so, it was a grievous fault,
And grievously hath Caesar answered for it.
Here, under leave of Brutus, and the rest, –
For Brutus is an honourable man,
So are they all; all honourable men, –
Come I to speak in Caesar's funeral.
He was my friend, faithful and just to me;
But Brutus says he was ambitious,
And Brutus is an honourable man.
He hath brought many captives home to Rome,
Whose ransoms did the general coffers fill:
Did this in Caesar seem to be ambitious?
When that the poor have cried, Caesar hath wept.
Ambition should be made of sterner stuff,
Yet Brutus says he was ambitious,
And Brutus is an honourable man.
You all did see that, on the Lupercal,
I thrice presented him a kingly crown,
Which he did thrice refuse. Was this ambition?
Yet Brutus says he was ambitious,
And, sure, he is an honourable man.
I speak not to disprove what Brutus spoke,
But here I am, to speak what I do know.
You all did love him once, not without cause;
What cause withholds you then to mourn for him?
O judgement! Thou art fled to brutish beasts,
And men have lost their reason!

(Act III   Scene 2)

William Shakespeare

First impressions

1   From this speech, what is your impression of: ● Caesar   ● Brutus
2   In the play, Mark Antony succeeds in making his listeners believe that it is Brutus who is ambitious and Caesar who was honourable. How does he achieve this?

Mark Antony uses a number of techniques which orators employ for persuasive purposes in their speeches. These 'tricks of the trade' are listed in the panel below.

Speaking persuasively

List of three
'zoos have supplied us with information about breeding, feeding and habitat'

Repetition
'no bed, no heating, no family'
60%, yes, 60% of polar bears...'

Alliteration
'safari parks offer safe, secure surroundings'

Based on personal experience
'I myself recently visited'
'I agree... I think... I believe... I admit... I am sure...'

Use of statistics or quotation
'A recent survey carried out by...shows...'
'£2 million is spent every year on...'

Use of rhetorical questions
'I wonder...?'
'Is it not true that...?'

Involvement of audience
'I am sure that each of you knows...'
'How would you feel if...?'

Ending strongly
'Think about it!'
Use a joke, a quotation, a catch phrase, or something very memorable.

Taking a closer look

1 Select short quotations from Mark Antony's speech which fulfil each of the techniques listed above. As you do this you will realise just how cleverly crafted this seemingly spontaneous speech is!

2 You could practise the same exercise on the following political speech made by Martin Luther King. Compare the two. Can you determine any differences between the literary example and this political speech?

> We must not allow our creative protests to degenerate into physical violence. Again and again we must rise to the majestic heights of meeting physical force with soul force. The marvellous new militancy which has engulfed the Negro community must not lead us to a distrust of all white people, for many of our white brothers, as evidenced by their presence here today, have come to realise that their destiny is tied up with our destiny and they have come to realise that their freedom is inextricably bound to our freedom. We cannot walk alone.
>
> And as we walk, we must make the pledge that we shall always march ahead. We cannot turn back. There are those who are asking the devotees of civil rights, 'When will you be satisfied?' We can never be satisfied as long as the Negro is the victim of the unspeakable horrors of police brutality. We can never be satisfied as long as our bodies, heavy with the fatigue of travel, cannot gain lodging in the motels of the highways and the hotels of the cities. We cannot be satisfied as long as the Negro's basic mobility is from a smaller ghetto to a larger one. We can never be satisfied as long as our children are stripped of their selfhood and robbed of their dignity by signs stating 'For whites only'. We cannot be satisfied as long as a Negro in Mississippi cannot vote and a Negro in New York believes he has nothing for which to vote. No, no, we are not satisfied, and we will not be satisfied until justice rolls down like waters and righteousness like a mighty stream.

I am not unmindful that some of you have come here out of great trials and tribulations. Some of you have come fresh from narrow jail cells. Some of you have come from areas where your quest for freedom left you battered by the storms of persecution and staggered by the winds of police brutality. You have been the veterans of creative suffering. Continue to work with the faith that unearned suffering is redemptive.

Go back to Mississippi, go back to Alabama, go back to South Carolina, go back to Georgia, go back to Louisiana, go back to the slums and ghettos of our northern cities, knowing that somehow this situation can and will be changed. Let us not wallow in the valley of despair.

I say to you today, my friends, so even though we face the difficulties of today and tomorrow, I still have a dream. It is a dream deeply rooted in the American dream.

I have a dream that one day this nation will rise up and live out the true meaning of its creed: 'We hold these truths to be self-evident; that all men are created equal.'

I have a dream that one day on the red hills of Georgia the sons of former slaves and the sons of former slaveowners will be able to sit down together at the table of brotherhood.

I have a dream that one day even the state of Mississippi, a state sweltering with the heat of injustice, sweltering with the heat of oppression, will be transformed into an oasis of freedom and justice.

I have a dream that my four little children will one day live in a nation where they will not be judged by the colour of their skin but by the content of their character.

I have a dream today.

This well-known speech was given by Dr Martin Luther King to a Civil Rights demonstration in Washington, U.S.A. on 28 August, 1963.

Dr King was the kind of speaker known as an orator. Orators try to affect the attitudes and beliefs of their audience by imaginative and emotional suggestions.

Dr King won the Nobel Peace Prize in 1964 for his leadership in using the principles of non-violent resistance in the struggle for racial equality. He was murdered on 4 April, 1968.

Is speech-writing a dying art?

Read the following article in which one writer seems to think so.

Read my lips: no new syntaxes

PRESIDENT BUSH made five attempts to define White House policy on taxation of the super-rich last week. This weekend, many people are still baffled. In part, it is a political confusion caused by conflicting pressures in the Republican Party. But in part, it is down to Mr Bush's celebrated inarticulacy.

He was in especially opaque form at Tuesday's press conference, which started the rot. This was what he said about his campaign support for Senator Jesse Helms, who had then failed to support his budget deal: 'But – so we're talking about the broad principles that unite us, and urge you vote not just for Jesse, but for others who – let's see how I get this properly – grammar, you know, the grammar – if we had more of whom we had – would – we wouldn't be in such a problem.'

Mr Bush's bizarre patterns of speech are a mixture of sports patois, technical jargon, acquired Texan, upper class New England nursery slang and a casual acquaintance with the traditional rules of grammar.

President Eisenhower, sometimes compared with Mr Bush, employed similarly baffling language. Once, a White House correspondent attempted revenge: he wrote, and circulated, a version of Abraham Lincoln's Gettysburg Address, as if spoken off the cuff by Ike. So here we offer George Bush's Gettysburg Address, with apologies to the incomparable Lincoln original.

LINCOLN at Gettysburg

Four score and seven years ago our fathers brought forth on this continent a new nation, conceived in Liberty, and dedicated to the proposition that all men are created equal.

Now we are engaged in a great civil war, testing whether that nation, or any nation so conceived and so dedicated, can long endure. We are met on a great battlefield of that war. We have come to dedicate a portion of that field, as a final resting place for those who here gave their lives that that nation might live. It is altogether fitting and proper that we should do this.

But, in a larger sense, we can not dedicate – we can not consecrate – we can not hallow – this ground. The brave men, living and dead, who struggled here, have consecrated it, far above our poor power to add or detract. The world will little note, nor long remember what we say here, but it can never forget what they did here. It is for us the living, rather, to be dedicated here to the unfinished work which they who fought here have thus far so nobly advanced. It is rather for us to be here dedicated to the great task remaining before us – that from these honoured dead we take increased devotion – that we here highly resolve that these dead shall not have died in vain – that this nation, under God, shall have a new birth of freedom – and that government of the people, by the people, for the people, shall not perish from the earth.

The BUSH liberty stuff

I'M NOT quite old enough to remember it – only kidding – but I think it was around 87 some years ago (have to be kinda careful ever since I got the day of Pearl Harbour wrong) that our fathers threw out the first pitch for liberty, started a whole new democratic ball-game on this continent, dedicated, as it was, to the all-men-are-equal thing.

Now we – caught up in this brother against brother – tremendous violence and bloodshed – we're – team-mate against team-mate, all this kind of thing – we're putting that Liberty experiment, that new, experimental kind of nation – unprecedented – we're putting that through the wringer. We have all come here – terrific battlefield of that conflict – hey, these brave men sacrificed with

the bases loaded that this nation might score at the bottom of the ninth – this is a wonderful thing we're doing – we've come to dedicate a part of this field to their memory.

But in a very real sense, we're pitching horseshoes after the boys have gone home for the pork rinds. The great thing about this is that these brave men who were engaged in this conflict – both living and deceased – have memorialised this ground more than we could ever hope – we that were on the bench or in the best seats throughout – can hope to elaborate upon or otherwise. The networks will give little more than a sound bit to our great eloquence here. But what happened here will be replayed in the world's memory forever.

Hey, it's up to us now to – in terms of the consecration thing – to carry on their work – rescue this nation from even deeper doo-doo – commit ourselves up to the neck for the thing for which they gave everything – so they will not have given it for nothing – all this kind of thing – that this nation, subject only to God's pocket veto, shall be given a new start in the freedom thing. So that – and read my lips – administration of you folks, by you folks, for you folks shall not go completely out of style.

The Independent March 1991

This is a bit of a cheat in that only one of these speeches was actually given, whilst the other is a pastiche of the way in which George Bush delivers his addresses to the people. Clearly, this journalist feels that speech-writing is not all that it used to be. What do you think?

Surveying speeches

Over the next week, listen to the news and other current affairs programmes. Note down any particularly good or bad examples of speech-writing. At the end of the week share these in a class discussion.

For writing

Try writing a short debate speech of 2 or 3 minutes in length, in which you use some of the devices listed in 'Speaking persuasively' on page 102. Write in favour of or in opposition to one of the following:

- 'The right of free speech is still one of our privileges.'
- 'The problem of unemployment can be solved by raising the school leaving age to 18.'
- 'Even at the end of the Twentieth century, a woman's place is in the home.'

Des res

Finding the right house to buy or rent can be a nightmare. But it is the estate agent's first job to persuade people to look around the houses on their lists and for this reason the descriptions that they write for publicity leaflets aim to make the residence seem as desirable as possible. Here is one example.

The official version

POSH ESTATE AGENTS

22 Heather Road, Baldon

22 Heather Road is a semi-detached brick cottage of surprisingly good proportions. The property is in need of extensive renovation but offers tremendous potential and is set in exceptionally good gardens.

Viewing of this attractive property is strongly recommended although we would warn potential purchasers that parts of the property may be unsafe and viewings are strictly at their own risk.

Baldon is a most sought after village being the final resting place of Sir Roger de Quincy and adjoining the grounds of Balderton Manor. A local post office and general stores are in the village as are two public houses and a village school, whilst more comprehensive facilities are available in the nearby town of Widdensford.
Viewing: by appointment only through the agents.

View of rear of property and garden

The accommodation comprises:

Ground floor

FRONT PARLOUR:	13' by 11'8" Fireplace (once stone). French windows
FRONT HALL:	Stairs to first floor.
REAR ROOM:	11'9" by 10'3" Fireplace
KITCHEN:	9'6" by 7'4" Deep sink
REAR HALL	
CLOAKROOM:	High level WC

First floor

BEDROOM 1:	12'3" by 11'6" French window onto balcony, Cupboard
LANDING:	9'4" by 7'6" Potential for shower room
BEDROOM 2:	11' by 12'10" Fireplace
Garden	70' by 20' In need of some attention Large garden stores

The buyer's alternative version

22 Heather Road, Baldon

22 Heather Road is small all round although there is planning permission available for an extension. You'll need one. The property is uninhabitable at the moment, in fact no one will give you a mortgage on it (cash sales only), but offers tremendous potential if you rebuild most of it. It is set in very long, thin gardens.

Viewing of this attractive property is strongly recommended. Don't take our word for it. We would warn potential purchasers that parts of the property may fall down around your ears and we can't insure you.

Baldon is a most sought after village although it has virtually no facilities. More comprehensive facilities are available in the town of Widdensford, eight miles away, so if you don't own a car forget it.
Viewing: don't go in there alone!

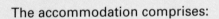

Interior view of Bedroom 1

The accommodation comprises:

Ground floor

FRONT PARLOUR:	13' by 11'8" Fireplace (once stone but bashed out with a sledge-hammer and replaced with cladding and a gas fire 40 years ago). French windows – frames need replacing
FRONT HALL:	Stairs to first floor – watch out for woodworm
REAR ROOM:	11'9" by 10'3" Fireplace with caved in chimney
KITCHEN:	9'6" by 7'4" Not enough room to swing a cat. Deep sink but only a single cold tap and no electricity
REAR HALL CLOAKROOM:	I wouldn't put my coat in here – it's an outside loo. High level WC?

First floor

BEDROOM 1:	12'3" by 11'6" French window. Balcony – exists in skeleton form. Cupboard. Just enough room for a double bed if the floor will hold it
LANDING:	9'4" by 7'6" Potential for shower room. By the way, where is the bathroom?
BEDROOM 2:	11' by 12'10" Fireplace – we need it – no central heating

Garden	70' by 20' Completely overgrown. Dilapidated shed can just be seen above the long grass, ferns etc.

Assignment

1 Write an estate agent's promotion aiming to persuade buyers to view:
- your house
- the scout/guide hut
- your school
- the local town hall

Include a general blurb to introduce the overall 'benefits' of the property and local services. Then go into details about specific rooms and features as above. Try to present the property in the best possible light.

2 Now write the alternative version giving a more realistic and perhaps less flattering view of the property.

With love...

In this technological age of telephones and fax machines, it might seem odd that people continue to write letters to one another on an informal basis. However, we do. This is partly because sometimes there are things that cannot be said, or do not come over as well, on the telephone. What other reasons can you think of for writing informal letters?

Read the following letters carefully. They are all examples of correspondence between real people from different periods in history.

My dear Cassandra

SLOANE ST. THURSDAY APRIL 18 [1811]

My dear Cassandra

I have so many little matters to tell you of, that I cannot wait any longer before I begin to put them down...

Mary and I, after disposing of her father and mother, went to the Liverpool Museum and the British Gallery, and I had some amusement at each, tho' my preference for men and women always inclines me to attend more to the company than the sight.

I did not see Theo till late on Tuesday; he was gone to Ilford, but he came back in time to shew his usual, nothing-meaning, harmless, heartless civility. Henry, who had been confined the whole day to the bank, took me in his way home; and after putting life and wit into the party for a quarter of an hour, put himself and his sister into a hackney coach...

I am sorry to tell you that I am getting very extravagant and spending all my money; and what is worse for *you,* I have been spending yours too; for in a linendraper's shop to which I went for check'd muslin, and for which I was obliged to give seven shillings a yard, I was tempted by a pretty coloured muslin, and bought ten yds. of it, on the chance of your liking it; but at the same time, if it shd. not suit you, you must not think yourself at all obliged to take it; it is only 3/6 pr. yd., and I shd. not in the least mind keeping the whole. In texture, it is just what we prefer, but its resemblance to green crewels I must own is not great, for the pattern is a small red spot...

We drank tea again yesterday with the Tilsons, and met the Smiths. I find all these little parties very pleasant...

Eliza is walking out by herself. She has plenty of business on her hands just now – for the day of the party is settled, and drawing near; above 80 people are invited for next Tuesday eveng. and there is to be some very good music, five professionals, three of them glee singers, besides amateurs. Fanny will listen to this. One of the hirelings is a capital on the harp, from which I expect great pleasure...

Saturday... If the weather permits, Eliza and I walk into London this morng. *She* is in want of chimney lights for Tuesday; and I of an ounce of darning cotton. She has resolved not to venture to the play tonight. The d'Entraigues and comte Julien cannot come to the party – which was at first a grief, but she has since supplied herself so well with performers that it is of no consequence; their not coming has produced our going to them tomorrow eveng. – which I like the idea of. It will be amusing to see the ways of a French circle...

Love to all.
Yours affec:
Jane

Jane Austen

Peter Rabbit

Eastwood Dunkeld
Sep 4. 93

My dear Noel,
I don't know what to write to you, so I shall tell you a story about four little rabbits whose names were —

Flopsy, Mopsy, Cottontail

and Peter

They lived with their mother in a sand bank under the root of a big fir tree.

Beatrix Potter

84 Charing Cross Road

MARKS & CO., Booksellers
84, Charing Cross Road
London, W.C. 2   4TH OCTOBER, 1965

Miss Helene Hanff
305 East 72nd Street
New York 21, New York
U.S.A.

Dear Helene,
It was good to hear from you again. Yes, we're still here, getting older and busier but no richer.

We have just managed to obtain a copy of E. M. Delafield's *Diary of a Provincial Lady,* in an edition published by Macmillan in 1942, a good clean copy, price $2.00. We are sending it off to you today by Book Post with invoice enclosed.

We had a very pleasant summer with more than the usual number of tourists, including hordes of young people making the pilgrimage to Carnaby Street. We watch it all from a safe distance, though I must say I rather like the Beatles. If the fans just wouldn't scream so.

Nora and the girls send their love,
                     Frank

HELENE HANFF   305 East 72nd Street   New York 21, N.Y.
                          SEPTEMBER 30, 1968
Still alive, are we?
I've been writing American history books for children for four or five years. Got hung up on the stuff and have been buying American history books – in ugly, cardboardy American editions, but somehow I just didn't think the stately homes of England would yield nice English editions of James Madison's stenographic record of the Constitutional Convention or T. Jefferson's letters to J. Adams or like that. Are you a grandfather yet? Tell Sheila and Mary their children are entitled to presentation copies of my *Collected Juvenile Works,* THAT should make them rush off and reproduce.

I introduced a young friend of mine to *Pride & Prejudice* one rainy Sunday and she has gone out of her mind for Jane Austen. She has a birthday round about Hallowe'en, can you find me some Austen for her? If you've got a complete set let me know the price, if it's expensive I'll make her husband give her half and I'll give her half.

Best to Nora and anybody else around.
Helene

Helene Hanff

Group discussion

1 Working in groups of 3 or 4, try to describe the tone, register and purpose of each letter. In other words, if you could hear the writer reading it aloud, how would they sound? Why has each letter been written? Who has it been written for?
2 a) What points of style and language do all these letters have in common?
    b) What differences are there between them?
3 What similarities are there in the layout of the letters?

Signing on and off in informal letters is very flexible indeed and sometimes extremely personal. It often gives the writer a chance to show affection towards their reader, as in Jane Austen's letter to her sister, Cassandra. Or the signing off line might be an expression of friendship, as the letters from Frank and Helene. How many more ways can you think of for signing on and off in informal letters?

For more on real and fictional letters see Unit 2 in the Forms of Narrative module in Book 4A, pages 14-19.

Writing informally

Write a letter to a child or a friend of your own age, telling them about:
● a recent family outing or event
● the latest news from your circle of friends
● another topic of your choice
Think about the way you will address them in the signing on line, your overall tone and how you will sign off.

Yours faithfully...

Examine the letters on these pages.

October 1991

Dear Colleague,

Please find enclosed a range of documents signalling forthcoming events and publications for 1992. There are certain items to which I would like to draw your attention.

Firstly, we are announcing the launch of the BFI/Open University distance learning package <u>Media Education: An Introduction</u>. This is the largest single project BFI Education has undertaken to date and, whilst designed for teachers completely new to the area of media education, we are sure that all people currently working in the field will appreciate the wealth of material the package offers. Furthermore, over the next 18 months, the Department is planning to run a number of INSET events around the country based upon this package.

Northern Ireland was incorporated into the terms of the BFI's Royal Charter in the summer 1991 and it is therefore particularly appropriate for BFI Education to hold the 1992 Easter School at the New University of Ulster, Jordanstown (near Belfast). Whilst we anticipate that the bulk of teachers attending will be from Northern Ireland, we hope that many teachers from England, Wales and Scotland will still be attracted.

The summer of 1992 will see the Education Department and the Television and Projects Unit within the BFI's Research Division organising and hosting the first major international conference and festival on Melodrama. The events will be held in London and will offer a unique opportunity for people working in many different fields and disciplines, e.g. Cinema Studies, Cultural Studies, Theatre Studies, Music and the Visual Arts, to discuss the wide ranging issues which surround the concept of Melodrama.

Finally, it is our intention in future mailings to include a Newsletter which will provide information on the latest institutional developments in the fields of cinema, television and video education <u>and</u> training.

I hope you have a successful 1992 and I look forward to meeting as many of you as possible at our events.

Yours sincerely,

Manuel Alvarado
Head of Education

British Film Institute
21 Stephen Street
London W1P 1PL

Telephone 071-255 1444
Telex 27624 BFILDNG
Fax 071-436 7950

NATIONAL FILM ARCHIVE

NATIONAL FILM THEATRE

LONDON FILM FESTIVAL

MUSEUM OF THE MOVING IMAGE

BFI PRODUCTION

BFI DISTRIBUTION

BFI PLANNING

BFI LIBRARY & INFORMATION SERVICES

BFI STILLS POSTERS & DESIGNS

BFI EDUCATION

BFI PUBLISHING

'SIGHT & SOUND'

M. J. GLASS Painting and Decorating

39 Bell End, Ladybank, Fife, Scotland Telephone:020 81 4516/82 5834

Dear Sir/Madam,

My name is Mike Glass. I have been running a highly competitive and personalised painting and decorating business for over 15 years now.

I take pride in providing a fast, efficient and clean professional decorating service.

I employ a small number of well trained, professional decorators, who are also personable, tidy workers who maintain a polite and helpful attitude. We work hard and I like to think we provide a better professional job.

I have a high number of satisfied clients who not only give us repeat business, but recommend us to others.

We are working in your area now!

We are currently decorating in your area and would welcome any enquiries from you. I would be happy to supply you with a free quotation for any interior or exterior work, any time.

My firm can supply you with any number of excellent recommendations on request.

PLEASE DO TRY US!

Yours faithfully,

M.J. GLASS
Managing Director

The LEISURE CIRCLE

Guild House, Farnsby Street, Swindon, SN99 9XX

Dear Member,

Unfortunately, you have been incorrectly charged £1.20 in respect of the OXFORD MINI HISTORY volume recently despatched. We have therefore arranged to credit your account with this amount to correct the mistake, and this adjustment will reflect on your next statement or the one following.

Please accept our apologies for any inconvenience caused.

Yours sincerely,

Debbie Green

Debbie Green
The Leisure Circle   C127

Looking at formal letters

1 How do these formal letters differ from the informal letters on pages 108-110? List the differences under the following headings:

Layout	Signing on and off	Tone

2 a) How many standard phrases can you find in these formal letters and any that you might have collected? (Look for phrases that are the same, or very similar in a number of letters.)
   b) Why do you think that standard phrases are used more often in formal letters than in informal ones, particularly where signing on and off are concerned?
3 a) What information is always provided in the layout of a formal letter?
   b) Why do you think this is needed?
4 What relationships are there between signing on and signing off here?

Standard letters

Many companies have to send out similar letters to hundreds of customers. In the past these all had to be typed individually and carbon copies taken for the files. Today things are very much simpler for the typist who has a word processor, because a **standard** or **skeleton letter** can be prepared. In a skeleton letter, the main text is standardised and blanks are left for the recipient's address, title, reference number, the date and any particular small changes of detail. Each time that particular type of letter is required the typist needs only to key in this small amount of information and then print it out. An example of a skeleton letter is given below.

EMPIRE CATERING LTD.   18 River Street, Bedford, Bedfordshire

OUR REF P/JDW/ep

15 October 1991

Miss A.P. Hart,
9 Reed Ave,
Dunstable
Bedfordshire

Dear Miss Hart,

CATERING MANAGER
Following your application for the above post we would like you to attend for interview on Friday 1 November at 2.30 p.m. When you arrive, please ask for me at Reception.

I would be grateful if you could telephone my secretary, Emma Thompson, on extension 4993, before Friday 25 October, to confirm that this interview time is convenient for you.

Yours sincerely

Sue Brown

Sue Brown
Personnel Manager

Do you think there are any disadvantages or problems with this type of letter? In general, what will be the recipients' reactions when receiving a letter like this?

Assignment

In a group of 3 or 4, prepare your own skeleton letter to do the following:
You are teachers in a school's Physical Education department and you are planning to take a party of children ski-ing next spring.

1 Prepare a skeleton letter to be sent to parents, informing them of details of the trip and asking for firm replies from those who would like their children to go.

2 Plan your letter, thinking carefully about the information you will need to include, and what action will need to be taken once the replies are received.
  ● Will you be asking for a deposit?
  ● Will parents be invited to attend a meeting?
  ● Will you sign off with 'yours faithfully' or 'yours sincerely'? (Make sure you know where to use the right one by checking the examples given on pages 111-113.)

3 Make a fair copy of your final draft, or put the letter into a computer or word processor.

Presenting yourself on paper

Often the letters we write need to show something of our personality. This is true of letters which are aimed at friends but can also be true of letters to people we hardly know, such as prospective employers.

Knowing the differences

1 It's obvious that the two types of letter mentioned above would look and sound very different from one another. With a partner, discuss how and why these letters would be different. List the differences under these headings:
   - Register/tone
   - Vocabulary
   - Content
   - Presentation
2 Write a letter in which you aim to tell the reader about yourself. Choose one of the following ideas:
   - a letter in response to an advertisement for a Saturday job
   - a letter of application for a place at college

   As you plan and write the letter make sure the register, vocabulary, content and presentation are appropriate to its purpose.
3 With your formal letter compile and attach a **C.V. (Curriculum Vitae)**, or résumé which sets out your achievements, qualifications and experience in a form that is easy to read. Your letter of application can then be shorter and you can concentrate on saying why you want the job/college place and why you think you are suitable.

   Include the following information in your C.V.

   Name, address, telephone number

   Marital status, date of birth

   Places of education, qualifications (or those you expect to get)

   Employment experience

   What you are doing at the moment, including part-time jobs

   Interests

   Additional information

   Referees

Professionally produced C.V.s are expensive, but you can achieve similar high-quality using a word processor or a desk-top publishing package.

When your C.V. is complete, make a couple of copies and keep them updated. You'll soon be needing them.

CURRICULUM VITAE

MICHAEL WEEKS

Address: 19 Bank Street   Date of Birth: 17. 9. 1972
           St Ives
           Cornwall

Education: The High School   Qualifications: GCSEs English C; History C; French B;
           St Ives   Maths B; Geography B; Physics B; Chemistry C 1988
           from 1983-1990   A-levels French C; Maths B; Geography D 1990

Work Experience:
Assistant chef at local café during summer holidays 1987

A load of junk

The average household receives a bundle of **unsolicited** or **junk mail** each week, i.e. mail that has not been requested. Many companies now use mail shots to persuade new customers to take up their unrepeatable offers, and this does not just apply to small or struggling companies either: for example, both electricity and gas boards have used mail shots.

Junk mail analysis

1 a) Make a collection of all the junk mail that arrives at your house this week. Do ask if you can have it first. There should be no objection in most cases – it has been nicknamed 'junk' mail because it usually ends up in the bin anyway!

   b) At the same time keep a tally of the genuine letters and try to work out what percentage of your household's mail is unsolicited.

2 Use your collection and the samples on these pages to answer the following questions about junk mail.

   ● Is this type of letter formal or informal?

   ● What tone is used? Comment on the approaches taken in one or two letters of your choice.

   ● Is it possible to generalise about the types of format or layout, signing on and off, etc?

   ● If the letters are addressed to someone who lives in your household, how can you account for it? Are any of these letters personal?

   ● What techniques do the companies use to attract the householder's attention in terms of: a) how the letter looks
   b) what the letter offers?

The language of junk mail can be very persuasive, and when a tear-off coupon or reply-paid envelope is included, many people send for more information when they would not usually have done so.

For more on persuasive language see Unit 4, pages 101-103.

Sir...

When people feel very strongly about an issue, they will often write to a newspaper in order that their opinions can be seen by others. The following selections of letters will give you some idea of the range of topics and the types of letter that appear in different newspapers.

Dog owners must be accountable

From Mrs Jane Hollins

Sir: I cannot believe no one has seen children playing with dogs until the latter are nearly driven wild. Fortunately the average 'home dog' can put up with a great deal of provocation. But some, such as pit bull terriers, are trained in savagery for the protection of their owner and home.

Everything should be done to end this situation; banning, muzzling or other measures. But looked at dispassionately, these dogs are the result of their heritage and training and are usually only performing their duty.

Yours sincerely,
JANE HOLLINS
Littlehampton, Sussex

The Independent May 1991

Register dogs rather than kill them

From Dr James Serpell

Sir: The Home Secretary's decision to ban so-called fighting dogs is ill considered and inappropriate ('American pit bull terriers to be banned,' 22 May). It is based on the erroneous assumption that because a dog has been bred for a particular behaviour it is therefore predestined to display this behaviour, regardless of circumstance.

All authorities on the breeding of working dogs, including the Kennel Club, would admit that many, if not the majority of, dogs which are bred for particular tasks – including gun dogs, working sheep-dogs or guide dogs for the blind – fail to make the grade in behavioural terms. There is no simple one-to-one correspondence between genes and behaviour, and all genetic predispositions are strongly modified by experience and training during development. If this is the case with other breeds, then it is also true of pit bull terriers. The majority of these dogs have never bitten or attacked anyone and unless they do so, they are innocent of any transgression.

Apart from being impossible to enforce, given the difficulties of defining either pit bull terriers or fighting dogs in general, the proposed destruction of these animals will do little to reduce the prevalence of dog attacks in Britain. Those seeking to own potentially dangerous dogs will simply look elsewhere (in the United States, for example, wolf-dog hybrids have become the latest fad).

The only effective deterrent to the ownership of dangerous dogs is legalisation that holds owners directly responsible for the actions (and welfare) of their dogs, reinforced by heavy fines, individual lifetime bans on the keeping of dogs and, where appropriate, the destruction of the offending animals. For such a law to be effective, however, it is essential that every dog is registered as belonging to a particular owner. Under such a scheme, it would be illegal to own an unregistered dog and every sale or transfer of ownership would require official notification. Registration fees could include compulsory third party insurance and be scaled according to the perceived aggressiveness of the breed.

Instead of using the tragic case of Rucksana Khan as an opportunity to find long-term solutions to the various problems posed by dogs in our society, Kenneth Baker has responded with an irrational, naïve and, above all, ineffective political gesture.

Yours faithfully,
JAMES SERPELL
Companion Animal
Research Group
Department of Clinical
Veterinary Medicine
University of Cambridge

The Independent May 1991

Dog registration

From Mr Nicholas Myerscough

Sir: I would like to agree with your sentiments regarding the control of dangerous dogs in your leading article today. A realistic dog registration scheme with a substantial fee funding a comprehensive network is the only logical solution. We should be trying to eliminate irresponsible owners as opposed to whole breeds.

However, as a practising veterinary surgeon, your propsal that vets 'sign safe dog exemptions' and face the legal consequences is completely unworkable. No veterinary surgeon will take responsibility for the safety of a dog when he or she is not in direct control.

It would save a great deal of time if the politicians and commentators came and asked the people at the sharp end of this problem rather than developing policy in splendid isolation.

Yours faithfully,
NICHOLAS MYERSCOUGH
Westway Veterinary Group
Newcastle-upon-Tyne

The Independent May 1991

AFTER a hectic stag night my mates stole my clothes from a hotel room.

A doorman four stone bigger than me lent me a pair of plus-four golf trousers and a polo-neck sweater to get me to the church where the vicar lent me an outfit of his without the dog collar.

BILL MURPHY, **Chelmsford, Essex**

■ MY Dad had to give me away twice as a bride. The vicar turned over too many pages of the prayer book and said: 'Let us start again.'

Mrs. E. YOUNGMAN **Harwich**

■ AT my hotel wedding reception, I was asked by a bridesmaid to mend a faulty loo flush.

While trying to fix it, the door slammed shut and in the darkness we couldn't get out. After banging and shouting, we were freed by guests – but no one seemed to believe our story.

JOHN MASSEY, **Shenfield, Essex**

■ AS my father took me down the aisle to my wedding, I thought what a lovely soloist. Then I realised it was my three-year-old bridesmaid behind me singing: 'Here comes the bride, all fat and wide.'

Mrs. E. CRAWSHAW **Bury, Lancs**

■ AT one family wedding all I could hear in the church was my granddaughter Tina saying: 'It's your turn now.'

To my horror she and her young cousin had a ludo board spread out on the seat and were throwing dice.

Mrs. H.C. PEACOCK. **Middlesbrough**

Daily Star July 1990

These letters also show you that the form of address is different to other letters (usually 'Sir', rather than 'Dear Sir') and that the tone and register of letters to newspapers is very specific. This is because the letter does not address one person only, in spite of being sent to the Editor. It is written with a view to being published and read by a wide audience. Often, as in the sequence about dangerous dogs, one letter or article can spark off a whole debate on the letters page.

Newspapers rarely publish very long letters, due to the limited space they have available, so letters are usually pithy and terse.

For writing

1 Browse through a selection of newspapers until you find a news item or article which interests you, or to which you object.
2 Either on your own, or with a partner, write a letter to the newspaper in question, giving your opinion on the matter. (You might even want to send it off when it's finished, but in that case it will need to be sent quickly.)
You may find it useful to refer back to Unit 4 on argumentative writing, pages 98-99, before you put your first draft of the letter together. Remember to keep your letter brief and to the point. Think about your intended audience, particularly as you redraft.

*C*harity event

From Comic Relief to Children in Need, fund-raising is big business. Everyday we are asked to dig into our pockets for another cause. Yet with cuts in government funding, wars, famine and natural disasters, there seems to be no alternative if we are going to help at all. And most of us do care personally about one or two causes in particular.

As a class, you are going to organise your own fund-raising event. It will involve a whole day of activities (or a whole week if you feel you have the stamina) and it can benefit the charity or charities of your choice.

Throughout this assignment, each keep a diary of your ideas, decisions and actions. Make notes on these as you go along as you will need to use your diaries in follow up activities. Planning the event in stages, as outlined on page 120, will help you in your organisation.

WWF WALK SPONSOR FORM

MIDLANDS, WALES AND SOUTH WEST

Every day up to 50 animal species face extinction. Since 1961 WWF has invested in over 5,000 projects in 130 countries to save Species in Danger...but much more needs to be done. This is your chance to help.

WALK

FOR SPECIES IN DANGER

The money you raise could:

- Contribute towards the £2 million WWF still needs to protect the African elephant.
- Fund a warden to monitor turtle nesting beaches in Greece

León Week 1991
October 11 – 19th

A week of events for Oxford's twin town in Nicaragua

OXFORD LEON ASSOCIATION

THE COMIC RELIEF, GOING LIVE EXCLUSIVE

HACK•PACK

Red alert to sniff out nose hounds

Prizes galore if you score!

THE biggest reward you will get for taking part will be the sheer fun of producing your own newspaper.

For the groups who produce the most interesting newspapers, there is some more excitement in store.

In each age category, there will be an overall winner.

These three winners (under 12, 13-15, and 16-18) will be featured on Going Live! in March next year. Selections from the winning entries will be printed in Radio Times and Fast Forward magazine.

So if you win, your first article will be read by at least TWO MILLION PEOPLE.

One representative from each winning group will also spend a day as a genuine

COMIC RELIEF today reveals the biggest newspaper event of all time.

Speaking from a secret

- Cartoons
- Competitions
- Reviews
- Travel articles
- Fashion features
- Sports coverage
- Crosswords and puzzles

119

Decide on the charity you wish to benefit from your event. Take everyone's suggestions into account, debate their merits and take a vote.

Brainstorm your ideas for the types of activities that you would like to plan for the event. Which ones are practical and which are not?

Divide your list of activities up amongst smaller groups and begin to think about what organisation the activity will involve.
◆ What are your needs?
◆ Who can help you?
◆ What will be your first steps?

Write short proposals for each activity in your groups. Outline how you intend to organise it.
◆ Who will be involved?
◆ What materials will you need?
◆ How long will it take?
◆ What publicity will be necessary?
◆ Are there any hidden costs?
◆ Will you need to obtain permission?
Can you envisage any problems? Ask for help if necessary.

Report back to the class and record any suggestions. Accept offers of help gratefully.

Co-ordinate all your plans and set up a schedule for the day (or week) of the event. Look carefully at diaries and timetables and come up with provisional dates. Write to people to make sure that these are convenient for them. Make a list of those you need to contact, e.g. the school principal/headteacher, the caretakers, person in charge of sports hall bookings, etc.

Notify in writing your headteacher and anyone else who needs to give you permission. (You may need to write persuasively here.)

Act on any letters or memos you receive as soon as you can. Book rooms or other facilities. Write to 'celebrities' or outside helpers who you want to involve. Contact the Charity organisation itself and let them know what you intend to do – they might be able to offer help.

Publicise the event. Will local shops or businesses act as sponsors? Could they display a poster? Set a budget for publicity so that you can keep an eye on the costs. Begin an advertising campaign, designing any posters, leaflets or forms that will be needed. Produce them in-house (using the school's facilities) if you can.

Write a detailed proposal for the event. Use your working diary to remind you of the steps you have taken and that will need to be taken.

Continue the publicity by producing newsletters, speaking to others through assemblies, generally persuading others to help and get involved. Write a press release and send it to the local paper. Make sure you explain within it the reasons for assisting your chosen charity. Check the last minute details and try to have an emergency plan in case key people have to cancel at the last moment.

After the event

1 Write an article for the school magazine or local press about the event and how it went.
2 Write letters of thanks to all those who have assisted you in even tiny ways.

Using your diary

You could write up your diary in any form you feel is suitable. For example:
● as an account of the day itself in the form of a report or from a personal viewpoint
● as an argumentative essay based on the question: 'Should the general public be asked to dig deeper into their pockets each year for causes which ought to be the responsibility of the Welfare State?'

Module 3 Non-literary Forms

Objectives

The material and activities included in this module aim to help you learn more about non-literary forms by:

◆ introducing you to a wide range of factual and information writing
◆ exploring the importance of tone, selection of information, and bias in these forms, and how this relates to their intended purpose
◆ providing you with the chance to experiment in your written work with journalistic and specialist writing

What is in a newspaper?

In Britain we read more newspapers than in any other country so 'news' is obviously important to us. But what is 'news'?

Newspapers are produced to sell, so the news must be of interest to the greatest number of people and must be about something they have not heard of before.

However, news does not have to be about something which happened today – if it was learned that a sports star had killed a man ten years ago that would be a big news story. While local newspapers will include national and international news most of their pages concern events and personalities in their area.

There are four main types of news stories:

- **Current affairs** covers politics, business, economics, and international stories, e.g. about countries at war.
- **Unusual events** e.g. if there is an air or rail disaster.
- **Stories about celebrities** such as entertainment stars, politicians, or the Royal family (most papers have a 'Royals' watcher).
- **Human interest stories** e.g. if the government cut its spending on books for the blind, the story might be about the effects on one blind person.

Jargon

Tabloid: small-sized newspapers like *Today* or the *Daily Mirror*.
Broadsheet: large-sized newspapers like *The Guardian* or *The Independent*.

What else is in a newspaper?

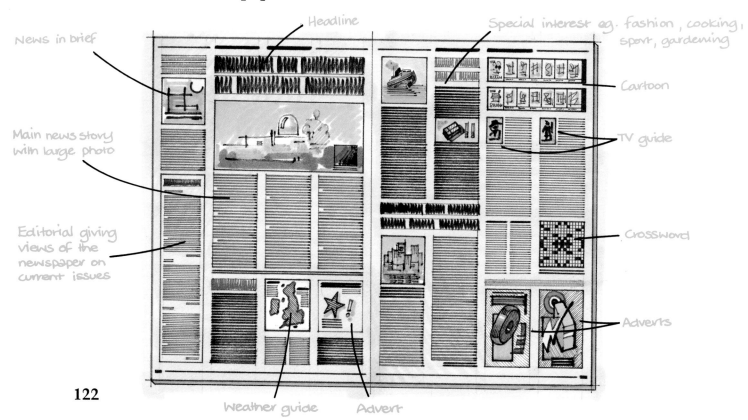

News in brief

Headline

Special interest eg. fashion, cooking, sport, gardening

Cartoon

Main news story with large photo

TV guide

Editorial giving views of the newspaper on current issues

Crossword

Adverts

Weather guide   Advert

Looking at content

With a partner make a copy of this chart and select one tabloid and one broadsheet newspaper. Record your results using a different colour for each paper.

| | News | | | | Advertisements | |
	Current affairs	Unusual	Human interest	Royal family	Classified	Others
Page 1						
Page 2						
Page 3						
Page 4						

Photos	Features	TV/ entertainment	Cartoons	Competitions	Agony/ gossip	Business	Sports

1 What do you think sells each of these newspapers?
2 What do you learn about how the newspapers are organised?
3 What conclusions can you draw about the readership of both newspapers?

Group discussion

'No news is good news.' It is often said that only 'bad' news is reported. Look through a selection of national and local newspapers and make a list of 'good' and 'bad' newspaper stories.
1 What do your lists tell you about your definition of good and bad news?
2 What do they tell you about the differences between local and national newspapers?

Writing about good and bad news

Write a short account, based on your discussion of this subject, of what you would consider good and bad news and how your list shows the differences between local and national newspapers you have studied. Why do you think these differences occur?

Discussing good and bad news

A newspaper editor once said 'News is not measured solely in importance.
If a member of the Royal family were stopped for speeding it would not get into the history books.'
1 Read a selection of tabloid and broadsheet newspapers and choose some stories you consider to be:
● important
● unimportant
2 How did you make your choices?
3 Do you agree with what the newspapers consider to be important stories?

Journalism

In this section you will be asked to write articles for a newspaper but first read the following advice from Roger Finn, the TV *Newsround* presenter.

- ◆ **The first sentence**   Put ten times more effort into this than anything else. Make it short and dramatic. Surprise your readers, make them curious.
- ◆ **Be clear**   Let readers know exactly what the story is about from the start. Put the most important facts right at the beginning.
- ◆ **The 5 W's**   Answer the five obvious questions about a news story: Who is involved? What happened? When did it happen? Where did it happen? Why did it happen?
- ◆ **Accuracy**   Get your facts right and never guess. Beware of feeling 'Well, I'm pretty sure that's right so I'll write it anyway.' I made that mistake when I wrote that Sidney was the capital of Australia.
- ◆ **Keep it brief**   Don't use complicated words if simple ones will do and above all don't bore your readers by making your story longer than it needs to be.
- ◆ **Be fair**   Remember that there are at least two points of view in any story. Your job is to present the whole truth so that your readers can make up their own minds.
- ◆ **Avoid clichés**   Especially if it is a sports story. Find new ways to describe familiar people and events.
- ◆ **Search for the special ingredient**   Once you've told the basic facts of an event, try to find a detail or quotation that makes your story special.

Most newspaper readers decide whether they are going to read something on the strength of the headline and the first sentence.

Badger baiters may be jailed   100%

Badger baiters and trappers will face imprisonment under the changes to the Criminal Justice Bill accepted by the Government last night.   70%

   The changes, based on a proposed amendment by Mr Peter Archer, the former Labour Solicitor General, come at a time of growing anxiety about the mal-treatment of badgers.   50%

   The present penalty for cruelty to badgers is a fine, although Ministers have announced an increase in the maximum from £2000 to £5000. Under the new clause magistrates can jail offenders for up to six months.   40%

The Daily Telegraph

NB The percentage figure represents numbers of readers who may read from beginning to end of an article.
So 100% may read the headline but only 50% get as far as the third paragraph. Because of this articles in newspapers give the main facts in the opening lines of a story and headlines become a vital part of attracting the reader. This is called **pyramid writing** because the number of readers diminishes from the broad 100% at the start of the article to a much smaller percentage at the end.

Writing your own article

Choose a local news story and write an article on it. Show the result to a partner who should check it against Roger Finn's tips and give you their opinion of how good a journalist you are!

   The section on pyramid writing shows that headlines have to be eye-catching and informative, so start your article with a striking headline. For more on headlines see pages 132-133 in this unit.

Tabloid and broadsheet styles

The following articles about the plight of the Amazonian Indians show you how tabloid and broadsheet newspapers emphasise different angles of a story.

WORLD CONCERN OVER BRAZIL RAIN FOREST

Indian tribes oppose dam

Altamira, Brazil (Reuter) – Indian tribesmen, wearing warpaint and brandishing spears, gathered in this Brazilian Amazon town yesterday to protest against planned hydroelectric dams which they say will drown the rain forest and disrupt their lives.

The five-day meeting, an unprecedented encounter in Amazonia, bringing together Indians, environmentalists and the foreign press, has captured worldwide attention because of the rapid destruction of the Amazon rain forest and fears that this will contribute to global warming.

The murder last December of the rubber tapper's leader, Chico Mendes, an outspoken campaigner for the preservation of the rain forest, has also focused international attention on the ecologically fragile region.

Hundreds of Indians, representing about 15 tribes, including Sioux from the United States, poured into the community centre in Altamira in the north-eastern state of Para for the meeting.

One tribal leader after another took the microphone to attack a planned complex of dams on the Xingu river, which they fear will disrupt the lives of some of the few tribes which remain.

And, as Senhor Gilberto Macuxi, representing the Indians of the northern state of Roraima, put it: 'Where there are no Indians the forests are destroyed.'

The Times 21 February 1989

Pop pow-wow for Sting the forest blaster

Backed by the sound of jungle drums, crusading rock star Sting is centre stage as he holds a pow-wow with an Indian chief in the Amazon.

The singer joined a protest by 500 of the Kayapo tribe fighting to stop the Brazilian government building a dam which will flood 65,000 square miles of rain forest.

It was the latest in a series of South American trips by Sting who is spear-heading a campaign to save the Amazon jungle. But amid the battle songs and war dances, he heard just how far progress has already marched into this neck of the woods as pop music boomed out from an Indian girl's ghetto blaster.

Today 23 February 1989

What do you think?

1 Which headline gives you the most information about the story?
2 Why do you think article 1 makes no reference to Sting when article 2 focuses on him.
3 Read article 2 carefully.
   a) Make a list of all the words which make you think of 'red indians'.
   b) In what ways does this give you a misleading impression of the Kayapo Indians?

4 Draw up a chart like the one below and use it to analyse each of the articles in more detail.

Writing your own analysis

Now that you have analysed the differences between these articles, write a brief account of your conclusions in which you discuss the importance of the way that language is used and the the way information is selected and ordered.

	Para 1 Subject	Para 1 Key words	Para 2 Subject	Para 2 Key words	Para 3 Subject	Para 3 Key words
Article 1						
Article 2						

Sub editing

Stories from around the world arrive in a newspaper's newsroom from two sources:

Press agencies   collect news and sell strictly factual accounts of events to newspapers who then rewrite the stories according to their readership and style. Famous press agencies are Reuters and the Press Association.

Press releases   are issued by organisations when they wish to have an event or a decision made public, e.g. when launching a new product.

Sub editors take the **raw copy** from the source, rearrange it into an article and give it a headline that they think will interest their readers.

Read the following piece of raw copy and the newspaper report which came out of it.

```
01/10  14:53  PAGE18  STARTREK  VER-07  BY-CH8  DEPTH-  13.9Cm  PAGE-

TOP OF STORY<
BRANDES PRESS AGENCY
By Ian Brandes, 1st October 1990, 0704 67415.
The new 'Captain Kirk' boldly journeyed to a place where no other Trekkie
has been before...to the political arena.
And British Shakespearean actor Patrick Stewart, alias Enterprise Commander
Jean-Luc Picard, phasered (hammered) 'Uncaring Britain' in an astonishing
attack. The bald superstar told a U.S. Star Trek fan magazine that he was
appalled by the rampant poverty and unemployment which existed in the U.K.
and was tearing families apart.
And he said: 'It has to be a terrible indictment on our society that there
are so many people living in misery.'
Stewart, who gives readings of Charles Dickens' 'Christmas Carol' to raise
money for the homeless, added: 'A report had been published in England about
families who were living on or below the poverty line. The figures of course
are stunning, for allegedly civilized Western countries.
'Dickens criticised the society he lived in, but it is still happening
today. Millions of people, that governments would rather ignore, are still
living in those horrendous conditions.'
ENDS...
```

New Star Trek hero Pat blasts at Britain

STAR TREK captain Patrick Stewart has blasted 'uncaring' Britain.

The British actor, Enterprise commander Jean-Luc Picard on TV, launched his attack in an American Star Trek fan magazine.

He said: 'It has to be a terrible indictment on our society that there are so many people living in misery.'

Patrick, 49, who gives readings from Charles Dickens to raise money for the homeless, talked of families living in poverty and added:

'Dickens criticised the society he lived in, but it is still happening today.

'Millions of people that governments would rather ignore are still living in these horrendous conditions.'

What do you think?

1 What information has been chosen for inclusion in the article from the raw copy?
2 What information has been left out from the article?
3 Can you give reasons for the order in which the information has been given?
4 Is the wording of the headline effective?

```
01/10  14:53  PAGE 18  PUPILS  VER-08  BY-CH8  DEPTH- 15.0Cm PAGE-
TOP OF STORY<
WESSEX NEWS
Twenty-three students from Reading in Berkshire have made history by being
the first pupils to be PAID to stay on at school.
Local companies have sponsored the sixth-formers to attend Highdown School
at Emmer Green in an exclusive scholarship scheme, the first of its kind in
the country.
There is no obligation on the students to join the sponsoring firm when their
further education ends.
The scheme, worth between 500 and 1,000 pounds per pupil, is proving to be
a hit both with the pupils and the businessmen who have made it possible.
Juliet Smith, sixth-form head at Highdown said 'The scholarships were
announced at the start of the school term. It works very well.
'It is very exciting. And there is no obligation at the end of the scholarship
for the companies to offer employment or for students to accept jobs there.
'It is not a facility to help firms find employees. We are very careful about
how it works.'
About fourteen firms are sponsoring students through a host of higher
education courses and A-levels.
A school spokesman said 'It will give our students a valuable insight into
what it is like to be in the workplace.'
ENDS mon 1.17
```

Writing your own articles

Study this example of a press agency report. You are going to write it up as a short newspaper article for:

- a broadsheet newspaper
- a tabloid newspaper

1 You will need to make a rough draft of the article first and ask your drafting partner for their opinion. For more on drafting partnerships see Unit 2 in The Process of Writing module, page 82.
2 Before you write up your articles look at this list of 'loaded' words commonly used by journalists. Use these in your work here and later in this unit where appropriate.

Each of these has a neutral equivalent, some of which are given here in brackets. Try to think of the neutral terms for the other loaded words in the list.

Militant	Contempt
Snatched	Blunder (mistake)
Hunted (searched)	Outcry
Battle	Soaring
Storm	Seized (took)
Row (discussion)	Axed
Slashed (cut)	

Is the news true?

All newspapers would claim that they give information to the public in a truthful and factual way. However, human nature and language itself makes this hard to achieve. Facts and the truth are often changed by the words used to express them.

These two articles tell the same story but there are differences in the way the story has been reported and in some of the facts that are presented.

Illness prompts burger caution

Chris Mihill
Medical Correspondent

The Department of Health yesterday warned people to cook beefburgers thoroughly after an outbreak of food poisoning at a McDonalds fast food restaurant

The warning, from Sir Donald Acheson, chief medical officer, follows an outbreak of a rare form of the illness in Preston. An investigation by the Public Health Laboratory Service found a link with beefburgers eaten at a local McDonalds. At least 14 people were taken ill last month, and there have been six subsequent reports of illness.

Sir Donald said: 'In recent years, human illness from this form of food poisoning [Eschericia coli 0157] has been showing a steady increase. Fortunately, the number of cases is still small – about 380 last year – but the organism can lead to bloody diarrhoea and, occasionally, go on to kidney failure.'

He added: 'This organism is heat-sensitive and can be readily destroyed by proper cooking. As far as the domestic consumer is concerned, there is no need for further precautions other than ensuring that the beefburgers are thoroughly cooked.'

The Department of Health says beefburgers made at home should be cooked until the juices run clear and there is no pink showing inside. People buying beefburgers in packs should follow the makers' instructions.

A spokesman for McDonalds said last night that only some of those who had become ill had eaten at the restaurant. 'Tests have been conducted in our Preston restaurant and in the premises of our meat supplier, and the presence of the bacterium that causes this particular type of food poisoning has not been detected.'

The Guardian 15 February 1991

BIG MAC BURGER BUG ALERT

Health warning after food poison outbreak

By JILL PALMER and STEVE WHITE

A BURGER alert went out last night after nine children who ate at McDonald's were hit by a terrifying food bug.

Three 'Big Mac' youngsters suffered rare, and potentially fatal, kidney damage. One victim was two years old.

In all, 20 people are feared to have been hit by the bug after eating burgers – not all at McDonald's – around the country.

Yesterday, the Government was so worried by the health scare its Chief Medical Officer, Sir Donald Acheson, ordered all Britain's fast-food chains to check that burgers were well prepared and cooked.

And he warned mums to make sure burgers were properly cooked at home. The Department of Health said it had found a 'highly significant association' between eating burgers which were not properly cooked and the strain of food poisoning.

Last night, McDonald's said it was cooking its burgers longer following discussions with catering companies and the Department of Health.

The bug broke out among customers of McDonald's in Friar Gate, Preston, Lancs.
All the victims, including a toddler, suffered severe diaorrhea.

Daily Mirror 15 February 1991

Group discussion

1 What impressions do you have of the scale of the problem from the headlines?
2 What are the differences in the factual information given in the articles?
3 What factors have decided the selection of the information in each case?
4 Which words are sensational? Look for words which exaggerate or emphasise in some way.
5 What opinion does each newspaper hold about this outbreak? Look at sentences which give opinion rather than fact.

For more on persuasive writing see Unit 4 in The Process of Writing module, pages 100-107.

Of course, the reporting of an event will also vary according to the nature of the observer, i.e. person A may witness a bank robbery from a completely different angle to person B.

Role play

1 Choose a group of 5 or 6 people to improvise a dramatic scene. For example, this might be a daring rescue, a protest about some local issue or an incident in the street.
2 As the scene is improvised, the rest of the class should watch and make notes.
  They are allowed to interview the participants at the end of the role play.
3 a) The observers then have fifteen minutes to prepare a news item, including a headline. They will have to decide what emphasis to give the event and write a news item which reflects that emphasis. For instance, a street incident might concentrate on an individual, the role of the police or the effects on the local community.

  b) The participants in the role play should write their eye-witness account of the incident.
4 Compare the newspaper reports and eye-witness accounts to see how many versions of the truth come out.
  ● Are there any differences in the factual information given?
  ● Which aspects of the story do different reports concentrate on?
  ● What aspects of the story do the different headlines pick out?
  ● Do the eye-witness accounts highlight any important facts that the reports do not mention?

The camera never lies

Is this really true? Look at these two pictures and talk about the messages they give you. In fact, the shots were taken at the same demonstration and the two groups pictured were not far from each other.

Loaded words

You have seen how **selection** in pictures and words can affect how the truth is presented.

In English there are many words which have roughly the same meaning but which have very different associations.

Shades of meaning

Compare these headlines:

GOVERNMENT BUYS LAND FOR DEVELOPMENT

MEADOWS GRABBED BY GOVERNMENT ORDER

1 What is the difference between 'buys' and 'grabs'?
2 What is added to the meaning of the second headline by calling the land 'meadows'?

The following words were used by the British press during the Gulf War in 1991.

We have Army, Navy and Air Force	They cower in their foxholes
We take out	Cowardly
We dig in	Their missiles cause civilian casualties
Our men are lads, professionals	Blindly obedient
Cautious	They fire wildly at anything in the sky
Loyal	Their planes are shot out of the sky
Brave	They destroy
Our missiles cause collateral damage	Their men are troops, brainwashed
We precision bomb	Fanatical
Our planes suffer a high rate of attrition	They have a war machine

Thinking about bias

1 The two columns of words have been mixed up. Sort them into two contrasting columns.
2 What do these phrases tell you about the reporting of the Gulf War?
  For more on the use of language during the Gulf War see the Knowledge about Language module, pages 14-15.

Editorials: comment and opinion

Editorial columns are written to comment on an important issue of the day. They are an opportunity for the newspaper to state an opinion openly and are written in persuasive language which often reveals political loyalties.
  Read the following editorial and think about the views it expresses.

Greenhousemongers

The world is at risk of untold catastrophe from the certain arrival of global warming, Mrs Thatcher warned when she opened the government's £7m climate research centre at Bracknell on Friday. She continued in this apocalyptic vein by predicting great migrations of people away from low-lying countries, such as Bangladesh, which would be flooded by a rise in the oceans, and from areas turned into desert be declining rainfall. The prime minister picked this up from the United Nations report on the greenhouse effect, which she welcomed as 'an authoritative early warning, an agreed assessment from some 300 of the world's leading scientists. They confirm that greenhouse gases are increasing substantially as a result of man's activities, and that this will warm all the Earth's surface with serious consequences for us all.' This is the UN report which also predicts that global warming could bring severe winter storms to Britain, the flooding of our coastal defences and malaria in southern England.

When Mrs Thatcher has the bit between her teeth there is no stopping her. This is fine when she's biting on the right bit, such as the market economy or a strong defence. But when it is the wrong bit, or at least one requiring more sober inquiry and consideration, such as the poll tax, then she can be a menace. With the greenhouse effect, Mrs Thatcher has fallen for the latest scientific faddism, and is pandering to the public's propensity to fall for the end-is-nigh predictions. As John Maddox, the editor of *Nature* magazine, wrote in *The Times*: 'Brooding on the prospect of global calamity seems to have become a passion. Now that the risk of nuclear warfare has receded, the threat of a general increase in the temperature of the surface of the Earth looks likely to take its place.' Ably assisted, he might have added, by the BBC's One World Week, in which normal journalistic judgement and inquiry was suspended in favour of environmentalist propaganda. There is no reason why the rest of us should do the same: it is time for a more hard-headed examination of the risks and costs.

There is no doubt that there is a natural greenhouse effect: sunlight which hits the Earth's surface is converted into infra-red radiation which cannot easily escape into space because of water vapour and carbon dioxide in the atmosphere. If it were not for this natural effect then the planet would be locked in an Ice Age. There is also no doubt that the atmosphere has changed since the Industrial Revolution: for example, there is now a lot more carbon dioxide thanks to increased burning of fossil fuels (especially coal and oil). The UN report rightly says that such emissions are substantially increasing greenhouse gases; on present trends carbon dioxide will have doubled by 2035. But it does not prove that this increase has so far raised temperatures; it merely predicts that it will in the future.

The Sunday Times 27 May 1990

What do you think?

1 Does the headline give you any clues about the opinion of this editorial?
2 Read the first sentence. How does its tone reinforce the headline?
3 Now make a note of any words or phrases, from the article as a whole, which are intended to persuade the reader in any way.
4 Make a list of all the references to Mrs Thatcher. What opinion does the editorial have of her on this issue?
5 Which sentences give the impression that the editorial is the voice of reason amongst the panic over the greenhouse effect?

Bias and persuasive language

If a writer either agrees or disagrees with the subject he is writing about this is called **bias** on a subject.

Road to folly

It was, said the police, a miracle that only one person died and 20 were injured when almost 100 cars collided on the M40 yesterday.

It would not have needed anything miraculous to have prevented the accident happening, though.

This new stretch of motorway cost £300 million to build yet the Department of Transport refused to install either lighting or fog warning lights.

This is not a new aberration. We have been misplanning our motorways since before the first stretch of the M1 opened in disaster in the late Fifties.

There are rarely enough lanes or proper lighting. The result is always measured in smashed vehicles and bodies. Then the Department relents.

But by then it is too late for those who have been involved in accidents.

The Department of Transport appears to employ the Sunday drivers of the civil service. It should replace them with professionals.

1 Look carefully at the editorial about the new M40 and make notes under these headings:
   ● **Bias** (who or what does the writer attack?)
   ● **Persuasive language** (what words or phrases make you think about the subject in a particular way?)

2 What is the bias in 'Greenhousemongers'?

Writing using bias

1 Take an incident that has happened in school in the last 24 hours and write two reports:
   ● one with a balanced view
   ● one with a biased view
2 Choose a recent issue in local or national politics and write a short article showing your bias on the subject. Use loaded language to reveal your opinions and to drive home your key points.

Today 16 February 1991

Headlines

Looking at headlines

England soccer ace heads into the pop league

THE GAZZ SINGER

Paul's new goal is a big hit for the vinyl score

1 What is the effect of the alliteration in this headline?
2 Identify the puns on:
   ● football
   ● pop music
3 Collect examples of headlines which use: alliteration or puns. Cut them out and label these features.

Headlines must be brief and this is often achieved by omitting parts of speech, e.g.

SEX CHANGE MARRIAGE BAR

4 What are the possible meanings of this headline?
5 Rewrite it so that its meaning is clear. Which parts of speech have you had to include to do this?

Reference to Berlin wall   *Russian army seen as harsh*   *Hints at careless act*

WALL OF STEEL THROWN AROUND REGA AMID ASSAULT FEARS

Hints at illegal act   *Shows tension in the area*

This headline uses words which create a particular impact through their implied meaning. Collect your own examples and display them with pointers showing meaning.

6 Label the implied meanings of the headlines you collected for question 3.

Comparing headlines

It is often possible to find bias in headlines.

POLICE SEIZE JOURNALISTS' TAPES

JOURNALISTS' TAPES TAKEN BY THE POLICE

1 Look at these two headlines about the same story and talk about the attitude to the police shown in each of them.
2 How is the attitude shown – look carefully at word order and word choice in each case.

Strangeways team gives warning of more riots if reforms are not made

Woolf says poor conditions led to prison riots

TELLY PLANS FOR THE MOD CONS
Prisoners at a riot hit jail may soon get their own telly.

QUICK END TO SLOPPING OUT AS PRISONERS GET NEW DEAL
The notorious practice of slopping out is to be ended within four years, Home Secretary announced yesterday.

SMALLER JAILS HOLD KEY TO GREATER JUSTICE

BAKER'S JAIL RIOT REFORMS

NO BARS TO GOOD PRISON REFORM

Woolf blue print for 'just jails'
The worst jail riot in British prison history has produced a blueprint for transforming the jail, described by reformers as the greatest step forward in penal policy this century.

Group discussion

Look at the headlines on page 132 about the need for prison reform and then in groups of 3 or 4, answer the questions that follow. (The Woolf Report was written by a government committee after the riots at Strangeways and other prisons in 1990.)

1 Sort the headlines into those that approve of the reforms, those that are neutral and those which are against the reforms. Identify words which made up your minds.
2 Who or what is featured in each headline and what emphasis does this give it?
3 Who are the headlines directed at?
4 Why should the story be reported in different ways?
5 Which headline is likely to make you read the article? Come to a group decision.

For writing

Read these newspaper articles and then write 2 or 3 headlines to go with each, showing different sides of the stories.

A Two baby duck-billed platypuses – the first to be bred in captivity in Australia for almost 50 years – emerged from burrows in the bank of a man-made lake at an Adelaide wildlife sanctuary yesterday.

Officials at the Warrawong sanctuary believe another four babies may still be inside the burrows.

The rare, egg-laying aquatic mammal confounded the first European visitors to Australia, and was treated as a hoax when specimens were first returned to Britain.

Dr John Walmsley, who founded the sanctuary in 1969, said yesterday that the platypus had long been extinct in the wild in South Australia, except for a colony introduced to Kangaroo Island. The last successful attempt to breed them in captivity was in 1943. A breeding programme, involving three females and two males from Kangaroo Island, began at Warrawong three years ago in ponds and lakes similar to the animal's native habitat.

The first babies, about 12 inches long, emerged after three months in burrows. The sanctuary hopes to build up a population of about 20 and release some in the wild.

B

More than 600 pages of Mark Twain's original pen-and-ink manuscript of his classic novel, *The Adventures of Huckleberry Finn*, lost from a New York library more than 100 years ago, have come to light in an attic in Hollywood.

The author gave the whole manuscript, of more than 1300 pages, to a library at Buffalo, New York, at the request of a local lawyer, James Fraser Gluck, in the 1880s but 665 pages later disappeared.

The missing pages have now been found by Mr Gluck's grand-daughter, a 62-year-old librarian in Hollywood, in a trunk of papers in her attic. The papers were left to her and a sister by an aunt.

The lost pages, covering the first half of the novel, written between 1876 and 1883, are in Twain's own hand, with many deletions, additions and changes on each page.

The rest of the manuscript has been safe in the rare books department of the Buffalo and Erie County Library since 1885.

The Daily Telegraph 15 February 1991

Gazzamania

This is the story of a modern-day hero.

'The 1990 World Cup in Italy saw the emergence of Paul Gascoigne as a world class player. Now known as Gazza, his outstanding ability, his cheeky clowning and his public display of emotion has touched the hearts of a nation. Since then Gazzamania has swept Britain. He's never out of the headlines, everything he does is news.'
> Channel Four, *Hard News* 19 October 1990

The hero steps onto the stage

'He's the best young talent to emerge from our country for a long time and I believe he is on the verge of greatness.' *Bobby Robson*

'He has proved himself to be one of the top midfield players in the world.' *Graham Taylor*

'Gascoigne is talented enough but he cannot resist playing the fool.' *The Times* 4 June 1990

'Gascoigne's first reaction is to lash out... his hot temper makes him a soft target at world level.'
> *The Sun* 7 June 1990

'If I keep going I know I can do this and that, have so much money in the bank...I know how good I am and what I can achieve.'
> Gazza, *The real me* video

What do you think?

1 Paul Gascoigne has made a video and recorded a pop song. What similarities are there between him and a pop star?
2 What do you think are the important elements in making a modern-day hero? Look at the evidence you are given here. You might think about whether Paul Gascoigne's fame rests on his talents as a player or on his commercial success.
3 It could be said that the media has created 'Gazza' by making sure that the interest in him is given full coverage: for instance whole magazines have been dedicated to him. Can you see any dangers in this? Is it right that the media makes money out of people in this way?

4 Think about the different ways in which Paul Gascoigne is presented on these pages. Try to identify the different audiences these images will appeal to.
5 Can you think of any other figures in sport or entertainment who have been built up in this way by the media?

For writing

1 Write a series of newspaper and magazine clippings from the year 2010 in which you report on the former hero of the 1990 World Cup.
2 Write an essay based on the material you are given here and any other information you have about Gazza, in which you discuss the power of the media to create and destroy heroes.

The spoils of success

‘ Paul's face adorns books, papers, magazines, posters and every other marketable product. ’
Match

‘ I get mobbed everywhere I go and it gets on my nerves. I wish people would realise I am only one of them. ’   Paul Gascoigne
Sunday Mirror magazine 28 October 1990

A change in fortunes

BELT UP GAZZA
Daily Mirror headline 1 October 1990

‘ Fame could crack me up. ’
Daily Mirror 20 October 1990

‘ Gascoigne was told last night – you are getting away with murder. ’ *Daily Star* 20 October 1990

‘ Gascoigne has said that he hates the press – he'd better watch out for the day the press hates him. ’
Radio 4 28 October 1990

MY LIFE IS HELL!
Gazza pays the price of the fame game
Daily Star headline, October 1991 after Paul Gascoigne is involved in Newcastle brawl.

‘ Sometimes I feel I haven't got a life of my own. It's getting to the stage where people want to fight me. They get a buzz out of it. ’
Gazza's comment in *Daily Star* article

You might compare the media treatment of some celebrities' careers to Shakespearean tragedy. Tragic heroes start by being brave and 'special' in some way but end in disaster. Below are some quotations from *Macbeth* which could well be applied to the media's image of well known personalities. Find out what happens to Macbeth and write a series of newspaper clippings which follow his career to its downfall.

> **Captain**: Brave Macbeth – well he deserves that name.
> **Witch**: All hail Macbeth, that shalt be king hereafter.
> **Macbeth**: I have no spur/To prick the sides of my intent but only/Vaulting ambition which o'er leaps itself/And falls on the other.
> **Lady Macbeth**: Are you a man?
> **Macbeth**: Out, out, brief candle/Life's but a walking shadow, a poor player/That struts and frets his hour upon the stage/And then is heard no more.

Assignments

1 Compare the front pages of two newspapers issued on the same day. Comment on the following in your written comparison:
- the type of stories
- the use of photographs
- differences in the stories reported
- advertising
- headlines
- the use of colour

What conclusions do you come to about the style of the newspapers you have chosen and the audience they are aimed at?

2 Using a range of different types of newspaper compare the treatment of either a human interest or a current affairs story.

Think about:
- where the story appears in each newspaper
- the length and detail of the article
- headlines
- the attitude of the newspaper to the story
- the use of photographs

3 Write your own perfect TV schedule for one day. This should include a watching guide and a recommendations panel, as well as times and channels.

4 Write a discursive essay in which you bring out the strengths and weaknesses of newspapers as a means of communication and compare these to other forms of media.

Advertising

How can I sell it?

The main purpose of advertising is to persuade someone to buy what you want to sell. Look at these classified advertisements and talk about how successful you think they are in attracting customers.

GREAT YARMOUTH, OAP spec., H and C, 10 bdrms, B/B, Cot and H.Ch. avail, Sp Ctre close, f info send SAE P.Burke, Saltings, Mere Road, Anside, Cumbria

AMSTRAD PC 1512 HD 20 (mono) with dBase III and Microsoft 3 inst. Will req. reloading of Amstrd MSDOS 3.2 Operating system. Rarely used. Tel. 026 33871

LGHT REMS 7 day service. Full ins. Comp rates. Care and personal service guaranteed. Anywhere in UK. Free est. P and Store on req. Tel 9891 7595

	Abbreviations	Persuasive words	Information needed
Guest house			
Computer			
Removals			

Looking at the classifieds

1 The language used in these ads is specialised in itself. In some places it reads more like a code. Try decoding these ads by filling in the table above, which helps to analyse the language in more detail.
2 Do these advertisements offer you all the information you would need about the items on sale?
3 How persuasive are ads like these?

Writing classified ads

1 In pairs write classified advertisements for the items pictured here in no more than 15 words, remember that each word will cost you money!
   Before drafting your ads:
   ● list the important features of these items
   ● brainstorm persuasive words which will help to sell them
   ● note down any other information needed, e.g. price, tel. no., etc.
2 Now try writing classified ads for one of these:
   ● subject lessons
   ● a lunchtime club
   ● a school drama production
   ● your form teacher
   You can probably think of abbreviations for lessons, clubs, etc. that are used in your school. Incorporate some of these into your ads.

Advertising yourself

1 Read about GREG in pairs and interview each other using the Datalink questions below, noting down your answers.

2 Use your answers as the basis for a piece about your partner for a dating page in a magazine.

Greg Mainey
(15)

Greg is not overly talkative, but he knows what he likes. 'Rugby, cycling, acid music and stuff like that.' He never watches the telly but he does read – Stephen King novels in the main. When he leaves school he's not sure what he wants to do – 'I haven't decided yet, maybe join the police force or something like that.' More than anything else he wants to be happy, and, yes, he likes girls. That's it.

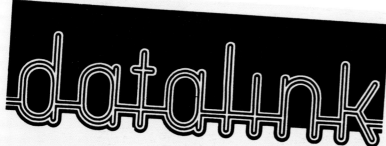

matching hearts *Nationwide* for more than a decade

Datalink .... Britain's most successful agency

FREE
COMPUTER TEST

During the last ten years nearly one million people have completed our questionnaires. So why not fill in this simple version. We will then send you, in complete CONFIDENCE, and with no obligation a full Colour Guide on the workings of Datalink, together with details of just ONE OF THE MANY Datalink Members who we feel you would like to meet.

FULL Names (CAPITALS) _____

Address _____

_____

START HERE

I am over 17

Occupation _____

Nationality _____

Your Sex (M/F) ___ Your Age ___

Your Height _____

Age range of person you wish to meet

Min _____ Max _____

YOUR PERSONALITY

Are You...

Shy _____
Nervous _____
Affectionate _____
Romantic _____
Intellectual _____
Tolerant _____

Outgoing _____
Self-Confident _____
Fun Loving _____
Ambitious _____
Creative _____
Generous _____

YOUR INTERESTS AND ACTIVITIES
If you enjoy the following please tick. If you dislike them please indicate with a cross. Otherwise leave blank.

Pop Music
Pub Evenings
Dining Out
Travelling
Theatre/Cinema
Walking/Cycling
Science/History
Watching TV

Classical Music
Dancing
Collecting Things
Spectator Sport
Poetry/Reading
Gardening
Conversation
Museum Visits

LKN

Please enclose 2 First Class Stamps

Image and motive in advertising

Jargon

Association: what you think of when you see a picture or read some words.
Image: the picture or words that are added to a product to give it particular associations.
Copy: any words used in an advertisement.
Motive: reason for wanting to buy the product.

Image making

A product on its own does not have an image.
This ginger beer bottle is given a traditional feel by its lettering but otherwise its associations are vague.

It is the job of an advertising agency to put the product in a setting to give it a certain appeal.

Looking at the image

1 What other objects are there in the box with the bottle?
2 Where has this box been kept before it was opened and the bottle found?
3 Why are all the objects in the box old?
4 What associations are the advertisers hoping we will have and how will they help to sell the product?

Brainstorming

Which of these two pictures would you use to advertise a battery razor?
What are the reasons for your choice?

Every picture tells a story

The picture and the copy work together in this advertisement to build up a youthful and romantic image which is also nostalgic.

Light – suggests dawn, have they been out all night?

Clothes – suggest they have been to a party. The girl is holding out her skirt to dry it, their hair is wet. Perhaps they have been for a swim? Young couple, beautiful and in love? Boy fire-maker and protector.

Car bonnet – indicates wealth and adds a nostalgic note.

Scuffed sand – suggests they have been dancing.

Fire – provides a focal point and highlights the couple.

Making a date:
Jacket from brother.
Car keys from dad.
Cotton from America.

For generations, they've been coming out here to the beach. Buddy Holly on the radio, a fire made from driftwood, a pair of cotton cords (perfect whether you're dressing up or down).

In America, we've spent years developing better cotton. We've nurtured different varieties, each designed to do a particular job perfectly. You can choose cotton that's blissfully warm, or crisp and cool; hard wearing and tough, or soft as velvet. But above all cotton that's comfortable.

So whatever the brand, you'll know you're going to be comfortable with it. Just as long as you look for the Cotton USA Mark.

THE PICK OF COTTON.

COTTON USA

Copy
First para: product introduced as an essential part of the situation, the motive is that it is as familiar as Dad, brother and making a date.
Second para: uses three images to reinforce the impact of the picture.
Third para: underlines the care of the producers and the usefulness of the product.
Fourth para: emphasis on comfort reinforces the cosy image of the picture.
Final line: pun on the word pick.

Taking a closer look

What effect do you think the following have on the reader:
- the type of print used
- the position of the image on the page
- the amount of space around the copy and the photograph
- If the logo and slogan are memorable can you explain this?
NB When skim reading a magazine the eye reads from top left to bottom right. How does this help to explain the positioning of the logo?

WE WON'T ASK YOUR CHILDREN TO PAY THE EARTH FOR TODAY'S ENERGY.

Environmental pressures have forced us all to think more about the world we leave to our children.

At British Coal we've been thinking particularly hard. And it's had reassuring results. You'd be surprised just how clean coal burning is today.

The world's modern coal-fired power stations aren't just more efficient, they can now eliminate 90% of sulphur emissions. An extensive programme of installing this technology (called flue gas desulphurisation) in British power stations has now started.

Coal-fired power stations generate 40% of the world's electricity, but contribute only 7% to total greenhouse gases (both of these figures come from OECD statistics).

And in Britain, coal produces over three quarters of our electricity. Modern coal plants are clean and safe to work in and live near.

The current technology is impressive enough. But future advances promise to provide us with 20% more electricity from the same amount of coal, reducing emissions still further.

The recent interim deal with the generators means British Coal will absorb all normal inflation, continuing to cut the real cost of coal to power stations over the next three years. Looking further ahead, long term contracts between British Coal and the electricity industry would guarantee prices well into the future.

Which all means that British Coal will be capable of generating electricity safely, cheaply and more cleanly during our own lifetimes. And those of generations to come.

Whichever way you look at it, it won't cost your family the earth.

For more information write to British Coal Marketing Department, Hobart House, Grosvenor Place, London SW1X 7AE, or ring 071-235 2020.

WAKE UP TO THE NEW AGE OF

British COAL

Analysing an ad

1 What kind of people are absent from this advertisement and why?
2 Who is it aimed at?
3 What is assumed here about class, family and children?
4 How does the copy help the picture in the advertisement?
5 What motive are we given to buy this product?
6 Script a brief conversation between the people in the advertisement.

For writing

Choose two contrasting magazine advertisements and write a detailed analysis of each. Does the advertisement have photographs or drawings? Can you see any reason for this choice? Think about the content of the pictures used and their position in the advertisement. What is the relationship between the copy and the pictures and how does the copy use language to persuade the reader? Who is the advertisement aimed at and does it give a clear motive for buying the product?

Slogans

Slogans are brief and catchy. They rely on:
- repeating the first letter in a series of words (alliteration)
- giving one word two meanings (punning)
- repeating a sound within a series of words (assonance or consonance)
- associating the product with a particular image

Thinking about slogans

1 Which of the above patterns can you identify in the following slogans?

> Gas. The heat of the moment
>
> Let the train take the strain
>
> Electricity – clean simplicity
>
> We're with the Woolwich
>
> Guinness is good for you

2 Try inventing some new slogans for the products mentioned in these examples. Remember they need to be brief and memorable.

Brand names

A product name is often associated with a particular appeal which is meant to make consumers buy the product.

Looking at brand names

Match these brand names with their appropriate appeal.

Product	Appeal
Goddess	Youth and energy
Jiff	Speed
Vitalis	Quality and value
Comfort	Beauty
Prudential	Care
Gold Blend	Effectiveness

2 Collect existing brand names for:
- breakfast cereals
- cars

Write them on a piece of paper and think about what appeal is given in the name.

For example, Ready Brek: the appeal is that of convenience and easy preparation, Ford Sierra: the appeal is that the name sounds mysterious and romantic.

3 a) Invent a brand name and catchy slogan for:
- a deodorant for men
- a chocolate bar
- a teenage magazine

b) Write a short account of your intended customer and the particular appeal of the product given by its name.

Motive and appeal

> An advertisement must give a clear answer to the question – why should the consumer buy the product being advertised, what is its appeal?

David Ogilvy, Advertising executive

Brainstorm

Look carefully at the setting and slogans for these advertisements.

1 Do they reveal certain attitudes towards men and women, the environment, children?
2 Are they directed at a particular age group?
3 Is the motive for buying given in the slogan or the setting or a combination of both?
4 On the basis of your responses to questions 1 to 3, fill in this chart.

Appeal	1	2
Parental care		
Tradition/nostalgia		
Genuine article		
Durability		
Glamour		
Compassion		

5 How is each of the motives in these advertisements created?

Writing about image and motive

Collect your own advertisements to show a range of motives. Use these as the starting point for a piece of writing showing how advertisers create a product's appeal through image, slogan amd brand name. Give a detailed account of how 2 or 3 advertisements work and use others in your collection to draw out general points about motive and audience.

Images of the Nineties

Advertising tries to reflect the attitudes of society, and in doing so often creates stereotypes. For instance, the 1980s became known as the decade of the go-getting, 'loads of money' Yuppie, partly as a result of advertising images. Advertisers are now presenting images which show a concern for the environment and what have been called 'caring values'. New stereotypes about men and women are also appearing in advertising.

Children and TV advertising

There are 8.5 million children in Britain. A survey carried out by the Wall's pocket money monitor (1990) shows that each child receives an average £1.49p pocket money per week, or £77.48p a year which adds up to a total of £660 million a year. This does not include money given by relatives and friends.

The following article, describes the effect on advertising of children's increased spending power and the growth of 'guilt buying' by parents.

Air the ad and spoil the child

'Kid consumerism' is a worrying new term which will strike fear into the heart of any right minded parent.

'Kid appeal' is already important and, according to a new report entitled 'Mums, kids and advertising', there is about to be a nationwide chorus of 'Please Mum, I want'. But advertisers should take note; the six year old of the 1990s will have to be targeted as carefully as the fussiest of shoppers.

The report promises a sharp rise in pre-teens following the 1960s boom generation starting their own families. By the year 2000 the population of under 16s will increase by around 1 million. Children are big business. Under 16s currently have an estimated £1 billion of disposable income in this country; food and toy purchases, although made by adults, are largely influenced by children; and the prospects for pre-teen spending seem rosier than ever.

Birth control and the desirability of a dual income has meant that women are leaving it later before having children. The increased demands on women, who often combine the roles of mother, earner and domestic skivvy, reduce the time available for children; to compensate, the theory goes, such parents are likely to spend more on their children. The older parent is also relatively well off and is able to indulge more readily in this 'guilt buying'.

With children spending only marginally less time watching TV than they do in the classroom, advertising can be an important part of selling to children.

Children are keen to keep in with their peer group and will not tolerate advertisements that are too 'whacky', according to the report. Research has also shown that children will instantly break eye contact with the screen when advertisements appear which they know are not aimed at them.

Pleasing a child audience is difficult for ad agencies.

'Favourite ads are nearly always adult orientated. Both kids and Mums liked the Persil advertisement. They felt that the character was real and they could identify with what was going on, says the report. On the other hand 'cutesy' advertisements such as the Bird's Eye Chick Sticks commercial was universally despised because it was felt to be patronising.

'The two golden rules when targeting children are: do *not* patronise them and do *not* try to be too hip and trendy,' says the report and goes on to make the point that children prefer adult humour. Their favourite seems to be the Carling Black Label Dambusters ad. Surveys have shown that 13-14 year olds drink alcohol regularly and this is an alarming factor for advertisers who have tried to lift lager advertising out of the range of under 18s with no success at all.

Telling children what is good for them might be an out dated idea but in the face of hard sell manufacturers some form of protection may be necessary.

The Observer October 1990

Discussing the article

In pairs, talk about these questions.
1 What is guilt buying?
2 Do you agree with the two golden rules for child-orientated advertising? Are there any others?
3 Can you think of examples of any TV advertisements which break these 'rules'?
4 Can you think of any TV advertisements which have influenced you to buy something? (It's difficult to admit this so be honest!)

Children's views

In a survey conducted by the IBA these advertisements were voted the most popular TV commercials by children aged between 4 and 13.

Top ads	Votes
Andrex	57
Trio	51
Transformers	47
Honey Smacks	35
My Little Pony	34
Smith's Crisps	33
PG Tips	23
Weetabix	23
Heineken beer	22
Carling Black Label	20
Milk	20

Group discussion

1 What conclusions can you come to about the ingredients needed for a TV advertisement to be successful with children from this survey?
2 a) Draw up a list of six questions and conduct your own survey on your friends' favourite ads. Find out what part of the advertisement is liked in particular: the music, the story-line, the animations, the voice over?
  b) Produce your own top ads list based on the results you get, giving reasons for each ad's popularity

Codes of practice

Here are some of the guidelines laid down by the ASA and the IBA in their codes of practice to control advertisements directed at children.

◆ Adverts should not encourage children to make themselves a nuisance to their parents, with the aim of persuading them to buy an advertised product.
◆ No advert should cause children to believe that they will be inferior to other people or be unpopular with them, if they do not buy a particular product or have it bought for them.

Points of safety

◆ Children should not appear to be unattended in street scenes unless they are obviously old enough to be responsible for their own safety.
◆ Children should not be seen behaving dangerously, e.g. leaning far out of windows, standing on the parapets of bridges, or climbing without adequate supervision or protection.

Points on broadcasting

◆ Cartoon characters or puppets featured in TV children's programmes must not recommend products or services of special interest to children.
◆ Alcoholic drinks and liqueur chocolates, must not be advertised during, before or after children's programmes.
◆ Adverts shall not encourage persistent sweet eating throughout the day nor the eating of sweet, sticky foods at bedtime.

Thinking about the codes

1 Which of these guidelines do you feel is most important in controlling advertising aimed at children? Give reasons for your choice.
2 What other guidelines would you recommend to protect children?
3 Can you think of any advertisements which come near to breaking the codes?

For writing

1 a) Read the statements below about children and advertising and talk in groups
     of 3 or 4 about this subject bringing in your own views and experience.
  b) One member of your group should make a note of what is said.
2 Use these notes as the basis for a short written account of the group's views on
  children and advertising.

> 'Learning about advertising is just a part of growing up – it is a way of learning about persuasion. Advertisements can make a child better equipped to cope with the world.'

> 'Greece has banned all toy adverts on TV and the EC is considering stronger measures to restrict this type of advertising.'

> 'Children are not stupid, they don't take much notice of adverts and see them mostly as just part of the entertainment on TV.'

> '95% of children have asked their parents to buy them a toy seen advertised on TV.'

> 'Advertisers can create desires and markets where none existed before.'

> 'The increase in teenage consumption of alcohol can be explained partly by the popularity of the Heineken and Carling Black Label advertisements.'

> 'It must be the best toothpaste if it's advertised on TV.'   *Nicholas, aged 8*

What do you think?

Read these more general complaints received by the ASA. In each case decide within
your groups whether the advertisement should be withdrawn.

FAST FORWARD BBC Enterprises Ltd 35 Marylebone High Street London W1M 4AA	**Complaint:** Objection to an offer which appeared on the front cover of *Fast Forward* magazine, which invited readers to 'JOIN THE NEIGHBOURS FAN CLUB FREE!'. Details given inside the magazine indicated that in order to obtain the free membership, readers were invited to enter a competition through which 5 free one-year memberships could be won. The complainant objected that this requirement should have been made clear on the front cover, particularly as the magazine is directed at children. **Conclusion: Complaint upheld.** The advertisers apologised for the complainant having been misled. They assured the Authority that steps had been taken to ensure that the wording of offers featured on the cover of the magazine were strictly checked in the future. The Authority noted the comments, but was concerned that greater care had not been taken in the preparation of the promotion, particularly as it was directed at children. The advertisers were reminded that promotions addressed to or likely to attract children should not take unfair advantage of their credulity or lack of experience. They were therefore requested to devise future offers accordingly.
Complaint from: Norwich	**Code extract:** Sales promotions should be designed not to cause avoidable disappointment.

BRITISH AIRWAYS PLC 200 Buckingham Palace Road London SW1W 9TA Agency: Saatchi & Saatchi Advertising Complaint from: Haywards Heath, West Sussex	**Complaint:** Objection to a national press and poster campaign which featured the strap line 'The World's Favourite Airline'. The complainant challenged the basis of this claim. **Conclusion: Complaint not upheld.** The advertisers stated that the claim was based on the fact that they flew more international passengers than any other airline and documentary evidence was submitted to this effect. The Authority considered this to represent adequate substantiation in support of the claim. **Code extract:** Without good reason, no advertisement should play on fear or excite distress.

Families

The stereotype of men as tough loners who are successful go-getters has recently been challenged in several TV advertisements.

Ad for Ford Granada car

Ad for American Express card

Thinking about the message

1 Who are these advertisements aimed at? Think about the age range, sex, job and lifestyle of the target audience.

2 What sort of images are the men given in these pictures: 'tough executive', 'caring dad', 'fast driver'?

3 According to these advertisements, what sort of people drive a car like this or have an American Express card? Why have these images been given to these products?

Representations of women and the family in advertising have changed over the years. Look at these ads for OXO which span several decades of advertising.

A

'my school lunch'

B

C

D

E

Group discussion

1 Which member of the family is missing in **B**?
2 What is implied about little girls in **A** and **B**?
3 What is the role of the father figure in **D** and **E**?
4 What do the pictures and the slogans tell you about female roles?
5 In what ways would you say some or all of these images are out of date?

Writing about representation

Look at the pictures C and E carefully. Script a conversation between the Oxo Woman of 1965 and her modern equivalent.

Stereotypes: men and women

'Advertisers create stereotypes to sell products more effectively. Women are often portrayed in a domestic setting whereas men are represented in fast cars and as successful businessmen. The reality is that more women work in Britain than any other EC country and the glamour of business success is enjoyed by only a few. Traditional roles for men and women are now being challenged and advertisers have begun to show men as caring fathers and women in executive suits. However, these are still stereotypes and may often produce feelings of guilt and inadequacy in both men and women who feel that they fall short of the ideal presented in advertisements.'

Noel McIntosh, Advertising agent

A

You never forget your first Raleigh.

Styles may change, but the joy of owning a Raleigh remains.
That secure feeling is still there, built into Raleigh bicycles for over 100 years along with rounded edges, non-slip pedals and sparkling paintwork.
The best memories are made to last; and so is a Raleigh.

Send to: Raleigh Industries, FREEPOST, Triumph Road, Nottingham NG7 1BR (no stamp necessary)
Please send me the Raleigh Fun Bike colour brochure
NAME
ADDRESS
POSTCODE
RALEIGH

B

YOU'LL NEVER REGRET BUYING SILK UNDERWEAR.

HITACHI

C

THE BOSS WAY OF LIFE.

BOSS

BOSS

BOSS NO. 1
THE FRAGRANCE FOR MEN

D

HIGH IN CALCIUM.

LOW IN FAT.

FREE FROM ARTIFICIAL ADDITIVES.

Hot Choc
Hot chocolate drink

THE DELICIOUS HOT CHOCOLATE DRINK FROM HORLICKS.

148

Looking at stereotypes

Look carefully at the advertisements on page 148 and consider the following points for each one.

1 What role is the man or the woman given?
2 How are the people or objects arranged in the picture and what messages does this give you?
3 What emphasis does the copy (the words) give the advertisement? Are any words repeated? Which words are particularly persuasive?
4 What motive are you given by the ad for buying the product?
5 Who is the ad aimed at? Make a chart like the one below to record the characteristics for each ad's target audience.

| | Target audience | | |
	Age	Sex	Occupation
Ad A			
Ad B			

6 Who or what are missing from the ad, e.g. people of a certain age, background, men, women, etc?

For writing

Collect your own examples of advertisements from TV, magazines and newpapers and analyse them closely as above. Write up your conclusions on how men and women are presented.

You could illustrate this with a completed version of the two figures below. Add labels to the figures to show the main features of the Ad man's woman and the Ad man's man.

Stereotypes of the future

Choose one of these products to represent men, women or both as they might appear in the year 2010:
● a breakfast cereal
● shampoo
● electricity
You could present this as a full page ad or perform it as a TV commercial, perhaps making a video of your performance.

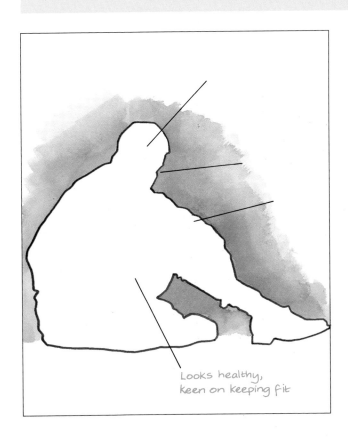

Looks healthy, keen on keeping fit

Has glamorous image

Writing for promotion

Promotional leaflets are written for a variety of purposes – to sell a product, to advertise a place or group of people, to raise money for a good cause or to give information on a political, medical or legal matter. All of them need to be written in a brief and easy-to-read way, and this depends on the words you use and the design of your leaflet.

Here are some tips.
◆ List the main points in one sentence lines and then present them with bullet points.
◆ Use cartoons, drawings or photos to back up your copy.
◆ Include a further information coupon or useful addresses.
◆ Choose contrasting typefaces for titles or key words.
◆ Use colour to highlight key points.

Here is the story of how one advertising agency prepared a promotional leaflet.

Stage 1: The brief

The brief comes through to the agency from the client.

 Abbey Street, Market Harborough, Leicestershire LE16 9BG
Tel: Market Harborough (088) 41040 Telex: 34291

Dear Sir,
We wish to promote our product in the following outlets: Self catering holiday homes, Camping sights, Holiday camps, Boating and caravanning centres. In particular we want a leaflet directed at the retailer. To ensure that they are aware of the profitable nature of Pot Noodles as a summer trade product.
Yours faithfully,

● This leaflet is directed at the retailer. What difference do you think there might be between addressing a retailer and the individual purchaser?

Stage 2: Preparing the copy sheet

The problem faced by the agency is that retailers get leaflets like this all the time, so it is important to catch their eye. Here are some considerations at this stage.

◆ Writing a good headline to gain the readers attention.
◆ How long the reader is prepared to read. If the leaflet is technical then more copy is needed.
◆ The use of bullet points will help the salespeople to point out the benefits to the retailer.
◆ The motive for buying must be central: in this case becoming part of a growing market and the quality of the product.

● What do you learn about writing copy from this stage?

For more on the way advertising copy is structured, see page 139 in this module.

Stage 3: Visualising

Once the copy is finalised the agency will try out several ideas for visuals, to gain the most successful combination of words and images.

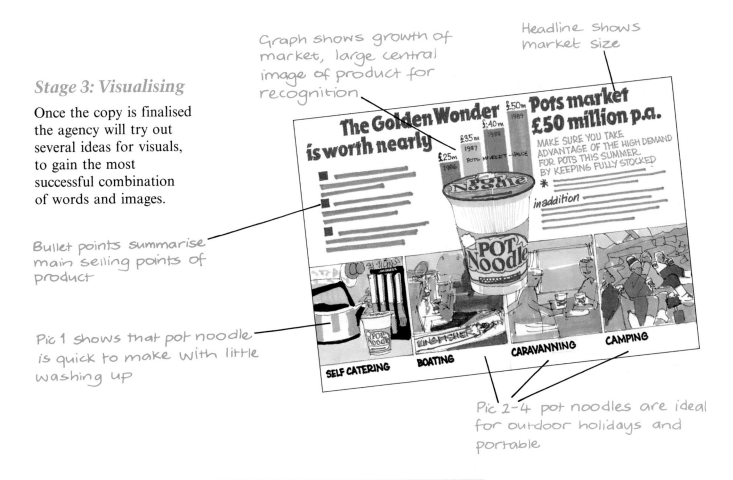

Graph shows growth of market, large central image of product for recognition

Headline shows market size

Bullet points summarise main selling points of product

Pic 1 shows that pot noodle is quick to make with little washing up

Pic 2-4 pot noodles are ideal for outdoor holidays and portable

● What do you learn about the importance of layout from this stage?

Stage 4: Getting the client's approval

Following a full costing of the leaflet and a 'proof' version of the leaflet, everything is returned to the client, in this case Golden Wonder, for their approval.

If this approval is given then the leaflet can be printed and distributed.

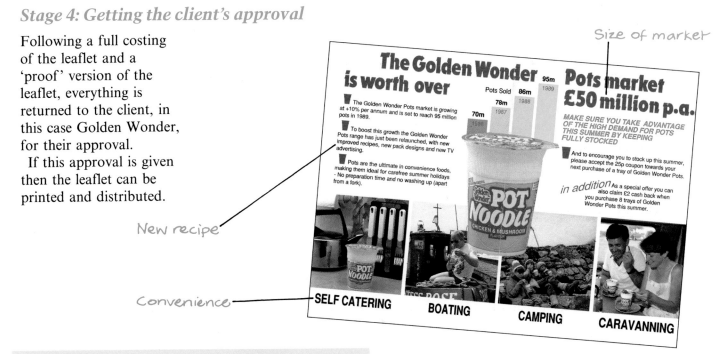

Size of market

New recipe

Convenience

● What objections might the client have at this stage?

For more on information writing see Unit 3 in
The Process of Writing module, pages 87-88.

Lettering and logos

Words can be given extra meaning according to the type of lettering used to write them.

Mobil

LIBERTY

Thinking about lettering

1 Do any of these names suggest the qualities of the products?
2 In what way does the typeface reinforce the message about them?

Holiday Express   **Holiday Express**

Holiday Express   HOLIDAY EXPRESS

HOLIDAY EXPRESS   **Holiday Express**

3 What sort of holiday would you expect from each of these holiday companies?
4 What sort of products or organisations might use each of these types of lettering?

Logos can also help to create a particular image.

5 What associations do these logos have?

All in a good cause

Here is a leaflet which deals with conservation

Clear headings, note repetition of 'so' to emphasise the point being made

Photo of human intervention, showing people in bad light

logo — simple and effective

Text with bullet points shows work of WDCS in easy-to-read form

Use of persuasive language

Dramatic photography showing animals in natural environment

Clear slogan to catch reader's attention

SO MUCH IN COMMON

Welcome to the awe-inspiring world of whales and dolphins. A diverse family of warm-blooded mammals whose grace and beauty are well-known and appreciated across all five continents. In contrast, we still know so little of the ways of life and intelligence of these magnificent creatures.

As the largest-brained animals on earth, whales are regarded by many as our ocean-going equivalents. Certainly, they hold a very special place in human history and whether subjects of worship, art, friendship, fear, love or commercial exploitation, whales have always inspired the deepest feelings.

Over the centuries, trade in whale products helped many nations prosper; countries now able to generate wealth and food without taking their awful toll. Now it's our turn to give life back to the whales and dolphins.

SO DIFFERENT IN NATURE

Pilot whale being killed · Faroe Islands (Denmark)

SO HOW CAN YOU HEL

"Of course, all this takes a great deal of time and money. But, most of all, it takes the will of people like you who care about whales and dolphins to make it happen.

So should we let them sink into oblivion and folklore? Or should we give them back their dignity, their freedom and their rightful place in the natural order of the world's rivers and oceans?

Sean R. Whyte · Director WDCS

Please show that you really care, either by joining the society or by supporting our work with a donation. We are a registered charity that devotes ALL its time and resource toward the conservation and protection of every known species of whale and dolphin. On the back of this leaflet, you'll find a few of the projects we're involved with. Overleaf, a way to make many more a reality.

Time is running out - it's in YOUR hands. Thank you".

WHALE AND DOLPHIN CONSERVATION SOCIETY

Humpback whale breaching (Photo courtesy of CCS)

WORKING THROUGHOUT THE WORLD

- WDCS exposed the cruel trade in live orcas (killer whales) captured off Iceland in nets.
- WDCS co-sponsored a study of the rare Hector's dolphin off New Zealand.
- WDCS paid for vital repairs to a whale rescue boat in Massachusetts, USA.
- WDCS is co-sponsoring a study of dolphins that are being harpooned off Peru.
- WDCS is co-sponsoring a preliminary survey of the threats facing several dolphin species off Chile's coast.
- WDCS published a special report on "Small Cetaceans - the forgotten Whales" and an educational guide "Whales and Dolphins of the World".
- WDCS co-produced a report on the maintenance of cetaceans (dolphins and whales) in British dolphinaria.
- WDCS is leading the UK campaign against dolphin killing by the tuna industry.

AND WITH YOUR HELP WE PROMISE TO DO MUCH MORE

WHALES AND DOLPHINS

Common dolphins (Photo courtesy of Marine Mammal Fund)

THEIR FUTURE IS NOW IN YOUR HANDS

WHALE AND DOLPHIN CONSERVATION SOCIETY

20 WEST LEA ROAD, BATH, AVON. BA1 3RL. Registered Charity 298656

MEMBERSHIP BENEFITS

- Twice a year you will receive our highly acclaimed colour magazine - "SONAR". Full of beautiful photographs of whales and dolphins, as well as reports from around the world.
- Updates in our regular newsletter on national and international developments and activities.
- Opportunities to join whalewatching expeditions.
- The pleasure and satisfaction of belonging to one of the world's leading whale and dolphin conservation groups.

Thinking about the leaflet

1. Read this leaflet and note down some of the persuasive words it uses, e.g. emotive phrases like 'awful toll'.
2. How do the writers of this leaflet make us sympathetic towards the whales and dolphins?
3. Look for parts of the leaflet where factual information is presented, e.g. where details of the work of WCDS are given.
4. What messages do the photographs give us about:
   - whales and dolphins ● human beings
5. Who do you think the target audience is? Does the leaflet assume any sort of knowledge of the subject?
6. Why is a photo of the director of WDCS included?

Assignment

Bearing in mind what you have learnt in this section about:
- features of design and layout
- writing persuasively
- writing for information

prepare and put together your own leaflet to promote a charity of your choosing.

153

Meeting the brief

Jargon

Account: the job given to the agency by the client.

Brief: the information given to an advertising agency by the client describing what is to be advertised.

Bullet point: dots or stars which precede items in a list of information.

Client: the company or Government department who wishes to have some advertising.

Copy: any words used in the advertisement.

Make up: the technique of arranging the type on the page either by cut and paste or a desk top publishing package.

Portfolio: all the finished work you present to your client.

Shoot: taking photographs to include in the advertisement.

This simulation will give you a chance to put into practice many of the techniques and skills you have tackled in this unit.

Form your own advertising agency

1 In groups of 4, first of all decide on a name and a logo for your agency. You might use your initials to make a word or acronym.

2 In order to produce a portfolio of work for your client each of you will have to take on one of these jobs and roles.

- The **Accounts manager** will take overall responsibility for working with the client and making sure that the team is working hard and cooperating. The Account manager is allowed the final decision if there is a disagreement.

  This member of your group is effectively the 'boss' and they should look out for any mistakes or contradictions between the words and the pictures in the leaflet. They will also contribute ideas for the content of the leaflet.

- The **Visualiser** is responsible for the visual parts of the advertisement, i.e. drawings, photographs, lines, bullet points, etc). They will have to have good ideas about how to present the product through pictures and design.

  This member of the group will have to be good at layout and have a strong visual sense. They also need to be able to work creatively with the Finished artist to achieve the best visual results.

- The **Copy writer** will produce the copy for the ad. In this case this means all the words which go into the leaflet, including slogans, persuasive descriptions, information, etc.

  Review the sections on copy on pages 150-152 before you write to ensure that you are using language for the maximum impact. Remember you only have a small space to put your point across – every word must count.

- The **Finished artist** will be responsible for drawing any illustrations the ad requires. They will also need to research any photos to be used in the ad. They have to work closely with the Visualiser, who will have strong ideas about the content of the illustrations and photos.

  This member should be a good illustrator: someone who is able to produce drawings, logos and bullet point designs which reinforce the copy.

Now read the brief that has been sent to your agency from the Ministry of Transport. You will be preparing a portfolio in the hope that the Ministry will hire you to do their advertising. Your teacher is the civil servant from the Ministry who will deal with any queries from the client or yourselves.

DEPARTMENT OF TRANSPORT AND INDUSTRY

Memorandum to advertising agencies

In the light of growing traffic congestion and recent events which have caused a shortage in the supply of oil, Her Majesty's Government are considering ways in which to reduce the population's use of the motor car, especially in urban areas.

Changing work habits and environmental factors have contributed to our determination to alter public perception about modes of transport. The Government therefore wishes to launch a major publicity campaign to persuade the public to utilise public transport services and their own fuel-free means of travelling – i.e. walking or riding a bicycle. The campaign should cover a range of media and agencies are asked to produce a package to include leaflets, whole page advertisements, radio announcements, jingles and TV advertisements.

We wish the car to be demoted in the public's mind and the benefits of more economical and environmentally friendly means of transport to be encouraged. The above objectives must be achieved in as entertaining and as attractive a way as possible.

For writing

In consultation with the DTI it has been decided that your primary task is to produce a leaflet for every household in the UK, but that you could also make plans for magazine and TV advertising to reinforce your 'mail-shot' campaign. All of these should be included in your portfolio.

Planning your campaign

In your teams, discuss the following in detail before any work on text or illustration begins.

1
- What media you are going to cover.
- What angle you are going to take, e.g. the damage caused by cars, the need for forward-looking people to stop using their cars, presenting the alternatives to cars in an attractive way.
- Who will be your target audience(s)? Define them by age, occupation, sex, etc.
- The slogan you will use. It must be memorable and a phrase which you can use in a range of media settings.
- Ways of getting your message across in a clear and persuasive way.

2 Once you have agreed on your aims and how you will aproach the campaign, you can work in your team roles towards producing material for presentation to the DTI. Arrange a meeting with the DTI representative to show him or her your initial visuals for the leaflet. (See Golden Wonder case study on pages 150-151 for an example of these.) Take on board his or her suggestions for changes and put forward your ideas for the TV and magazine campaigns.

3 When you have completed your final leaflet and ads for other media, make a display of your work and if possible a video of your TV commercial.

Specialist writing: techniques

Making it clear

When you are writing in subjects like Science, Geography, History and English you use different forms and styles of writing. For example, in Science you would generally write in brief sentences which convey scientific information in the form of a report or 'write up'. In contrast, you would use a more descriptive form of writing if you were asked to write about the experience of being a soldier in the trenches during the First World War in History. Many subjects with a factual basis deal with giving instructions. For example, in Home Economics you will be asked to read cooking instructions and to write your own.

In this and the following unit, you will write on several different subjects and in many styles. As you do this, remember these key points.

- Look at all the available information and select the material you will include carefully.
- Organise your material under paragraph headings and put them into a logical sequence. For instance, if you are writing about rainforests, a paragraph about the traditional life of the Indians might be followed by a paragraph on how modern man has used the same environment. The contrast here will make its own point.
- Use linking language, like that featured in this unit on pages 160-161, to give your writing shape and direction.
- Decide who your audience is and what the purpose of the piece of writing is. For example, do not be too technical if you are writing for the 'general public' and make sure that the argument or knowledge you are trying to convey is clear to the reader.

For more on structuring your writing see Unit 2 in The Process of Writing module, pages 76-77.

Science experiment

Some students in Year 10 were asked to report on their experience of dissecting a sheep's eye. They chose to do this in a variety of ways, as accounts **A**, **B** and **C** show.

A   The first step of dissecting the eye was to take off the cornea and conjunctive. Before the eye was touched it lay in the cottonwool, a dead, deep black pupil, gazing unseeingly at the ceiling. When its transparent protection was wrenched away it left the iris bare and brown. Now it was to be attacked: the scalpel dived into the eye and scraped the iris off, not smoothly but in bits and pieces. Underneath the vitreous humour lay. It was tipped into the human hand, sloppy and jelly like. Then the lens was pulled out, and for the first time the eye was more like a machine to me than something that was living. The lens was round, smooth and perfect. Through it things are upside down. Now all that remained was the retina, empty like a shell.

Subject: Science
Task: To dissect a sheep's eye
Activity: Comment on the stages of your dissection, including observations on texture and colour.

B   Mark and I started off by cutting off all the disgusting fatty bits from around the side of the eye. Once that was done we had to start the gory job of cutting open. First of all we had to get the see-through cornea off the front of the eyeball. This was very difficult because we couldn't get started, and in the end

156

it took about five minutes to get it off. Then the aqueous humour poured out. Now the iris had to come out – it looked very slimy and black – and when it did come out it was like a rolled up pancake. Now we had to be extra careful because the lens was next, using the tweezers. These had to be placed on either side of the lens and it popped out unharmed. It was very clear with a lovely oval convex shape. One part of the suspensory ligament was still attached like a black slug. To get out the vitreous all you had to do was turn the rest of the eye over and the vitreous would pour out into your hand in a sort of bag with a ring of black muscle around it. It looked just like jelly. So now there was a perfect view of the retina with its various shades of purple pigment and criss-crossed red blood vessels. In the middle the blind spot was clear with the optic nerve behind it. This is what should have happened, but unfortunately me and Mark were not good enough at dissecting because all we got was the cornea, the iris was splattered in tiny bits in the aqueous humour: the lens was found in three bits in unrecognisable shapes with no trace of the vitreous humour or the suspensory ligaments. In short it was a complete disaster.

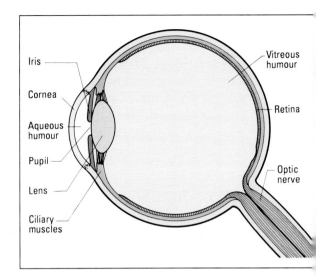

C Ode to an eye

Rotting, Putrefying,
Devoid of life.
Cloudy, Opaque,
All unseeing,
The eye wobbles
On the dissecting board.
The Scalpel strikes...
Aqueous humour
sprays into the
Dissector's eye.
The dark, brooding iris
No longer shows
The slit-like pupil.
The bag that holds
The vitreous humour,
bursts, and with a squelch,
Deflates, and leaves a pool
of slimy transparent jelly
All over the desk.
Inside the retina
Is green and shimmering.
Turning to blue
In the changing light,
Like an empty shell
On the sea shore of sight, –
Bereft of vision.

Taking a closer look

1 Now it is your turn to dissect these pieces of writing. Make a chart like the one below, giving yourself enough room for notes.

	A	B	C
1st or 3rd person Stage Scientific information Personal reaction Descriptive words			

2 Who is each piece written for? What features of the language used helped you to decide?
3 In **A** verbs like 'wrenched' and 'attacked' are used. What does this tell you about the writer's attitude to the experiment?
4 What evidence is there in **B** that the writer has mixed feelings about the experiment?
5 Which piece is the most successful at conveying:
   ● scientific information
   ● the experience of dissecting an eye
6 Apart from the way it is set out, what is 'poetic' about **C**?

For writing

Write a brief account of how in your view each piece is suited to the task set by the teacher.

Processes and structures

It is sometimes difficult to make sense of factual writing. There seem to be so many facts that readers lose track of what is being described. Do not despair! This sort of writing is often done to a formula and this section will help you to read and understand factual writing.

Factual writing often describes:
- the **process** by which something is made, like paper or aluminium
- how something is **structured**, like an eye or an aeroplane

Thinking about processes

Read this description of how rubber is processed and then copy and complete this chart which offers the information in another way. You will have to think of a way to include the alternative processes of crepe rubber, heveacrumb and concentrated latex.

Place	Stage	Action	Change that occurs
At the tree	Wintering		
	Tapping	Cutting bark to release latex Collected in small cups on tree	
Rubber factory	Coagulation	Add formic acid	Soft, spongy blocks

Rubber processing

The fully grown rubber tree is a large, smooth-barked tree with branches springing out at some height from the ground. It sheds its leaves annually despite its equatorial habitat. This is known as **wintering**, and during this period of a few weeks, the tree yields less latex. The **latex** is a white milky liquid which oozes out when the bark is cut. It contains about 60 per cent water, 35 per cent rubber hydrocarbons and several minor mineral constituents. **Tapping** is the carefully controlled cutting of the bark to release the latex.

Rubber trees are usually tapped on alternate days, using a special knife. Tappers start their work early in the morning and tap about 300 trees each. The latex runs out into small cups attached to the tree and is collected by the tappers. On wet days tapping is not done as the rain-water dilutes the latex.

The collected latex is first **coagulated** into soft, spongy blocks by adding formic acid or acetic acid. This makes it solid and more easily handled and it is passed through rollers to squeeze out water, and produce **sheets** which are then cut into standard sizes. The rubber sheets are **smoked** in a specially constructed smokehouse for several days in order to preserve them. Smoked sheet rubber is brown in colour rather than white.

There are several other ways of processing the rubber. For instance, the sheets may not be smoked but simply dried and rolled very thin through pairs of rollers moving at different speeds to produce the very fine crinkly sheets known as **crepe rubber**. Alternatively, the rubber may not be coagulated at all but be exported as

latex. If this is the case the latex is **concentrated** to remove some of the unwanted water, either by a centrifugal process, or by evaporation, and is preserved by adding ammonia. Concentrated latex has many advantages as an export product for it is more easily handled than sheets, being carried in special tanker-trucks, rail-wagons and ships. It can also be used almost immediately by consuming firms for making such things as foam rubber cushions and mattresses.

The latest processing method is to produce **heveacrumb**. This is done by adding a mixture of chemicals to the rubber so that when it is passed through rollers it does not form a sheet but a mass of crumb-like pieces. Heveacrumb dries very quickly and is thus produced fast and relatively cheaply. It can be produced in 5 to 6 hours instead of the 5 to 6 days taken to make smoked sheets. The crumbs are pressed together into bales for transport, and packed in poly-thene bags. Heveacrumb is adaptable to a wide range of uses by consumers and has become an increasingly important product in the rubber industry.

1 Read this description of the heart and then draw up and complete a chart like the one shown here. Think up a way of showing how blood circulates through the heart and around the body. This could be done by inserting coloured arrows on your chart.

Description	Function	Action	Effect
Hollow bag of cardiac muscle in four chambers (x2 atria/auricles x2 ventricles)		CM contracts CM relaxes (one contraction and one relaxation = a heart beat	
Bicuspid/tricuspid valves	To control blood flow from atria to ventricles		
Semi-lunar valves		Open and close	Blood moves out of heart along arteries

The heart

The heart is a hollow bag with walls made of a special kind of muscle, called **cardiac muscle.** When cardiac muscle contracts it squeezes blood out of the heart into blood vessels which carry it to all parts of the body. When the cardiac muscle relaxes the heart fills with blood that is returning from its journey around the body. One contraction and relaxation of the heart is called a heart-beat. In humans, the heart normally beats from 60 to 70 times a minute. During exercise this may increase to about 150 times a minute.

The space inside the heart is divided into four compartments, called **chambers.** The two top chambers are called **atria,** or **auricles,** and their walls contain a thin layer of cardiac muscle. The two lower chambers are called **ventricles,** and their walls are made of a much thicker layer of cardiac muscle.

The heart contains a number of valves. These control the direction in which blood flows through the heart. The **bicuspid** and **tricuspid valves** ensure that blood flows only from the atria into the ventricles. The lower edges of these valves are held in place by tendons and muscles. Semi-lunar valves are situated at the points where blood flows out of the heart. The semi-lunar valves ensure that blood cannot flow back into the ventricles once it has left the heart...

Blood is driven around the body mainly by the pumping actions of the heart. But the flow of blood is greatly assisted by arteries and veins as well.

Arteries divide to form smaller vessels called **arterioles** which have a thinner muscular/elastic layer. Arterioles divide many times to form a dense network of **capillaries** which have walls only one cell thick. Capillaries eventually join together into **veins,** which carry blood back to the heart.

Arteries
Arteries have thick walls made mainly of muscle and elastic fibres. Each heart-beat forces blood into arteries at high pressure, which stretches the artery walls outwards. Between heart-beats elastic and muscle fibres in the arteries press inwards on the blood, forcing it away from the heart. Blood must flow in this direction because the semi-lunar valves stop it flowing back into the heart. This wave of stretching and contraction in arteries causes the 'pulse' which can be felt in the wrist and neck.

2 Now turn back to the accounts of dissecting an eye and make a table for the structure of an eye using the information you are given.

Looking at the language

These two pieces of factual writing on rubber and the heart have particular features. Read through them again and find examples of the following:
- use of the passive voice
- ways in which the words are given emphasis
- use of facts and figures to explain the subject

Language links

The problem with this piece of writing is that it contains too many 'thens' and 'ands'. Whatever sort of information writing you are doing it is helpful to have a variety of linking words to use in your work.

Cholera: a waterborne disease

Cholera is a dreaded disease. It affects the lining of the intestine and causes diarrhoea, cramps, dehydration and, frequently, death. What is more, death is often rapid. In the 19th and early 20th centuries fatal epidemics spread throughout the world. For instance, during the four major epidemics which reached Britain, 300,000 people died of cholera.

Cholera was most common where living conditions were poor.

In such areas, houses were overcrowded, rubbish accumulated and sewage treatment was inadequate. Most people in those days thought that cholera was caused by 'miasma' and 'effluvia, from marshes. Consequently any attempt to curb the disease failed. The real problem was that drinking water was contaminated with untreated sewage. Despite ideas about the origin of cholera, John Snow, a doctor, suspected that contaminated drinking water had something to do with the spread of the disease. For this reason, in 1854 he mapped the homes and water supply of victims of cholera in part of London, and found that all the victims obtained their water supply from a single pump in Broad Street. One night he removed the handle from the pump and so prevented people from using it.

As a result, fewer people caught cholera, and his theory was shown to be correct. However people were slow to accept that water quality was crucial to health. In fact, the idea that germs caused disease was not fully established until later in the 19th century through the work of such great scientists as Louis Pasteur in France and Robert Koch in Germany.

Catalyst September 1990

Looking at the links

1 Some of the linking words have already been underlined. Identify the rest in this passage.
2 Talk about how each linking phrase is used in the extract.
3 Who do you think the audience is for this passage? How can you tell?
4 What is each paragraph about? What does this tell you about how this passage is organised?
5 Where do you think this piece of writing first appeared? What is it about the writing that gives you this impression?

Establishing links

Read this letter and then decide which of the linking words, given as choices below, should occupy the gaps. Be prepared to give reasons for your final choices.

Dear Sir,

I am writing to express my opinion about what you suggested in your article called 'Dole Giveaway', **[1]** that the Social Security system was being abused by people doing casual work while drawing benefit, and that **[2]** it should be reduced or **[3]** abolished.

[4], let me say that I am the unemployed head of a family of six, and that all four of my children are at school, **[5]** I am entitled to draw only the minimum benefits. **[6]**, we are always short of money. **[7]**, unemployment is running at 15% in this area, so there is little chance of finding a job, at least not at my age (54). I **[8]** feel that I am entitled to full support from the state. **[9]** when I was working, I paid taxes, like everybody else. **[10]** I still have to pay VAT even now!

[11], many people that I know are out of work, though most of them would prefer to be working. None of them have any money to spare, but **[12]** I know of only one man who abuses the system. **[13]** I know of many who, for some reason or another, do not draw their full entitlement.

[14], I would like to ask if the author of the article has ever been out of work himself. **[15]** I think that he had better keep his opinions to himself until he knows what he is talking about.

Yours faithfully,

Adam Smithson

1	for example namely therefore in other words	7	As a result All the same However For instance What is more On the other hand	11	Alternatively Even Secondly On the other hand
2	thus for this reason so on the other hand			12	even in spite of that by the way although
3	what's more at any rate even at last	8	therefore by comparison for example because	13	In that case Alternatively For example On the contrary
4	In the first place Next Furthermore In fact	9	Otherwise After all Equally By the way	14	To sum up Finally Therefore In the end
5	yet though however because	10	At any rate That is to say In other words Incidentally	15	In that case If so Therefore If not
6	By comparison In spite of that				

Using linking words

Rewrite the field trip description that opened this section using suitable linking words instead of 'then' and 'and'. Reorder the information given if you feel that is appropriate.

Looking at usage

In pairs, explain how you would use each of these linking words. Take turns to explain:

for example	after all
equally	on the other hand
namely	secondly
incidentally	for this reason
however	although

Summary

Whether you are writing up experiments or giving an account of a historical event, you are selecting important and relevant information.

Out of bounds

Jan: Where were you at dinner time?

Liz: I had to sit outside the Head's office, didn't I?

Jan: What happened, then?

Liz: Dizzy caught me and Donna out of school at break.

Jan: What happened?

Liz: You know the bit by the path, you know, at the back of the Sports Centre, not at the school side but over near where the Junior is. I don't usually go over there but there were these boys, Darren was one of them, oh yeah *and* Gary, well quite a few of that lot, I'm really sick of all them, they think they're so hard. You know Deb, John's sister, well she's only this tall and Darren and that lot got her on the way home – pulled her about and took her bag and that. Anyway, I didn't want to be seen dead with them, especially Gary, so Donna and me went off to the Sports Centre at break. She wanted to tell me about this new bloke. It was really freezing. We were gassing away when I realised that old Mrs Todd was staring straight at us from the Junior. I could see her get on the 'phone so we ran round the side of the Centre – straight into Dizzy. By the time he'd taken us into school Mr Nelson knew all about it.

Making the selection

Liz is describing something that has happened to her but obviously does not include *everything* that has happened or been said.

1 Write an account of no more than four sentences about Liz's experience.

2 What are the differences between your written account and her spoken account?

3 Talk about how you selected the information. How did you decide which parts to leave out, for example?

To be able to scan a piece of writing and sum it up briefly is a useful skill for GCSE and in working life. Read this extract from Neil Armstrong's personal recollections of the first moon landing.

A *Apollo II, carrying Neil Armstrong, Lieutenant-Colonel Michael Collins, and Colonel Edwin Aldrin, was launched on 16 July. At 03.56 BST on 21 July Armstrong stepped off the ladder of lunar landing vehicle, Eagle, on to the Moon. [1969]*
NEIL ARMSTRONG: The most dramatic recollections I had were the sights themselves. Of all the spectacular views we had, the most impressive to me was on the way to the Moon, when we flew through its shadow. We were still thousands of miles away, but close enough, so that the Moon almost filled our circular window. It was eclipsing the Sun, from our position, and the corona of the Sun was visible around the limb of the Moon as a gigantic lens-shaped or saucer-shaped light, stretching out to several lunar diameters. It was magnificent, but the Moon was even more so. We were in its shadow, so there was no part of it illuminated by the Sun. It was illuminated only by earthshine. It made the Moon appear blue-grey, and the entire scene looked decidedly three-dimensional.

Summary: the view of the Moon, illuminated by earthshine, from the window of the spacecraft. Armstrong describes the light effects from the Moon's shadow as it eclipses the Sun.

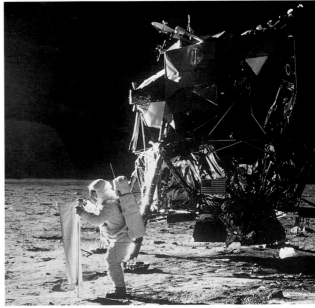

Tips on making a summary
- Read the passage twice and decide what it is about.
- Then decide: what information is repeated
  what is only descriptive
  what are examples to make a point
- Eliminate all of these
- Decide which information you will select and which order it will go in.

Writing *a summary*

Now read this extract from the same account by Neil Armstrong and make a summary of it.

B *[Later]* The Moon was a very natural and pleasant environment in which to work. It had many of the advantages of zero gravity, but it was in a sense less *lonesome* than Zero G, where you always have to pay attention to securing attachment points to give you some means of leverage. In one-sixth gravity, on the Moon, you had a distinct feeling of being *somewhere...* As we deployed our experiments on the surface we had to jettison things like lanyards, retaining fasteners, etc., and some of these we tossed away. The objects would go away with a slow, lazy motion. If anyone tried to throw a baseball back and forth in that atmosphere he would have difficulty, at first, acclimatising himself to that slow, lazy trajectory; but I believe he could adapt to it quite readily...
  Odour is very subjective, but to me there was a distinct smell to the lunar material – pungent, like gunpowder or spent cap-pistol caps. We carted a fair amount of lunar dust back inside the vehicle with us, either on our suits and boots or on the conveyor system we used to get boxes and equipment back inside. We did notice the odour right away.

Rainforests

When you read a piece of specialist writing, whether it is geographic, scientific or historical, you will come across facts and figures and sometimes, opinions. These will form the basis of your knowledge of a subject.

Read this selection of information on the subject of tropical rainforests. You should also refer to the newspaper articles about Sting and the rainforest in Unit 1 on page 125.

The rainforest environment

The Amazon rainforest (or Amazonia) covers a huge lowland area drained by the River Amazon and its tributaries. This vast river rises in the Andes mountains to the west of Amazonia and, with its many tributaries, carries an enormous volume of water and load of silt into the Atlantic Ocean.

The area lies across the equator, which means that the mid-day sun is nearly overhead throughout the year. We have already discovered that a high sun results in a lot of energy being received by the surface of the earth and the lower layers of the atmosphere. Daytime temperatures are high throughout the year. Weather conditions are almost the same every day. The sun rises at about 6 a.m., and the early morning mists soon disperse. As the sun gets higher in the sky and temperatures rise, a lot of water evaporates from the rivers and forests. As the air rises it cools, and the water vapour condenses to produce great masses of cloud. By afternoon there is usually a torrential downpour, often with thunder and lightning. The clouds then break up, and at about 6 p.m. the sun sets and night begins. The regular evaporation and rainfall means that the weather is always humid and sticky as well as hot, and there are no summer and winter seasons as we know them.

Any climate with average monthly temperatures over 25 °C and a rainfall of over 2000 millimetres spread throughout the year will result in vegetation similar to that of Amazonia. The tallest trees rise like giant pillars to over forty metres high, and are close enough together for their crowns to overlap. From above the trees seem to form a continuous canopy. Beneath this layer are other layers made by smaller trees, while there are masses of creepers and rope-like lianas looping and hanging from the trunks and branches. In places in the greeny gloom of the forest floor there are open spaces, but often there is a cover of bushes and undergrowth which is difficult to move through. Thousands of different sorts of birds, reptiles, insects and animals inhabit the jungle environment.

With the little change in climate there is no particular season for the trees to flower and fruit. Individual trees lose their leaves at different times, so the forest as a whole remains evergreen. The floor is covered by a thick, spongy layer of decaying leaves, and it is humus from these that provides the vegetation with food. Such rich plant growth suggests the soil is rich, but this is far from true. When the tree cover is removed, the heavy rainfall and heat soon wash plant food out of the thin reddish soils, and there is every danger of it being lost completely by erosion.

The pattern of forest regeneration

The rainforest is capable of regeneration when gaps in the canopy occur. Certain pioneer species grow first, but most die within 15 years. Gradually mature-phase species return and the forest is completely restored.

Bulldozing of all vegetation has serious consequences. The soils may become irreversibly impoverished or eroded. In the end, all that may replace what was once spectacular forest is scrappy, low-grade scrub.

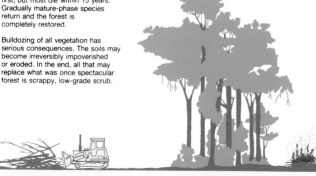

Low-grade scrub | Total forest destruction   Uncut forest | Uncut forest | Forest cut and burned | Farm in use (2–3 years) | Two years later: pioneers established | After 15 years, small primaries emerge | After 60 years, primaries dominate | After 100 years, as uncut forest

RAINFOREST IN OUR BACKYARD

The 'jungles' cover large areas of Brazil, Central America, Central Africa, India, Madagascar, Southeast Asia and Indonesia. An environment largely hostile to people, they have remained sparsely populated. They were a resource which remained unexploited until the Twentieth century when growth in population, shortage of land and poverty encouraged the people of these developing countries to move into the rainforests. Until recently the rainforests had been home only to the native groups, who had lived for generations in harmony with their 'home' environment, and small groups of pioneers, such as rubber tappers. Both groups had an interest in conserving the forest, for they depended on its well-being. In more recent years, however, the pioneers have included prospectors in search of tin and gold. These people were not so concerned for the forest. Their activities were small-scale but they awakened governments to the fact that the rainforests could make money and so the land was opened up to a new wave of settlers. The poor farmers, driven out of regions like northeast Brazil by poverty, lack of land and difficult environmental conditions, such as drought, were encouraged to settle along the new roads which were driven through the forest. The trees were felled; the valuable timber (about 10%) taken away for export and the rest burned. The farmers then set about trying to grow crops on land which had been shared out from a map, regardless of the quality of soils or the relief. The lesson they learned was that the lush vegetation of the rainforests was not due to rich soils. In fact most of the nutrients in the system were stored in the trees. Once exposed to the heavy rains the nutrients left in the soil were soon washed away (**leaching**) leaving low- grade agricultural land.

Trapped by the poverty created by the failure of small-scale farming these people have often been forced to sell their land to the large landowners, such as cattle ranchers, who have grassed the areas which were once lush forest. These landowners form the last wave of colonisation, that of big business – mining companies, logging firms, hydro-electric power schemes – all of which destroy the forest in return for short-term financial gain.

Wide World GCSE Geography review September 1990

Rubbertappers' leader gunned down in his backyard

Fighter for Amazon ecology murdered

THE leader of Brazil's rubbertappers and internationally known defender of the Amazon rain forest, 44-year-old Francisco Mendes, has been assassinated at his home in Xapuri, in the state of Acre.

He died instantly after being shot in the chest as he went out into his backyard. Two men were seen running away from an empty house next door, but local police failed to capture them.

Chico Mendes, as he was known, had received many death threats because of his fight to save the forest from destruction. He was president of the Rural Workers' Union in Xapuri, leader of the National Rubbertappers' Association, and founder of the Union of Forest Peoples, an alliance of Indians and rubbertappers.

Mendes led the rubbertappers, whose existence depends on the survival of the forest, in *empates*, the physical blockade of machines sent in by land-owners to clear the trees for cattle farms.

In Washington last year, at a prize-giving ceremony, he denounced the involvement of large American companies like Xerox and Georgia Pacific, the Dutch company Bruynzeel and the Japanese Tyomenka in rain forest devastation:

'By buying expensive mahogany furniture, you Americans are helping to finance the destruction of the last forest reserves on the planet,' he told his audience.

He successfully urged the World Bank and the Inter American Regional Bank not to finance the highway planned to link Acre's capital, Branco, to the rest of Brazil, until serious environmental protection measures had been taken.

These activities earned him the hatred of those in Acre for whom roads, sawmills and cattle farms mean progress and above all profit. For them he was no more than an agitator.

Several attempts had already been made on Chico Mendes's life. A few months ago the military police warned him that a gunman had been hired to kill him and provided him with a bodyguard. He never announced his movements in advance.

Union leaders in Acre suspect two brothers, who are members of the right-wing landowners organisation UDR, of involvement in the killing.

The Guardian 24 December 1988

'Our lands have not been demarcated. That is why we are being invaded by the whites who are taking gold from our lands and are bringing diseases and contaminating the Yanomami. We call the white man's diseases *xawara*. These diseases kill our people.

'At first we didn't know that the miners were invading our land. Now we know: those who live near the miners and ranchers, the Yanomami of the Ajarani, the Catrimani, the Demini, the Couto do Magalhaes and the Erico. There are Yanomami that know that it is bad for them and are sorry because they are striken with illnesses. There are others who think it is good because they receive machetes, axes, pans and matches that they use in the forest.

'But we, who know that the miners deceive us, are telling the others. So that they know what is happening. The miners want to take our Yanomami women to keep them and they are deceiving us and stealing our gold.

'I am telling you this because I am worried and angry. I want you to know of our situation, to understand our worries and to join our struggle.

'We Yanomami want the demarcation of our Yanomami Park. A continuous area, that is very important for us Yanomami.'

Statement issued by Davi, Yanomami from Toototobi, Carreira, Yanomami headman of Wakathaotheri, and Rubi, Yanomami from the lower Catrimani, at a meeting at Surumu, 7 to 9 January 1985.

Survival International News No 9 1985

Amazonia: life in the jungle

The forests are part of a vast area more than ten times the size of England – Amazonia in South America. The Indians are from one of the few tribes that remain in these hot, humid jungles. No one quite knows where their ancestors came from, or when they first appeared in these huge forests.

Most of the things they used were made from forest materials, and these quickly decay, leaving little trace of the past. They also move from place to place in the forests, so remains of past villages are hard to find. It is thought that Indians have been living in this way in the Amazon forest for thousands of years.

The Indians adapted very cleverly to the jungle environment, and they managed to make use of every aspect of it without causing any major change. They obtained food by hunting animals, fishing in the many rivers, gathering wild produce and growing crops such as manioc, maize, yams, groundnuts and bananas. They grew these crops in patches of forest cleared by the 'slash-and-burn' method.

When there were only a few people this did no permanent damage to the forest. After a few years new 'gardens' would be made and the old ones revert to jungle. Many different sorts of fish and animals were caught, such as wild pigs, monkeys and tapir, with harpoons, spears, nets, blow-guns and dogs.

All the resources they used were from the surrounding forest. Wood was used for house frames, simple furniture and weapons, while clay was made into pottery.

● In particular, the access of new technologies has created totally new possibilities in the use of their environments. Steel tools, which have now replaced the traditional stone axes throughout Amazonia, have made the labour of slash and burn agriculture about four times as efficient. Metal cooking pots and arrow points, shotguns, drills, needles, mirrors, scissors, beads, cloth, fish-hooks, nylon etc. all soon become integral parts of the Indians' economies, until suddenly the Indians find that they can no longer survive independently of the outside world.

To pay for these new necessities the Indians must produce a surplus, creating wholly new demands on what was previously a self-sufficient and self-limiting system. What begins as a simple transaction, machetes in exchange for manioc, axes for artefacts, sets in motion a whole process of social and economic change in the Indian societies. From being isolated, autonomous, independent, self-sufficient peoples with subsistence economies, the Indians became dependent, accessible and manipulable and linked to the market economy of western civilisation. The ineluctable process by which tribespeople become peasants is initiated. The change in orientation of the Indians' economies also has the effect of severely disrupting the relations with the natural environment.

Extract from school textbook: *A Sense of Place*

Taking a closer look

1   The information you are offered divides into two categories:
    ● environmental   ● human
    Before you do the longer written assignments work with a partner to identify the important information given about both categories.

2   Reread *The rainforest environment*. Draw your version of the diagram below and label it using information from all the pieces given here.

3   Reread all the information about the people of the rainforest. Think about ways of representing these people. For instance, you will need to contrast the traditional life of the Indians with the life which is now replacing it. You will also have to present the three main groups of people involved: the Indians, the Farmers/Rubber tappers and Big business. You could present this information as a spider diagram, a chart or by means of an illustration.

4   Find evidence of bias in *Rainforest in our backyard* and discuss the attitude of the writer to the subject.
    For more on bias see Unit 1, pages 130-131.

5   In what way is *The rainforest environment* similar to the description of the heart or the process of producing rubber on pages 158-159?
    ● Look at the way the information is organised in paragraphs and the way the writer uses commas in the article.
    ● Is the passive voice employed?

6   What audience is each of these passages about the rainforest intended for and how do you know?

Assignments

1   Write about the rainforests in the form of a report that would be suitable for:
    ● primary school children   ● the uninformed reader

2   Write a letter to a newspaper expressing your views on the treatment of the rainforest and its people.

3   Prepare your own article on this subject for your school magazine.

The Sidney Street siege

Here are three accounts of the same event which took place in London in 1911.
Read these passages and decide which of them is:
- an eye witness account
- a newspaper article
- an historical description

A While mainland Europe was not unused to the activities of various anarchist groups, their presence in Britain was almost unknown. This may be partly because no legislation was ever passed against anarchists, however this liberalism did not prevent the shocking and violent events of a cold day in January in the year 1911. Following the killing of three policemen by the mysterious anarchist known as Peter the Painter and his gang, the murderers sought refuge in a building in Sidney Street, just off the Mile End Road in London. Police and army units were despatched by the then Home Secretary, Winston Churchill. Shots were exchanged and another policeman was wounded. At this point, Churchill ordered reinforcements and arrived at the scene to direct operations. Thousands of rounds of ammunition were fired in the conflict which followed but eventually a fire was detected at the back of the besieged building. Two charred bodies were retrieved from the ruins but the whereabouts of the third gang member was never established. Churchill reflected the public's sense of shock when he said, 'Who would have imagined a scene like this in England?'

B

I took a taxi, and drove to the corner of that street, where I found a dense crowd observing the affair as far as they dared peer round the angle of the walls from adjoining streets.

Immediately in front of me four soldiers of one of the Guards' regiments lay on their stomachs, protected from the dirt of the road by newspaper 'sandwich' boards, firing their rifles at a house halfway down the street. Another young Guardsman, leaning against a wall, took random shots at intervals while he smoked a Woodbine. As I stood near him, he winked and said,'What a game!'

It was something more than a game. Bullets were flicking off the wall like peas, plugging holes into the dirty yellow brick, and ricocheting fantastically. One of them took a neat chip out of a policeman's helmet, and he said, 'Well, I'll be blowed!' and laughed in a foolish way. It was before the war, when we learned to know more about the meaning of bullets.

A cinematograph operator, standing well inside Sidney Street, was winding his handle vigorously, quite oblivious of the whiz of bullets, which were being fired at a slanting angle from the house.

I found myself in a group of journalists.

'Get back there!' shouted the police.

But we were determined to see the drama out. It was more sensational than any 'movie' show. Immediately opposite was a tall gin palace – *The Rising Sun.*

A publican stood in the doorway, sullenly.

'Whatcher want?' he asked.

'Your roof,' said one of the journalists.

'A quid each, and worth it,' he said.

At that time, before the era of paper money, some of us carried golden sovereigns in our pockets, one to a 'quid'. Most of the others did, but, as usual, I had not more than eighteenpence. A friend lent me the neccesary coin.

It was a good vantage point, or O.P., as we should have called it later in history. It looked right across to the house in Sidney Street in which Peter the Painter and his friends were defending themselves to the death.

We could not see the soldiers, but we could see the effect of their intermittent fire, which had smashed every pane of glass and kept chipping off bits of brick in the anarchists' abode.

The thing became a bore as I watched it for an hour or more, during which time Mr Winston Churchill, who was then Home Secretary, came to take command of active operation, thereby causing an immense amount of ridicule in next day's papers. With a bowler hat pushed firmly down on his bulging brow, and one hand in his breast pocket, like Napoleon on the field of battle, he peered round the corner of the street.

In the top-floor room of the anarchists' house we observed a gas jet burning, and presently some of us noticed the white ash of burnt paper fluttering out of a chimney pot.

'They're burning documents,' said one of my friends.

They were burning more than that. They were setting fire to the house, upstairs and downstairs.

'Did you ever see such a game in London!' exclaimed the man next to me on the roof of the public house.

For a moment I thought I saw one of the murderers standing on the window sill. But it was a blackened curtain which suddenly blew outside the window frame and dangled on the sill.

A moment later I had one quick glimpse of a man's arm with a pistol in his hand. He fired and there was a quick flash. At the same moment a volley of shots rang out from the Guardsmen opposite. It is certain that they killed the man who had shown himself, for afterwards they found his body (or a bit of it) with a bullet through the skull. It was not long afterwards that the roof fell in with an upward rush of flame and sparks.

The detectives, with revolvers ready, now advanced in Indian file. One of them ran forward and kicked at the front door. It fell in, and a sheet of flame leaped out. No other shot was fired from within. Peter the Painter and his fellow bandits were charred cinders in the bonfire they had made.

Philip Gibbs

C Fight with anarchists
Houndsditch assassins trapped.
Two killed in Stepney.
Seven hours' siege by Scots Guards and Police.

A house in Stepney, to which the Houndsditch murderers had been traced, was surrounded yesterday by a large detachment of police and military. The criminals were fully armed and well supplied with ammunition. Shots were exchanged for nearly seven hours until the building caught fire and the men within either shot themselves or were burnt to death.

At an early hour in the morning a number of detectives and police attempted to arrest the fugitives in a tenement building in Sidney-street, Mile End Road. The ground floor of the building was cleared, but two desperate men, who were at first believed to be 'Peter the Painter' and 'Fritz,' but who have not been definitely identified, offered armed resistance. Early in the morning they severely wounded a police sergeant, and continued to hold at bay all who approached their quarters by firing with automatic pistols from two windows that overlooked Sidney-street.

So desperate and prolonged was their resistance that not only had the police force to be strongly augmented, but detachments of Foot Guards were summoned from the Tower, and finally a section of Royal Horse Artillery from St. John's Wood Barracks was sent for. From 7 in the morning until nearly 2 in the afternoon desultory firing was taking place against the windows of the house within which the desperadoes were sheltered. Sometimes, when a response came from them, the fire became brisk and almost heavy, but the attack failed to dislodge them. By 12 o'clock the Home Secretary and many officials of the City Police and Scotland Yard were at the scene of this extraordinary encounter.

At half-past 12 it was seen that the back of the premises was on fire. The Fire Brigade was summoned, but the fire was allowed to burn unchecked in the hope that it would force the defenders to take to the open. By half-past 1 o'clock the house was fairly ablaze, and one of the besieged appeared at the door. He was greeted with a heavy fusillade, and from his cries it was judged that he was wounded.

At a quarter to 2 o'clock shots were heard from the back of the house. It is believed that the defenders, finding escape impossible, had turned their pistols upon themselves. A few minutes later the floors of the burning house fell in, and the inmates, whatever their condition, were buried in the burning *debris.* The Fire Brigade then set to work and subdued the fire. Among the half-burned refuse they discovered the charred remains of two men. One body was pulled out just before 3 o'clock by the back of the building, and the second was recovered about 8 o'clock last evening.

One of the bodies is said to be that of Fritz Svaars (?), but the other, though it has not been identified, is believed not to be that of 'Peter the Painter'.

During the street fusillade two persons are said to have been wounded by ricochet bullets, and several among the large crowd of sightseers had narrow escapes. Inspector Quinn, of Scotland Yard, shook a spent bullet out of his coat.

Looking at style

1 Deciding which passage is which depends on recognising different styles of writing (having a headline may have also helped to identify one of them!). Talk about these differences and record the results of your discussions in a chart like the one shown here.

2 Which passage did you find the most enjoyable to read? How did you come to a conclusion about this?

3 Which is the oldest piece of writing? Identify the phrases and idioms which gave you an impression of the piece having being written a long time ago.

For more on differences in styles of writing, see The Process of Writing module, pages 62-64.

Newspaper article	Eye witness account	Historical description
1 precise times	1 comment/ chat	1 puts event in context
2 little ref. to individuals	2 vivid memories	2
3	3	3
4	4	

Role play

1 Make a flow chart of events in Sidney Street on the day of the siege using all the evidence available to you.
2 Then, in small groups, imagine that you are on the roof of the pub, *The Rising Sun*. Act out the scene as it unfolds before you.

Hot seating

In a group of 4, take the parts listed below and each of you prepare a list of ten questions to ask one of the other characters. Hot seat each other to discover more about the people involved in the siege.

- an anarchist
- a guardsman
- a journalist
- a member of the public

Writing about history

Here is an example of how history can be presented in the form of a cartoon. Using the facts and information you are given about events of Sidney Street siege in 1911 make a story-board using the device of a modern-day narrator like the one in the story of the two princes in the Tower below.

Extract from
Prove It!

Women's rights

The feminist movement has made people more aware of the way attitudes and language itself can be used to discriminate against women. Read the following selection of facts and opinions about the moves made towards equality for women over the last 150 years.

'...we continue to detest the injustice and barbarity of the laws which govern women's existence in marriage, the family and society.'
George Sand, Indiana 1832

'...any woman born with a great gift in the Sixteenth century would certainly have gone crazed, shot herself, or ended her days in some lonely cottage outside the village, half-witch, half-wizard, feared and mocked at.'
Virginia Woolf

Women's dates

1837 Women had *very* few legal rights, but until they were married, they had total control over any property they owned, could enter into legal contracts and sue or be sued. Married women were not allowed to keep their own property; any funds earned went to the husband; a wife owed absolute fidelity to her spouse, and she was forced to cohabit even if he beat her or committed adultery.

1857 With the Divorce Act the procedure for divorce became easier but women had to prove adultery and desertion, bigamy, incest, or cruelty. A husband needed only to point to her adultery and file for divorce. After this a woman was entitled to receive maintenance from her spouse but a father had absolute authority over his legitimate children and even if he died, a wife had no guaranteed right to serve as testamentary guardian.

1870 The Married Woman's Property Act enabled a woman to keep her own earnings.

1882 She gained complete control over her property.

1884 The Matrimonial Causes Act gave her total personal freedom.

1886 A mother finally gained the right to possible guardianship of her children.

By the **1880s**, a husband and wife were seen as possessing separate identities.

1919 Sex Discrimination Act. This gave women the right of entry to most professions.

1928 Women's right to vote. Women over 21 were now given the vote; this was largely as a result of World War One when women were able to prove their ability to do many traditionally male jobs.

1970 Equal Pay Act. Women had to be paid the same rate as men if they were doing similar work.

1975 Equal Opportunities Commission. This was set up to wipe out notions of women as second class citizens; further it sought to diminish discrimination and prejudice which limits girls' expectations and ambitions.

1978 Equal Opportunities Commission Annual Report
- Women earn two-thirds as much as men in a week.
- Women are still in small occupation groups and low-paid jobs.
- Women are lower on promotion scales than men.
- Out of 293 jobs the Department of Trade only appointed 12 women.

1990 Tax emancipation. Married women permitted by law to be taxed separately from their husbands.

Male writers' response to women writers at the turn of the century

In Aldous Huxley's story *The farcical history of Richard Greenow* the hero has a writer's block due to a fellow, female, writer who is depicted as a vampire tigress who preys on the young man and takes all his creative ideas. Male writers of the turn of the century were particularly vicious about women writers: D.H. Lawrence thought that the world was being taken over by 'Cock sure women at the expense of hen sore men', James Joyce said that women's style was 'namby pamby marmalady drawersy' and Henry James has a female character in one of his stories who 'could invent stories by the yard but who couldn't write a page of English'. Women critics have speculated that this criticism of women writers was due to their (male writers) dependence on women patrons and publicists. However the characterisation of women as 'dangerous' and destructive may be traced back to The Bible and reflects a (male) cultural misogyny one of the consequences of which has been to stifle the creative output in women and exclude them from an artistic milieu taken for granted by men.

Marilyn French's novel *The Women's Room* (1977) is the story of a woman who escapes a suburban marriage and discovers, through her hard won independence and her female friendships, the exhilaration of liberation. Marilyn French has said that the success of her book was because it was one of the first books that 'spelt the truth about how a lot of women felt… The reason they were unhappy was not because they were neurotic or bad, but because these were cultural facts about what happens to women. They were able to see that a male dominated society was keeping them in their place, was not allowing them to be empowered either intellectually or economically.'

So what's all the fuss about?

The Plain Speaker: And what are you working on at the moment?

The Linguist: Well, I'm writing a paper on language and gender.

The Plain Speaker: You mean all that stuff about sexist words that feminists carry on about? Now that's something that really irritates me, all this nonsense about chairperson and *he* or *she* and *Ms.* If women want to chair meetings that's OK by me, but I don't see why they can't just be called chairmen and shut up about it. And quite frankly the next time someone adds or *she* when I've used *he,* I'll explode!

It's a waste of time, those extra words, and what's more important, it distracts attention from what I'm talking about. When I'm talking, I want to be able to say what I want to say in the quickest and simplest and most straightforward way. I don't want people putting words into my mouth and telling me I shouldn't say this and can't say that – or injecting sex into everything, insisting on a *she* for every *he!*

The Linguist: But if people aren't reminded that *he* could be *she,* it might not occur to them. I remember how taken aback you were when your daughter said she couldn't be a doctor because she was a girl. And how you said she must have picked up such an idea at school because she would never have heard any such nonsense at home.

The Plain Speaker: But what's that got to do with *he* or *she?* That was just some nonsensical idea she picked up from somewhere, which we nipped in the bud before it went any further. We told her in no uncertain terms that it was nonsense. Being a girl wouldn't stop her being a doctor, but not working hard enough at school jolly well would!

M.A: How did you decide to become a writer? You're Black, female and a Trinidadian...

R.G: I wanted to be an actress. But I didn't look exactly like Hilda Simms and that was the type they liked, very pale and very pretty hair...

M.A: Pretty hair? You mean hair like white folks?

R.G: Yeah. Like white folks. I decided to write my own play and put myself into it. I had my first play done off Broadway. From then on I considered myself a playwright. But the canvas proved too restrictive. I decided to try the short story. And then that too was restricted...

M.A: I want to go back to 'pretty hair'. It's of particular interest that you, whom I know personally to have been engaged in the projection of the concept of Black beauty long before the phrase 'black is beautiful' became popular, would use the phrase 'pretty hair' meaning straight hair, white folks' hair. That shows the profound power of the self destructive-image –

R.G: – that we are burdened with, even in the West Indies where I was born. We were taught that you didn't go round with a person who was 'pickey headed'. We have to fight through a lot of things, and the first is the self image that was given to us. We've had to struggle through a lot of things that other people generally don't. It's particularly true in the Western hemisphere. Isn't that why we both straighten our hair?

M.A: There is that contradiction in knowing that one is gorgeous and lovely, in good health and about the size one wants to be, and feels sexy and sensual, that one is attractive. There is that and at the same time there is the contradiction of it. And then to be Black and female as opposed to being white and male is a total contradiction. A double contradiction.

R.G: We were demeaned yet always had to aspire to freedom – the heights. Our ambition was nurtured by the Western society – the same society which said that you're female. You're Black. You can't climb here. That probably made us strong.

Article about *The Late Show* presenter Sarah Dunant

'Men on TV come with an authority that's given to them because they are male. They don't have to be attractive to keep it. But tell me about an old, not very attractive female newsreader. There isn't one. The women are young, 'good looking', done over for the box.'

'When I started TV... I was a severe Oxfam dresser. The producer took me aside. Major battle. And for the second programme I was dressed up. I saw myself and I was terribly upset. Then I realised that, like a good feminist, I was looking at the image rather than listening to the words.'

The Guardian 20 February 1991

Article by Suzie Mackenzie, on the writer and therapist Suzie Orbach

Fat Is A Feminist Issue, or FiFi, as she now fondly calls it, drew directly on her experience of being overweight: 'Well, never exactly obese but several sizes larger than I am today.' It put forward the theory, quite simply, that fat was a response to women's powerlessness in the world.

Fat she says, 'represents one way of saying,"Screw you." It makes the space that women crave in society.' The most revolutionary idea was that many women actually unconsciously desired to be fat because it protected them. The root cause of the tenacity of fatness was women's own fear of being thin.

'Thin equals sexy equals someone else's fantasy' is the equation she uses in her book. And there was another interesting strand to this idea. If you were thin, she suggests, other women would envy you. You may be desired by men, but your sisters would consign you to the reject pile and women, she believes, cannot flourish without the love and approval of other women.

The Guardian 21 February 1991

What do you think?

1 In groups of 4 or 5, discuss what you learn about 'feminist' attitudes from these extracts.
2 Do you think that women are still disadvantaged or is the idea of women fighting for their rights out of date?

Assignments

1 Read the various views presented here carefully and then write a discursive essay about what you have learned about feminism. If you have found this issue interesting, you may like to do some further research into it before you plan your piece of writing. You could try reading more about some of the people mentioned here or look at the way women are portrayed currently in the media.
2 Write a short account of the varying styles and tones of the pieces in this selection. Some are quite 'angry' and strongly argumentative, while others seem more relaxed and 'chatty'. Try to account for the style of each piece in terms of its audience and purpose. You may find it helpful to complete a chart like the one below before planning your account.

For more on argumentative writing see The Process of Writing module, pages 94-99.

Title	Tone	Example	Purpose
Angelou/Guy	chatty/ relaxed	'Yeah. Like white folks.'	A transcript of a conversation between two writers for those studying/ interested in their work.
On Marilyn French	objective	Marilyn French has said...	An account of the effect of a feminist novel on women of the time.

Here's one I made earlier

In this section you will be asked to think about the language of recipes and to develop your own recipe-writing style.

Middle East
Hab el jose (walnut balls)
(makes 15-20)

150g (5oz) walnuts, ground;
50g (2oz) breadcrumbs;
$\frac{1}{2}$ x 5ml spoon ($\frac{1}{2}$ tsp) ground cumin;
1 x 15ml spoon (1 tbs) tahina paste (available in health food shops);
$\frac{1}{2}$ x 5ml spoon ($\frac{1}{2}$ tsp) cayenne or chilli powder;
50g (2 oz) sesame seeds;
a little olive oil;
pinch of paprika;
1 x15ml spoon (1tbs) fresh mint, finely chopped (optional);
salt and pepper.

Start by making a mixture with the walnuts, breadcrumbs and cumin. Put them into a bowl, and add enough tahina to make a soft paste. Flavour with the cayenne or chilli powder and salt and pepper. Shake the sesame seeds on to a plate. Grease your fingers with olive oil and take up small pieces of the paste, shaping them into walnut-sized balls by rolling them between your palms. Then trail each of the walnut balls in the sesame seeds to coat them. Before serving, arrange the hab el jose on a plate and sprinkle the paprika and mint over them.

Nigeria
Wake-ewa (black-eyed beans with sauce)
(serves 4-6)

450g (1lb) black-eyed beans, soaked and cooked;
1 large onion;
4 x 15ml spoon (4 tbs) oil;
1 x 5ml spoon (1 tsp) chilli powder;
1 x 5ml spoon (1 tsp) ground cilantro (coriander);
1 x 5ml spoon (1 tsp) thyme;
3 tomatoes, chopped finely;
1 x 5ml spoon (1 tsp) sugar;
salt.

First cut the onion in half. Grate one half and then slice the rest finely. Warm the oil in a pan and soften the onion slices in it.
Meanwhile, combine the grated onion, chilli, cilantro and thyme in a bowl with the tomatoes and add this to the cooked onion slices. Continue to cook the mixture gently for 10-15 minutes, stirring constantly.
After this add the beans, mash them a little with a fork and then add the sugar and salt. Mix everything well and cook for 5-10 minutes to heat all the ingredients before serving with salad and rice.

Looking at the language

Make a note of the words in these recipes which tell you what to do. Common examples of these are: 'Bring to the boil...' 'Sprinkle with...' 'Add...' These are likely to be instances of the imperative, which is often used in instructional writing.

Hold on to your collection of instructions as you will need them again
when you finish reading this poem. For more on writing instructions see
The Process of Writing module, pages 89-91.

Daily London recipe

Take any number of them
you can think of,
pour into empty red bus
       until full
and then push in ten
          more.
Allow enough time
to get hot under the collar
before transferring into
multi-storey building.
Leave for eight hours
and pour back into same bus
      already half full.
      Scrape remainder off.
When settled down
tip into terraced houses each
carefully lined with copy of
The Standard and *Tit Bits*
Place mixture before open
television screen at 7pm
and then allow to cool
in bed at 10.30pm
May be served with
working overalls
or pinstripe suit.

Steve Turner

For writing

Write your own poem in the form of a recipe.
Once you have chosen a theme, brainstorm ideas about it with a
partner, e.g. if your recipe poem is about shopping in a supermarket,
you will need to think about the sights, sounds, smells, and feelings
of that experience before you write about it.
   Make sure that you use some of the imperative instructions you
gathered from reading the food recipes.

Recipes can be more than just lists of instructions. Look at this recipe
and the one for Baked Bananas on page 178. Talk about the ways in
which the authors make the recipes personal.

Pumpkin soup

1 medium sized pumpkin
1 pint milk
2 tbs honey
salt and pepper to taste

I took a pumpkin and when I'd taken out all the
seeds, I cut up all the nice orangey flesh. This
went into a saucepan with some water and
bubbled away gently for about quarter of an
hour. I checked to see that it was soft, and when
I thought it was about right I mashed it up with
a potato masher until all the lumps had disappeared, sloshed in the milk and put it back on
the stove.

While this was cooking I rinsed the pumpkin
seeds well and then spread them out on a baking
tray. I wanted to toast them gently in the oven.
After about another five minutes or so I trickled
in the honey to give it a nice flavour and added
some salt and pepper. By this time too the seeds
were all crispy and brown and smelled delicious.
Everything was ready for my guests who particularly enjoyed eating the creamy soup because I
sprinkled it with the golden pumpkin seeds, and
gave them some crusty French bread to mop
it up with.

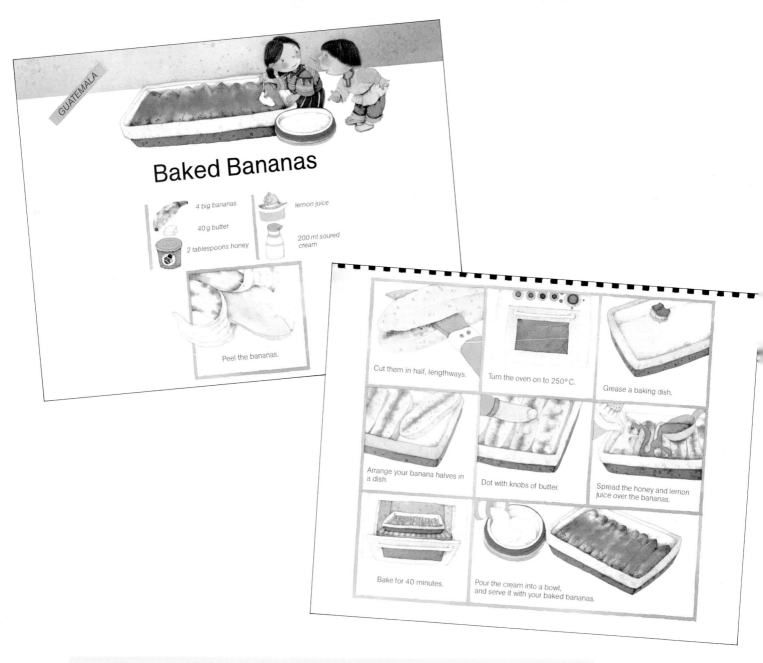

Baked Bananas

4 big bananas

40 g butter

2 tablespoons honey

lemon juice

200 ml soured cream

Peel the bananas.

Cut them in half, lengthways.

Turn the oven on to 250°C.

Grease a baking dish.

Arrange your banana halves in a dish.

Dot with knobs of butter.

Spread the honey and lemon juice over the bananas.

Bake for 40 minutes.

Pour the cream into a bowl, and serve it with your baked bananas.

Group discussion

1 What is the audience for each of these recipes? How did you arrive at your conclusions?
2 How would you describe the tone of the Pumpkin soup piece?
3 Which recipe of the two would be the easier to follow? Why?

Rewriting recipes

Rewrite the Pumpkin soup recipe, taking out all the chatty lines and leaving only the instructions. What differences does this make? Which version do you prefer?

Writing your own recipe

Now write your own recipe, basing it on a particular meal you remember as enjoyable. Include details about how you got on with each stage of the cooking and about your guests' reactions to the meal.

178

Newspaper launch

This assignment will give you the opportunity to use many of the skills you have gained in this module. You will need to work in a group of 6.

You will be asked to produce one edition of your own newspaper together with an informative piece of writing which describes the process. You can use either a desk-top publishing package or a cut and paste method.

Brainstorming your aims

Will your newspaper:
- give brief, dramatic news accounts with an emphasis on entertainment, competitions, etc?
- offer serious, balanced comment on current affairs and a focus on a specific aspect of newspapers? e.g. sport, the arts, the environment
- influence public opinion by giving views and comments with a particular slant? e.g. if the politics of your paper are Green this will affect your selection and treatment of the news.

What other aims do you have? Which paper currently on the market is most like you see yours as being?

Make some early decisions on:
- the name of the newspaper
- whether it is national or local
- whether it is a Tabloid or a broadsheet
- the type of advertising you will include
- the number of pages it will make. Put together a 'dummy' (see page 180) and plan the paper page by page
- the front page design and layout

Brainstorming content

Which of these will you include?

Brainstorming readership

- Who are you writing for?
- What are their politics? Do they vote Conservative/Labour/Liberal Democrat/ Green/Other?
- What sort of subjects are they likely to be interested in?

International news	Sex
Royal Family	Sport
Environment	Women's issues
Home news	Politics
Travel	Competitions/puzzles

- What jobs do they have?

Managers	Manual workers
Doctors	Teachers
Home makers	Shopkeepers
Skilled workers	Self-employed

- What do they spend their money on?

DIY	Family	Eating out	Books
Fashion	Investments	Foreign holidays	

- What is their age range/sex/social class?

Teens	Male	Working
19-35	Female	Middle

The answer to these questions will give you some idea about what items to write and the views to adopt when writing the news. Feature articles in which you will have to write as specialists, need to be decided on next.

Brainstorming your jobs

You will need an editor, who will have final say on which items are included.
This might be your teacher or one member of your group.
Here are some other roles you will either have to share or to allocate to specific
people.

Reporters for:
- local/national/international news
- features (money, fashion, stars, medical, home, children)
- sport
- gossip
- women's issues
- science or historical features
- TV/entertainment

You will also need:
- Advertising copywriters
- Photographers (or photo researchers)

The dummy: Newspapers arrange the layout of articles, advertising, photographs on
a 'dummy' version of the newspaper. This is then filled in by pasting on the contents
of the paper. Here is an example which you could imitate for your newspaper.

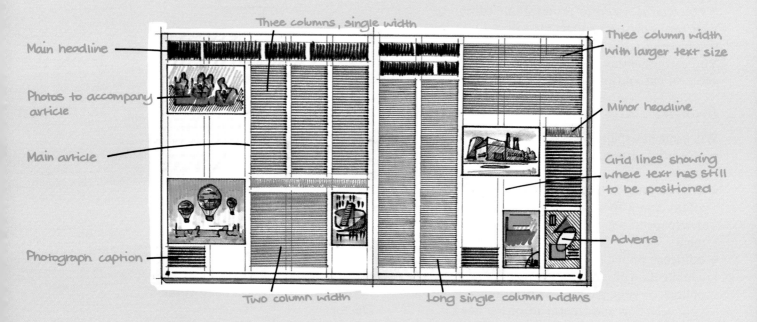

Main headline
Photos to accompany article
Main article
Photograph caption
Three columns, single width
Two column width
Long single column widths
Three column width with larger text size
Minor headline
Grid lines showing where text has still to be positioned
Adverts

Final decisions

- How are you going to gather your news? A good start would be to read local or
  national newspapers and to listen to the news programmes on the Radio and TV.
- What proportion of the paper will be occupied by pictures and headlines as
  opposed to text?
- Are you going to include an editorial column on an important issue of the day?
  What view will you take?
- What features will you include? Do you have any experts on your staff? This will
  need the sort of writing that is looked at in Units 3 and 4 on Specialist writing.
- Decide on a deadline when all the articles have to be in and design can begin.
  Decide on a second deadline when the edition will be complete.

Index of authors and extracts

Acknowledgements

The authors and publisher are grateful for permission to include the following copyright material:

Module 1: Knowledge about Language

John Agard: 'Listen Mr Oxford don' from *Mangoes and Bullets* (Serpent's Tail, 1985). Reprinted by permission of Caroline Sheldon Literary Agency. **Lesley Alexander**: 'The Magpied Piper of Newcastle on Tyne', first published in *Northumbrian No 37*. Used with permission. **Michael Alexander**: extract from *Beowulf* (pp. 93-4), translated by Michael Alexander (Penguin Classics, 1973), © Michael Alexander, 1973. Reprinted by permission of Penguin Books Ltd. **BBC**: for an extract from a Hampshire Dialect recording from *English With an Accent*, 1971, Mono Rec. 173. **James Berry**: extracts from *A Thief in the Village*, © 1987 James Berry (Hamish Hamilton, 1987). Used with permission. **John Cleese and Connie Booth**: 'A Touch of Class' from *The Complete Fawlty Towers* (Methuen, 1977). Reprinted by permission of David Wilkinson Associates. **Stella Gibbons**: from *Cold Comfort Farm*, © Stella Gibbons 1932. Reproduced by permission of Curtis Brown Ltd., London. **Guardian News Service Ltd**: for Benjamin Zephaniah, 'De Kings Speech', *The Guardian*, 7 November 1990. **Nicolás Guillén**: 'Such a white soul...' from *Man-making Words: Selected Poems of Nicolás Guillén* (Robert Marquez & David Arthur McMurray, 1972). **Barry Hines**: from *Kes* (1968). Reprinted by permission of Michael Joseph Ltd. **The Independent**: for extract from an article by Dr John Honey in *The Independent on Sunday*, 17 March 1991; for extract from 'Dealing with political pollsters' by Miles Kington, *The Independent*, 26 July 1987; for extract from 'Military words weasel a way into the language' by Edward Lucas, *The Independent*, 22 January 1991. **Lucy O'Connor**: *Tom's Spooky Night*, © Lucy O'Connor 1992. Used with permission. **George Bernard Shaw**: extracts from *Pygmalion*. Reprinted by permission of the Society of Authors on behalf of the Bernard Shaw Estate. **R.C. Sherriff**: from the play *Journey's End*, © R.C. Sherriff. Reproduced by permission of Curtis Brown Ltd, London. **Kamal Singh**: 'Six O'Clock Feeling' from *Black Poetry*, ed. Grace Nichols (Blackie, 1988).

Module 2: The Process of Writing

British Film Institute: for publicity letter, courtesy of Manuel Alvarado, Head of Education. **Bruce Chatwin**: from *In Patagonia* (Picador). **Comic Relief**: for *Hack Pack* extracts. **Graham Greene**: from *Our Man in Havana* (Heinemann, 1958). Reprinted by permission of David Higham Associates Ltd. **Helene Hanff**: from *84 Charing Cross Road*. Reprinted by permission of André Deutsch Ltd. **Guardian News Service Ltd**: for Geoff Hannan, 'The Power and the Glory', *Education Guardian*, 9 October 1990; for Edward Pilkington, 'Support or Sabotage', 'Hue and Cry' and 'Uncertain Future for the Hunters', *Education Guardian*, 15 January 1991. **The Independent**: for a selection of letters first published in *The Independent*, 23/24 May 1991; for 'Stores Join "Green" Fight', *The Independent*, 5 March 1991; for 'Read My Lips: No New Syntaxes' by John Lichfield, *The Independent*, March 1991; for 'Flyers Stuck in a Downward Dive' by Steve Pinder, *The Independent*, 5 March 1991; for 'Of All the Towns in All the World' by Adel Darwish, *The Independent on Sunday*, 30 September 1990. Used with permission. **Leisure Circle**: for permission to reproduce The Leisure Circle logo and letter. **Robins Cinemas Ltd**: for permission to reproduce cinema programme 29 June to 29 August 1991. **RoSPA**: for permission to reproduce advice on 'What to do if fire breaks out'. **Christopher Rush**: 'The Pen is Mightier than the Sword' and extract from 'Tutti Frutti' from *Into the Ebb* (Aberdeen University Press). Used with permission of the author and publisher. **Dave Smith**: 'Fit for the Finish' from *Health and Fitness Magazine*, May 1991. '*Step-by-step Instructions for Wiring a Plug*', compiled from material supplied by the Electricity Association. **William Carlos Williams**: 'This is Just to Say' from *The Collected Poems of William Carlos Williams 1909-1939*, Vol. 1. Reprinted by permission of Carcanet Press Ltd.

Module 3: Non-literary Forms

Thanks are due to the following for permission to reproduce advertising material, slogans and logos in this section.

The publishers would like to point out that the use of slogans, logos and ads from various companies in no way implies endorsement of a particular product, nor does it indicate any direct promotion by the companies concerned of their products to schoolchildren.

American Express. **Bartle Bogle Hegarty Ltd** (Audi). **British Aerospace PLC**. **British Coal Corporation**. **British Gas PLC**. **British Railways Board**. **BT Corporate Relations**, Corporate Design Unit. **Brook Bond Foods** (Oxo). **Burton Gold Medal Biscuits Ltd** (Wagon Wheels). **Cable & Wireless PLC**. **Ogilvy & Mather Ltd** (Cotton USA). **Cotton Council**. **Datalink**. **Fox FM**. **Electricity Association**. **Guinness Brewing G.B.**. **H.J. Heinz Company Ltd**. **Hitachi Sales (U.K.) Ltd**. **Great Universal Stores** (The Complete KIT). **IBM**. **Liberty of London Prints Ltd**. **McIntosh Associates** (Golden Wonder). **R. Whites**. **Mobil Holdings Ltd**. **Ogilvy & Mather Advertising** (Ford Granada; Hot Chocolate). **Proctor & Gamble** (Hugo Boss). **RAF crest**, © British Crown copyright/MOD. Reproduced with the permission of the Controller of Her Britannic Majesty's Stationery Office. **Raleigh Industries**. **Thames Water Utilities Ltd**. **J. Walter Thompson Company Ltd** (Lux). Photo: Terence Donovan. **Varta Batteries Ltd**. **Woolwich Building Society**. **Whale & Dolphin Conservation Society**.

Thanks are also due to the following:
Philip Allan Publishers: for 'Cholera: A Waterborn Disease' from *Catalyst: GCSE Science Review*, Vol. 1 No. 1 September 1990; 'Rainforest in Our Backyard' from *Wide World: GCSE Geography Review*, September 1990. **Channel Four Television**: extract from *Hard News*, 19 October 1990. **Daily Mirror**: 'New Star Trek Hero Pat Blasts at Britain', *Daily Mirror*, 2 October 1990; 'Big Mac Burger Bug Alert' by Jill Palmer & Steve White, *Daily Mirror*, 15 February 1991. **Ewan McNaughton Associates**: 'Platypuses Break Their Duck' by Christopher Milne, and 'Huckleberry Finn Manuscript Found in Hollywood Attic' by R. Barry O'Brien, both first published in *The Daily Telegraph*, 15 February 1991; 'Badger Baiters May be Jailed'. All copyright The Daily Telegraph PLC 1991. **Guardian News Service Ltd**: 'Illness Prompts Burger Caution' by Chris Mihill, *The Guardian*, 15 February 1991; 'Fighter for Amazon Ecology Murdered' by Jan Rocha, *The Guardian*, 24 December 1988; brief extract from a much longer article entitled 'Of Friends and Feminists' by Suzie Mackenzie, first published in *The Guardian*, 30 January 1991; from 'Facing Facts' by Luke Jennings, *The Guardian*, 20 February 1991. **Michael Joseph Ltd**: extract from *First Men on the Moon: A Voyage with Neil Armstrong, Michael Collins and Edwin*

Aldrin, by Gene Farmer and Dora Jane Hamblan (1970). **McIntosh Associates**: quote on stereotypes by Noel McIntosh. **The Observer**: 'Air the Ad and Spoil the Child' by Emily Bell (adapted), October 1990. **Oxford University Press**: 'Amazonia: life in the jungle' from Rex Beddis, *A Sense of Place*; extracts from B.S. Beckett, *GCSE: Biology* and *Illustrated Biology*; extract from *Prove It!* by Anne Stanyon. **Times Newspapers Ltd**: 'Greenhousemongers' from *The Sunday Times*, 27 May 1990. **Today Newspaper**: 'Pop Pow-wow for Sting the Forest Blaster', *Today*, 23 February 1989 and 'Road to Folly', editorial *Today*, 16 February 1991. **UNICEF**: baked bananas recipe from *The Little Cooks*. **Virago**: extract from *Writing Lives* edited by May Chamberlain, featuring Maya Angelou and Rosa Guy.

The illustrations are by **Mike Allport** p.24/5, 35/ 37, 57; **Felicity Roma Bowers** p.176; **Tony Chance** p.20, 101, 136, 149, 162, 176; **Frances Cony** p.11, 26; **Gerard Gibson** p.48, 168; **Robin Harris** p.33; **Carmelle Hayes** p.16, 177; **Sarah Hopkins** p.27; **Paul Hunt** p.44/5; **Sian Leetham** p.38, 52, 53; **Christopher Logan** p.122, 180; **Katrina Longden** p.13; **Diane Lumley** p.37; **Peter Melnyczuk** p.71; **Nilesh Mistry** p.86; **Oxford Illustrators** p.89, 167; **Chris Riddell** p.69; **Julie Roberts** p.7, 9, 29, 50, 53, 62, 67, 97; **Rachel Ross** p.73; **Duncan Storr** p.4, 5, 32, 40/1, 84.

The handwriting and diagrams are by **Elitta Fell**.

The publishers would like to thank the following for permission to reproduce photographs:
Allsport UK Ltd/Phillip Brown p.134 (top), **Allsport UK Ltd/Billy Stickland** p.134 (bottom); **Alpha/Paul Harris** p.126; **BBC News and Current Affairs** p.105, 129 (both); **BBC Photography Library** p.93 (both); **Camera Press (UK) Ltd** p.172 (right), **Camera Press (UK) Ltd/American Photo Synd** p.92, **Camera Press (UK) Ltd/B. McCreeth** p.134 (middle), **Camera Press (UK) Ltd/A. Varley** p.135; **Channel 4/All Arts** p.56 (bottom left); **Martyn Chillmaid** p.55 (all), 82, 138 (both); **Colorific Photo Library Ltd** p.103; **Michael Dudley** p.46, 178; **Mary Evans Picture Library** p.108; **Fletcher and Boyce** p.30; **The Image Bank/Lisl Dennis** p.85, **The Image Bank/Peter Frey** p.158; **The League Against Cruel Sport** p.95; **Duncan Phillips** p.2, 106, 107; **Paul Popper Ltd** p.125, 133 (both), 163, 172 (left); **Paul Roberts** p.179; **David Simpson** p.137; **Syndication International** p.22, **Syndication International/Library of Congress** p.104; **Victoria and Albert Museum Picture Library** p.56 (all except bottom left); **Frederick Warne, Penguin Books Ltd** p.109.